THE FANATIC'S GUIDE TO
S E C FOOTBALL
BY
FRANK AND RITA CANTRELL WENZEL

TABLE OF CONTENTS

FOREWORD

You may be asking, "Who are we to write a book about Southeastern Conference football"? That's exactly the question we got when we approached the SEC with our idea. After all, we aren't professional journalists or photographers. We are just fans. A school administrator husband and a minister wife who both love all aspects of Southeastern Conference football: the game, the fans, the color, excitement, history and tradition.

We saw the need to have a book like this after we attended a game in an unfamiliar city and came away realizing we had not enjoyed the experience to the fullest because we were ignorant of many things: how to get around, what to see and do, where to park, and so on. After a search of available materials, we realized that no such book existed. That's when the idea was born. We would travel to each of the twelve SEC member school campuses (plus five other cities where SEC football is played) research the football heritage of each institution, interview hundreds and hundreds of fans, take over 2,600 pictures and put it all together in a book that could be used and enjoyed by fans whether on the go to a game or sitting on their couch at home.

Guiding us in our efforts were the three goals we set for the project. We wanted to EXCITE fans by writing about the great family of schools in the SEC, each with its proud heritage and tradition. We wanted to EDUCATE readers about the many interesting and often important aspects of SEC member schools. Finally, we wanted to ENABLE those who use our book to attend games with increased confidence and enjoyment.

Now, after 2 years, it is finished. There is much more we could have included, but we leave those things for the second edition. (We could even write a book about writing this book!) However, we will keep traveling and meeting fans and learning about the SEC. We will improve upon our work and look back at our first effort with humor. It has been a wonderful adventure. We hope you enjoy the book and that it helps you to experience the adventure for yourselves!

Frank and Rita Cantrell Wenzel

CREDITS

Robert "Bo" Stanford and American Printing Company, Birmingham, Alabama
Mike Suchcicki, Pensacola, Florida - Original artwork for the cover and "Fanatic's Map"
Ron Stallcup, Pensacola, Florida - Colorist for the cover and "Fanatic's Map"
Mark Whitworth and the Southeastern Conference Office
Tracy Washington and the Collegiate Licensing Company
The Sports Information Offices of all twelve SEC schools
The Chambers of Commerce and Visitors Bureaus for the area maps
Bob Smith, Childersburg, Alabama - Photo cropping and layout
Pat Connell and Margie Wise for their administrative assistance
Frank Wenzel - All photographs (except for the aerial photos)
Rita Wenzel - Typesetting and layout

ISBN 0-9639067-3-9

This book is dedicated to God,
for the vision, guidance, wisdom and courage
to follow our dreams,

in loving memory of our parents,
Frank and Ethel Hermecz Wenzel
and
Cecil and Louise Reynolds Cantrell,
who showed us The Way;

and to:

The many fans who were interested in our project
and took the time to answer our questions,

Bob and Becky Smith for their belief in this book and us,

Charles R. Dixon, Jr., Richard S. Goodwin and R. Kirk Flowers
for their partnership so it could finally be printed,

John, John Coleman and Jonathan Cantrell
who first heard about our dreams and didn't think we were crazy,
and
Clay and Rusty Loveday for whom we dream,

Bud and Ina Wenzel Flowers,
who dubbed us "the dynamic duo" twenty-three years ago and have
proceeded to help keep us dynamic with their love and prayers,

Hubert and Lona Wenzel Phillips,
for their faith and belief that we could "do all things through Christ,"

Simone Lipscomb,
Kirk and Tammy Flowers,
Lance and Janet Lipscomb,
Chris and Kelly Flowers Tibbs,
Kerry and Christy Flowers,
who always said "you can do it" and helped to keep us going!

And finally, for Emily, Sydney, Brett, Ashton
and Baby Tibbs (due in November),
through whom **"the tradition continues."**

What makes Southeastern Conference football special? Is it our history as Southerners which has resulted in an "us against them" mentality? Is it the need to advance our sectional pride which others once sought to lay so low? Is it the South's love of the outdoors and combativeness? Is it our more traditional view of sex (the conquest) and gender roles? Is it all of the above? Yes, and MORE!

Football to the Southerner is an excuse to party, to be with friends in the good and the bad times. It is a way of keeping score with life--- a fantasy---yet too real.

When they've taken away prayer in schools, when they sell liquor on Sunday, when Dixie is no longer played and the Rebel flag is not unfurled, when they finally find a cure for kudzu . . . when all the things that made the South the South have passed away . . . football will remain!

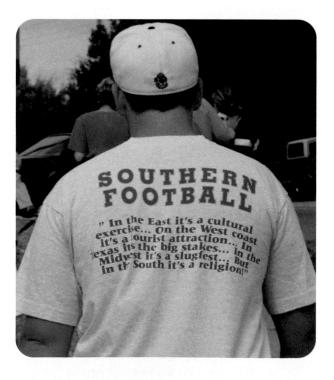

This t-shirt (which we "followed" after a game in Athens) says it all!

In 1992 nearly 1 out of 5 people who attended a Division 1A football game in the United States was attending a Southeastern Conference game. Though that seems like a large number, there are many fans who rarely travel to "away" games and many more who have never left the comfort of their living rooms!

This book was written for ALL those people! It includes information about the history, tradition and development of football at each school. The "Fan Scan" section shares tidbits from our interesting fan interviews. There is also a complete section about the growth and development of the Southeastern Conference as well as some superlative statistics. Even the correct color matching numbers are here so that you can distinguish between the reds, blues, oranges and golds of the twelve teams! Travel tips which we learned "the hard way" are included to help you better enjoy your whole gameday experience.

Although we were able to interview over 2,000 fans during the past two years, we know that is only a small percentage of people who follow and support SEC football. We hope **you** will take time to complete the "Fan Scan" included in the book and return it to us so that the future editions will be even more representative of what you, the fans think and feel. Since this is "**The** Fanatic's Guide to SEC Football," we would like to hear about your travel experiences and how you celebrate football. Perhaps you would even share your special gameday recipes!

It was fun to learn more about the SEC and its member schools. It was a joy to meet other fans and listen to them talk with pride and fervor about their team. It was an education and adventure that we want to share with you. So, sit back and prepare to have fun while you learn . . . and don't forget to take us with you to your next game . . . at home or away!

The following is a sample of the kind of questions which we asked those fans whom we interviewed for this book. We hope you will take the time to complete this survey and return it to us so that we can add your opinions to those we have already received.

Please answer the questions with regard to YOUR FAVORITE SEC SCHOOL and don't forget to name your school in the space provided below.

When you return your completed "Fan Scan" we would also appreciate any additional suggestions or comments to help us improve the next edition of "The Fanatic's Guide to SEC Football."

Thank you for your help . . . and we'll see you at the game!

(Put the name of your favorite SEC School here.)

1. Which SEC school do you consider your biggest rival?_____

2. What are your favorite "traditions" associated with football at your school?

3. What makes your school unique in the SEC?

4. Which of these SEC campuses have you visited to see a football game?

    ____Alabama   ____Georgia   ____Mississippi State
    ____Arkansas   ____Kentucky   ____South Carolina
    ____Auburn   ____LSU   ____Tennessee
    ____Florida   ____Ole Miss   ____Vanderbilt

5. How far have you traveled to see your school's team play?_____

6. How many games do you see your team play each year?
    1 - 4 _____   5 - 7 _____   10 or more_____

7. Besides your school's band, which SEC schools do you feel have the best band?
    1st_____ 2nd_____

8. If you had to pick another SEC school to attend as a student which one would it be?
    _____ Why?_____

9. Which SEC school would you be most upset to hear your child had decided to attend?
    _____ Why?_____

10. Besides your school's mascot, what is your favorite SEC mascot?_____

11. Are you a member of the Alumni Association? _____

    Other booster/scholarship group? Which one? _____

12. Do you usually wear school colors to the games? _____

13. What is your favorite place to stay in the area? _____

14. What is your favorite place to eat in the area? _____

15. What food(s) do you most associate with "gameday"? _____

    _____

16. What is your favorite way to spend the day on campus waiting for a game?
    _____Tailgating   _____Sightseeing in the area
    _____Visiting friends   _____I usually arrive just in time for the game
    _____Other (describe) _____

17. What is your age group? ____0-25 ____26-36 ____37-50 ____51-65 ___66+

18. Are you: ____Male ____Female

19. Are you: ____Student ____Alumnus ____Faculty member ____Just a fan!

20. How long have you been a fan? _____

21. What do you MOST enjoy about attending your school's football games?

22. What do you LEAST enjoy about attending your school's football games?

23. Do you favor the new conference alignment (East and West Divisions)?
    ___Yes   ____NO   ____NO OPINION

24. Do you like the idea of a championship game to determine the SEC champ and Sugar
    Bowl representative? ___Yes   ____NO   ____NO OPINION

THANK YOU for taking the time to answer our questions! If you would like us to keep in touch with you for more information and updates to "The Fanatic's Guide" please give us your name, address and phone number.

NAME:_____

ADDRESS:_____

_____

PHONE: _____

QUESTION	AL	ARK	AU	FL	GA
Who is your biggest rival in the SEC?	Auburn	Alabama	Alabama	Georgia	Florida
What is your favorite tradition?	Winning	Whooo, Pig! Sooie	Tiger Walk, Tailgating & War Eagle	Mr. 2 Bits	Tailgating
What makes you unique in the SEC?	Winning tradition	Mascot & Fans	Small town, Friendly & Colors	Fans	Tradition
What SEC school has the best band (other than yours)?	TN	FL	TN	TN	AL
Which other SEC school would you attend?	Vanderbilt	Alabama & LSU	Tennessee	Vanderbilt	Florida
Which SEC school would you not want your child to attend?	Auburn	Ole Miss	Alabama	Georgia	Florida
What is your favorite SEC mascot (other than your own)?	UGA	UGA & Bully	UGA & Albert	UGA	Colonel Reb
Do you wear school colors to the games?	67%	94%	89%	88%	100%
What is your favorite gameday food?	Hot dogs	BBQ	Chicken	Chicken	Chicken
What do you most enjoy on gameday?	Winning	Atmosphere & Fans	Atmosphere & Fans	Winning	Winning
What do you least enjoy on gameday?	Drunks	Parking & Traffic	Traffic	Losing	Losing
What is your favorite place to stay in the area?	Sheraton Capstone	Hilton & Park Inn	AU Hotel & Conference Center	Holiday Inn	Ramada Inn
What is your favorite place to eat in the area?	Dreamland BarBQ	AQ & Kirby's	Ryan's	Outback Steakhouse	The Grill
Do you favor the new conference alignment?	Y-52% N-44% *NO-4%	Y-56% N-6% *NO-38%	Y-50% N-38% *NO-12%	Y-38% N-35% *NO-26%	Y-54% N-20% *NO-26%
Do you like the idea of a championship game?	Y-74 N-22 *NO-4%	Y-78% N-11% *NO-11%	Y-56% N-33% *NO-11%	Y-78 N-17 *NO-5%	Y-73% N-25% *NO-2%

NO - No Opinion

"FAN SCAN" SURVEY RESULTS

KY	LSU	MISS	MSU	USC	TN	VAN
Tennessee	Ole Miss	Miss. State	Ole Miss	Georgia	Alabama	Tennessee
Tailgating	Mike circling the field	The Grove	Cowbells	2001	Running through the T	Tailgating
Fans	Fans	Traditions	Fans	Location	Fan support	Academics, private school & small size
TN	AL	AL	AL	GA	AL	TN
Vanderbilt	Alabama & Florida	Alabama	Auburn	Georgia	Florida	Alabama
Tennessee	Ole Miss	Miss. State	Ole Miss	Auburn	Alabama	Tennessee
None!	Smokey	UGA	Albert	UGA	UGA & Mike	Big AL
94%	87%	68%	85%	78%	91%	80%
Chili	Jambalaya	Chicken	BarBQ	Chicken	Chicken	Burgers
Tailgating	Death Valley Atmosphere	Friends	Friends	Game	Friends	Friends
Losing	Losing	Losing	Nothing	Losing	Losing	Losing
Hyatt	Hilton	Holiday Inn	Motor home	Embassy Suites	Hyatt	Holiday Inn
Applebee's, Outback & O'Charley's	Ralph & Kacoo's	Downtown Grill	Tailgate	California Dreaming	Bayou Bay, Regas & Calhoun's	Houston's
Y-72% N-6% *NO-22%	Y-43% N-24% *NO-43%	NOT ON SURVEY	Y-79% N-14% *NO-7%	Y-71% N-6% *NO-23%	Y-50% N-50$ *NO-10%	Y-66% N-17% *NO-17%
Y-94% N-0 *NO-6%	Y-71% N-21% *NO-8%	NOT ON SURVEY	Y-86% N-14% *NO-0	Y-94% N-6% *NO-0	Y-36% N-50% *NO-14%	Y-83% N-0% *NO-17%

NO - No Opinion

SEC FOOTBALL IS . . .

FALL . . .

FUN . . .

FOOD . . .

FAMILY . . .

FRIENDS . . .

F
E
U
D
S . . .

...*FANTASTIC!!!*

THE SOUTHEASTERN CONFERENCE
1992 IN REVIEW
What a year for SEC football!

The conference celebrated its 60th birthday.

Four member institutions celebrated
their football centennials:
Alabama, Auburn, Georgia and South Carolina.

New league members, Arkansas and South Carolina,
competed in their first season of SEC football.

The SEC followed a football schedule based on new
divisional alignment for the first time.

The first Conference Championship Game was played
(Alabama 28, Florida 21).

For the 11th time in the last 12 years at least half of the
SEC's teams appeared in post-season bowl games,
winning five, loosing one.

The SEC had the best winning percentage against
non-conference opponents of any
collegiate football conference -- 75% (27-9).

Billy Brewer of Ole Miss became the Dean of SEC
football coaches on the eve of his 11th season
following the resignations of Tennessee coach,
Johnny Majors (1977-1992), and Auburn's,
Pat Dye (1981-1992).

Alabama's Gene Stallings won SEC and National
Coach of the Year honors.

Alabama won the National Championship
by defeating Miami in the Sugar Bowl, 34-13, uniting
SEC fans in pride for their league.

SEC HISTORY

Although the SEC officially celebrated its 60th birthday in 1992, the league can trace its roots back to the late 1800's and the formation of the Southern Intercollegiate Athletic Association (SIAA). Football was beginning to rival baseball as a college sport and basketball was in its infancy. With the growth in team sports came the need to standardize rules and manage competition. It was only natural that organizational efforts would be made among the schools to meet this and other needs.

When the SIAA was formed on December 22, 1894, almost all of the present-day members of the SEC were playing football (11 were playing by 1895 and Florida began in 1906). The SIAA had seven charter members: Alabama, Auburn, Georgia, Georgia Tech, North Caolina, Sewanee and Vanderbilt. Within a year twelve more schools had joined and by 1920 the Association claimed 30 member institutions from Texas to Virginia!

In December of 1920 at a meeting in Gainesville, Florida, presided over by Professor S. V. Sanford of Georgia, fourteen of the larger schools in the SIAA reorganized as the Southern Conference. Charter members of this new league included: Alabama, Auburn, Clemson, Georgia, Georgia Tech, Kentucky, Maryland, Mississippi State, North Carolina, North Carolina State, Tennessee, Virginia, Virginia Tech and Washington and Lee. Efforts to limit the size of the new conference were unsuccessful. By 1928 there were twenty-three members! By that time Florida, Louisiana State, South Carolina, Tulane, Vanderbilt, VMI, Sewanee and Duke had joined.

Once again reorganization proved necessary. On December 8-9, 1932, in Knoxville, Tennessee, the thirteen members west and south of the Appalachians realigned as the Southeastern Conference. The ten member schools from the eastern seaboard remained in the Southern Conference.

Membership in the SEC has been fairly stable over the decades. On December 13, 1940, Sewanee withdrew. On June 1, 1964, Georgia Tech quit the league, followed by Tulane on June 1, 1966. But in 1990, the first new members were added: Arkansas on August 1 and South Carolina on September 25! At the end of sixty years the SEC boasts twelve strong teams, just one less than at the beginning. Speculation continues that two other institutions will be brought into the league since the divisional alignment has made a larger conference more workable.

Within a few years after the founding of the conference, it became apparent that strong leadership and direction were needed within the league to deal with the growing complexity of intercollegiate sports. So, in 1940, the office of Conference Commissioner was created. Jackson, Mississippi, served as the first headquarters for the league's staff. In 1948, the office moved to Birmingham, Alabama, where it remains today. Altogether, six commissioners have led the SEC to its position of pre-eminence among intercollegiate athletic conferences. By every yardstick, from attendance, to national championships, to revenue, the SEC is the envy of its rivals!

SEC HEADQUARTERS

After forty-three years in Birmingham, the SEC finally has a home befitting its status as the premier conference in America. In October, 1991, the staff of twenty-four saw their offices moved into a specially constructed, two story building in downtown Birmingham. The thirty thousand square foot facility was provided by the city and insures ample room for the diverse operations of the conference including certifying athletic eligibility, managing championship events, monitoring NCAA and SEC compliance, coordinating officiating assignments, negotiating television contracts, distributing conference revenue and coordinating all media and public relations activities.

The new headquarters building is located at 2201 Civic Center Boulevard just off Interstate Highway 20-59. It is adjacent to the Birmingham-Jefferson Civic Center. The most impressive feature of the building is the foyer entrance which is highlighted by a two story rotunda where school banners are hung and displays honoring the current league champion in each of the eighteen conference sports may be found. The rotunda gracefully links the two galleries where exhibits centering on the twelve member institutions and the league's history are showcased. A research library is also housed within the facility.

When football was introduced into the Southeastern U.S. in the latter part of the nineteenth century it moved like Sherman through Georgia. Unlike the earlier one, this "northern invasion" was most welcome.

Kentucky was the first of the present-day members of the SEC to participate in football back in the 1880's. It was not until 1891 however, that Kentucky, Tennessee and Vanderbilt all began to play on a regular basis. For that reason, these three schools all celebrated their 100th season of football in 1991. Four more schools reached their centennial year in 1992: Alabama, Auburn, Georgia and South Carolina.

In 1993 Ole Miss celebrates "A Century of Heroes" and LSU looks back on "A Golden Century." Arkansas will blow out 100 candles in 1994! Mississippi State will achieve the century mark in 1995, but Florida, the last of the SEC schools to hit the gridiron, will have to wait until 2006!

The SEC consistently leads all football conferences in every aspect of attendance: total attendance, average attendance and percentage of capacity! 1992 was no exception.

Although many games were "sellouts" with capacity crowds, tickets were generally available before gametime at or below face value, or somewhat above for "big" games where ticket scalping is legal or permitted. The only game we encountered where tickets were very scarce and prohibitively expensive was the Sugar Bowl.

We report this to encourage those fans who are not season ticket holders, or who may not have secured a ticket in advance, to go to the game anyway. Do not be deterred from supporting your team in person. The worst that could happen is that you might have to watch or listen to the game with tailgaters who choose to remain outside the stadium. But if we were gamblers, we would bet that you could find a ticket! In our opinion, this live experience, complete with campus atmosphere, is much more rewarding than staying home and being a couch potato.

1992 SEC HOME ATTENDANCE

RANK	TEAM	AVERAGE	PERCENTAGE OF CAPACITY
1	TENNESSEE	95,924	104.4
2	FLORIDA	83,945	101.2
3	GEORGIA	83,194	97.4
4	ALABAMA	75,696	98.8
5	AUBURN	72,936	85.6
6	LSU	67,221	83.9
7	SO. CAROLINA	63,728	88.0
8	KENTUCKY	54,146	93.7
9	ARKANSAS	44.751	84.1
10	MISS. STATE	39,420	95.7
11	VANDERBILT	38,178	93.1
12	OLE MISS	36,464	80.8

The largest crowd to witness an SEC game in 1992 was in Knoxville at the Tennessee-Alabama game on October 17, which attracted 97,388 fans. The smallest crowd was the 22,500 spectators present for the Ole Miss-Louisiana Tech game at Oxford on November 14.

Which SEC team provided the biggest fan draw around the league? In 1992 it was Alabama who won that distinction by packing the stands wherever they went. Four of Alabama's SEC opponents who played the Tide on their home turf reported their biggest conference attendance. Three teams can thank Georgia for their largest league crowd of the year, while Tennessee brought the most fans to two stadiums. LSU, Auburn, Ole Miss and Kentucky each were responsible for one school's largest SEC home crowd.

Altogether, seven different conference teams helped achieve attendance records at their sister institutions--strong evidence of the SEC's competitive health and balance!

With the growth of the league to twelve member schools,the SEC has divided into two six-team divisions and mandated an eight game conference schedule in football. The 1992 season was the inaugural one for this new arrangement.

A 5-2-1 schedule format is followed which is designed to allow each school to play all five of its division opponents along with two permanent and one rotating non-division opponent each year. Schools play each rotating non-division opponent two years (at home and away) before rotating to another cross-conference foe. This format guarantees that each school will play every member of the league at least twice during an eight year period.

Eastern Division	Western Division
Florida	Alabama
Georgia	Arkansas
Kentucky	Auburn
South Carolina	LSU
Tennessee	Ole Miss
Vanderbilt	Mississippi State

SEC 1992 FINAL STANDINGS

EASTERN DIVISION

	SEC	Pct.	ALL	Pct.
*FLORIDA	6-2	.750	8-4	.667
*GEORGIA	6-2	.750	9-2	.818
TENNESSEE	5-3	.625	8-3	.727
SO. CAROLINA	3-5	.375	5-6	.455
KENTUCKY	2-6	.250	4-7	.364
VANDERBILT	2-6	.250	4-7	.364

*Eastern Division Co-Champions

WESTERN DIVISION

	SEC	Pct.	ALL	Pct.
*ALABAMA	8-0	1.000	12-0	1.000
OLE MISS	5-3	.625	8-3	.727
MISS. STATE	4-4	.500	7-4	.636
ARKANSAS	3-4-1	.438	3-7-1	.318
AUBURN	2-5-1	.313	5-5-1	.500
LSU	1-7	.125	2-9	.182

*Western Division and SEC Champion

THE SEC IN POST 1992 SEASON BOWL GAMES

Florida Citrus Bowl
Georgia (9-2) 21, Ohio State (8-2-1) 14
Hall of Fame Bowl
Tennessee (8-3) 38, Boston College (8-2-1) 23
Liberty Bowl
Ole Miss (8-3) 13, Air Force (7-4) 0
Outback Steakhouse Gator Bowl
Florida (8-4) 27, North Carolina State (9-2-1) 10
Peach Bowl
North Carolina (8-3) 21, **Mississippi State (7-4) 17**
USF&G Sugar Bowl
Alabama (12-0) 34, Miami (11-0) 13

Alabama
Permanent Non-Division (2): Tennessee, Vanderbilt
Rotating Non-Division (1):

1993 at So. Carolina	1996 Kentucky	1998 Florida
1994 Georgia	1997 at Kentucky	1999 at Florida
1995 at Georgia		

Arkansas
Permanent Non-Division (2): South Carolina, Tennessee
Rotating Non-Division (1):

1993 at Georgia	1996 Florida	1998 Kentucky
1994 Vanderbilt	1997 at Florida	1999 at Kentucky
1995 at Vanderbilt		

Auburn
Permanent Non-Division (2): Florida, Georgia
Rotating Non-Division (1):

1993 at Vanderbilt	1996 So. Carolina	1998 Tennessee
1994 Kentucky	1997 at So. Carolina	1999 at Tennessee
1995 at Kentucky		

Louisiana State University
Permanent Non-Division (2): Florida, Kentucky
Rotating Non-Division (1):

1993 at Tennessee	1996 Vanderbilt	1998 Georgia
1994 So. Carolina	1997 at Vanderbilt	1999 at Georgia
1995 at So. Carolina		

Ole Miss
Permanent Non-Division (2): Georgia, Vanderbilt
Rotating Non-Division (1):

1993 at Kentucky	1996 Tennessee	1998 So. Carolina
1994 Florida	1997 at Tennessee	1999 at So. Carolina
1995 at FLorida		

Mississippi State
Permanent Non-Division (2): Kentucky, South Carolina
Rotating Non-Division (1):

1993 at Florida	1996 Georgia	1998 Vanderbilt
1994 Tennessee	1997 at Georgia	1999 at Vanderbilt
1995 at Tennessee		

Florida
Permanent Non-Division (2): Auburn, LSU
Rotating Non-Division (1):

1993 Miss. State	1996 at Arkansas	1998 at Alabama
1994 at Ole Miss	1997 Arkansas	1999 Alabama
1995 Ole Miss		

Georgia
Permanent Non-Division (2): Auburn, Ole Miss
Rotating Non-Division (1):

1993 Arkansas	1996 at Miss. State	1998 at LSU
1994 at Alabama	1997 Miss. State	1999 LSU
1995 Alabama		

Kentucky
Permanent Non-Division (2): LSU, Mississippi State
Rotating Non-Division (1):

1993 Ole Miss	1996 at Alabama	1998 at Arkansas
1994 at Auburn	1997 Alabama	1999 Arkansas
1995 Auburn		

South Carolina
Permanent Non-Division (2): Arkansas, Mississippi State
Rotating Non-Division (1):

1993 Alabama	1996 at Auburn	1998 at Ole Miss
1994 at LSU	1997 Auburn	1999 Ole Miss
1995 LSU		

Tennessee
Permanent Non-Division (2): Alabama, Arkansas
Rotating Non-Division (1):

1993 LSU	1996 at Ole Miss	1998 at Auburn
1994 at Miss. State	1997 Ole Miss	1999 Auburn
1995 Miss. State		

Vanderbilt
Permanent Non-Division (2): Alabama, Ole Miss
Rotating Non-Division (1):

1993 Auburn	1996 at LSU	1998 at Miss. State
1994 at Arkansas	1997 LSU	1999 Miss. State
1995 Arkansas		

The first Conference Championship Game was held December 5, 1992, and saw Western Division champ, Alabama, win a thriller over Eastern Division representative, Florida, at Birmingham's Legion Field. (The SEC and Birmingham have an agreement to play the next four title games there) As the victor, Alabama received an automatic invitation to the USF&G Sugar Bowl. This was the first time a championship game was used by a Division IA conference to determine the title winner.

The need, as well as the possibility for such a game, grew out of the expansion of the SEC from ten teams to twelve. When a conference has that many members, fairness and competition, as well as fan interest, are better served if two teams have a shot at the championship rather than just one. Under NCAA regulations, a conference with twelve or more members may play a twelfth game to determine its champion, provided a divisional alignment has been used in the regular season.

The participants in the championship game are determined by the best overall SEC winning percentage in each division after the mandated eight game regular season conference schedule. In the event of a tie for a divisional championship, the following procedures are used to break all ties and determine the divisional representative in the Championship Game:

A. Two Team Tie
1. Head-to-head competition between the two tied teams.
2. Records of the tied teams within the division.
3. Head-to-head competition versus the team within the division with the best overall (divisional and non-divisional) conference record and proceeding through the division. Multiple ties within the division will be broken from first to last.

4. Overall record versus non-division teams.
5. Combined record versus all common non-divisional teams.
6. Record versus common non-divisional team with the best overall conference (divisional and non-divisional) record and proceeding through the other common non-divisional teams based on their order of finish within their division.
7. Vote of the Athletic Directors whose institutions are not involved in the tie.

B. Three (or More) Team Tie
(Once the tie has been reduced to two teams, go to the two team tie breaker format)
1. Combined head-to-head record among the tied teams.
2. Record of the tied teams within the division.
3. Head-to-head competition versus the team within the division with the best overall (divisional and non-divisional) conference record and proceeding through the division. Multiple ties within the division will be broken from first to last.
4. Overall record versus non-division teams.
5. Combined record versus all comon non-divisional teams.
6. Record versus common non-divisional team with the best overall conference (divisional and non-divisional) record and proceeding through other common non-divisional teams based on their order of finish within their division.
7. Vote of the Athletic Directors whose institutions are not involved in the tie.

One interesting aspect of the Championship Game itself is the first-time-ever (for a Division IA conference) provision for a tie breaking system. In the event of a tie at the end of regulation play in the Championship Game, NCAA Rule 3-1-3 (Extra Periods) will apply. An extra period shall consist of two series with both teams putting the ball in play at their opponent's 25 yard line. Each team retains the ball until it scores or fails to make a first down. The team scoring the greater number of points during regulation and the extra period(s) shall be declared the winner.

Florida Gator team members receive encouragement as they take the field prior to the second half of the '92 Championship game.

The Florida Band warms the chilled crowd at the inaugural Championship Game.

Bama players warm up for the final test on their way to the 1992 SEC title.

Flags fly in the frigid wind as the Alabama band performs at the '92 Championship Game.

	ALA	ARK	AUB	FLA	GA	KY
	W-L-T	W-L-T	W-L-T	W-L-T	W-L-T	W-L-T
ALABAMA	----	3-0-0	33-23-1	*18-8-0	33-22-4	30-1-1
ARKANSAS	0-3-0	----	0-1-1	1-0-0	3-2-0	0-1-1
AUBURN	23-33-1	1-0-1	----	37-30-2	45-44-7	20-5-1
FLORIDA	*8-17-0	0-1-0	30-37-2	----	*25-43-2	26-17-0
GEORGIA	22-33-4	3-2-0	44-45-7	*44-25-2	----	35-9-2
KENTUCKY	1-30-1	0-0-0	5-20-1	17-26-0	9-35-2	----
LSU	14-37-5	23-13-2	15-11-1	18-18-3	12-7-1	31-11-1
MISSISSIPPI	6-32-2	*19-19-1	6-11-0	9-7-1	9-21-1	23-11-1
MISS STATE	11-63-3	3-0-0	18-46-2	16-29-2	5-12-0	*8-13-0
SO CAROLINA	0-8-0	0-1-0	1-2-1	3-7-3	9-34-2	1-2-1
TENNESSEE	27-41-7	3-1-0	18-22-3	15-7-0	10-10-2	56-23-9
VANDERBILT	18-48-4	1-2-0	*19-14-1	9-15-2	16-35-2	*32-30-4

	LSU	MISS	MSU	USC	TN	VAN
	W-L-T	W-L-T	W-L-T	W-L-T	W-L-T	W-L-T
ALABAMA	37-14-5	32-6-2	63-11-3	8-0-0	41-27-7	48-18-4
ARKANSAS	13-23-2	*20-18-1	0-3-0	1-0-0	1-3-0	2-1-0
AUBURN	11-15-1	11-6-0	46-18-2	2-1-1	22-18-3	*13-19-1
FLORIDA	18-18-3	7-9-1	29-16-2	7-3-3	7-15-0	15-9-2
GEORGIA	7-12-1	21-9-1	12-5-0	34-9-2	10-10-2	35-16-2
KENTUCKY	11-31-1	11-23-1	*13-7-0	2-1-1	23-56-9	*29-32-4
LSU	----	45-32-4	51-32-3	12-1-0	3-17-3	16-7-1
MISSISSIPPI	32-45-4	----	52-31-6	4-5-0	18-39-1	34-31-2
MISS STATE	32-51-3	31-52-6	----	0-1-0	14-22-1	7-6-2
SO CAROLINA	1-12-0	5-4-0	1-0-0	----	2-7-2	2-0-0
TENNESSEE	17-3-3	39-18-1	22-14-1	7-2-2	----	*55-26-5
VANDERBILT	7-16-1	31-34-2	6-7-2	0-2-0	*27-55-5	----

*Disagreement between schools about series record

SOUTHEASTERN CONFERENCE
ALL-TIME FOOTBALL STANDINGS
1933-1992

CURRENT MEMBERS

TEAM	SEASONS	TOTAL GAMES	W - L - T	PCT.	1992 SEC RECORD
ALABAMA	59	400	279-101-20	.723	8-0
TENNESSEE	59	360	217-124-19	.629	5-3
GEORGIA	60	359	210-136-13	.603	6-2
LSU	60	365	196-148-21	.566	1-7
OLE MISS	59	355	186-154-15	.545	5-3
AUBURN	59	379	195-167-17	.537	2-5-1
FLORIDA	59	351	167-169-15	.497	6-2
ARKANSAS	1	8	3 - 4 - 1	.438	3-4-1
SO CAROLINA	1	8	3 - 5 - 0	.375	3-5
KENTUCKY	59	359	113-234-12	.331	2-6
MISS STATE	59	365	114-240-11	.327	4-4
VANDERBILT	58	367	97-252-18	.289	2-6

FORMER MEMBERS

GEORGIA TECH	31	194	115-70-9	.616	--
TULANE	33	195	69-113-13	.387	--
SEWANEE	8	37	0 - 37 - 0	.000	--

NOTE: Sewanee withdrew after the 1940 season, Georgia Tech after 1963 and Tulane after 1965. During World War II Alabama, Auburn, Florida, Kentucky, Ole Miss, Mississippi State, Tennessee and Vanderbilt suspended football in 1943; Vanderbilt through 1944. Appointed conference games of 1954, '58, '64, '65, '66, '67, '68, and the Alabama-Ole Miss games of 1980 and '81 are not included in these records or total points.

TOP 10 ALL-TIME SEC COACHING LEADERS
(Victories as an SEC Head Coach Since 1933)

1. Paul "Bear" Bryant (Kentucky, 1946-53; Alabama 1958-82) ... 292
2. Vince Dooley (Georgia, 1964-88) 201
3. Johnny Vaught (Ole Miss, 1947-70, 1973) 190
4. Ralph "Shug" Jordan (Auburn, 1951-75) 176
5. Wally Butts (Georgia, 1939-60) 140
6. Charlie McClendon (LSU,1962-79) 137
7. Johnny Majors (Tennessee, 1977-92) 115
8. Bob Neyland (Tennessee, 1933-34, 1936-40, 1946-52) 112
9. Doug Dickey (Tennessee, 1964-69; Florida 1970-78) 104
10. Pat Dye (Auburn, 1981-92) 99

SEC CHAMPIONSHIP COACHES (Includes Ties)

Paul "Bear" Bryant (14)	Kentucky (1) 1950; Alabama (13)1961,64,65,66,71,72,73,74,75,77,78,79,81
Johnny Vaught (6)	Ole Miss 1947, 54, 55, 60, 62, 63
Vince Dooley (6)	Georgia 1966, 68, 76, 80, 81, 82
Bob Neyland (5)	Tennessee 1938, 39, 40, 46, 51
Pat Dye (4)	Auburn 1983, 87, 88, 89
Frank Thomas (4)	Alabama 1933, 34, 37, 45
Wally Butts (4)	Georgia 1942, 46, 48, 59
Bill Alexander (3)	Georgia Tech 1939, 43, 44
Johnny Majors (3)	Tennessee 1985, 89, 90
Bernie Moore (2)	LSU 1935, 36
Paul Dietzel (2)	LSU 1958, 61
Doug Dickey (2)	Tennessee 1967, 69
Bobby Dodd (2)	Georgia Tech 1951, 52
Allyn McKeen (1)	Mississippi State 1941
Red Drew (1)	Alabama 1953
Bowden Wyatt (1)	Tennessee 1956
Ralph "Shug" Jordan (1)	Auburn 1957
Charlie McClendon (1)	LSU 1970
Fran Curci (1)	Kentucky 1976
Bill Arnsperger (1)	LSU 1986
Mike Archer (1)	LSU 1988
Bill Curry (1)	Alabama 1989
Steve Spurrier (1)	Florida 1991
Gene Stallings (1)	Alabama 1992

ACTIVE HEAD COACHES
(Victories as an SEC Head Coach Through 1992)

Billy Brewer	Ole Miss	62
Bill Curry	Alabama & Kentucky	37
Gene Stallings	Alabama	31
Ray Goff	Georgia	29
Steve Spurrier	Florida	28
Jackie Sherrill	Mississippi State	14
Gerry DiNardo	Vanderbilt	9
Curley Hallman	LSU	7
Sparky Woods	South Carolina	5
Phil Fulmer	Tennessee	4
Danny Ford	Arkansas	—
Terry Bowden	Auburn	—

30 / THE FANATIC'S GUIDE TO SEC FOOTBALL

SEC FOOTBALL TITLES
BY TEAMS

CURRENT MEMBERS

ALABAMA (20)	1933, [1]34, 37, 45, 53, [5]61, 64, 65, [6]66, 71, 72, 73, 74, 75, 77, 78, 79, [8]81, [10]89, 92
TENNESSEE (11)	1938, [2]39, 40, [3]46, [4]51, 56, 67, 69, 85, [10]89, 90
GEORGIA (10)	1942, [3]46, 48, 59, [6]66, 68, [7]76, 80, [8]81, 82
LOUISIANA STATE (7)	1935, 36, 58, [5]61, 70, 86, [9]88
MISSISSIPPI (6)	1947, 54, 55, 60, 62, 63
AUBURN (5)	1957, 83, 87, [9]88, [10]89
KENTUCKY (2)	1950, [7]76
MISSISSIPPI STATE (1)	1941
FLORIDA (1)	1991
VANDERBILT (0)	—

FORMER MEMBERS

GEORGIA TECH (5)	[2]1939, 1943, 1944, [4]1951, 1952
TULANE (3)	[1]1934, [2]1939, 1949
SEWANEE (0)	—

[1] Alabama & Tulane tied (1934)
[2] Tennessee, Georgia Tech and Tulane tied (1939)
[3] Tennessee & Georgia tied (1946)
[4] Tennessee & Georgia Tech tied (1951)
[5] Alabama & LSU tied (1961)
[6] Alabama & Georgia tied (1966)
[7] Georgia & Kentucky tied (1976)
[8] Alabama & Georgia tied (1981)
[9] LSU & Auburn tied (1988)
[10] Alabama, LSU & Auburn tied (1989)

SEC ALL-TIME BOWL GAME RECORDS
(Through Post 1992 Season Bowls)

	W	L	T	TOTAL
ALABAMA	25	17	3	45
ARKANSAS	9	15	3	27
AUBURN	12	9	2	23
FLORIDA	9	11	0	20
GEORGIA	15	13	3	31
KENTUCKY	5	2	0	7
LSU	11	16	1	28
MISSISSIPPI	14	11	0	25
MISSISSIPPI STATE	4	4	0	8
SOUTH CAROLINA	0	8	0	8
TENNESSEE	18	15	0	33
VANDERBILT	1	1	1	3

For the next two years the following contracts/agreements are in effect between the SEC and the Bowl Coalitions.

USF&G SUGAR BOWL -- SEC Champion will play a Coalition One Team.

Date:	Saturday, January 1	Stadium:	Superdome (77,000)
Time:	7:30 PM (CST)	TV:	ABC
Site:	New Orleans, LA	Teams:	SEC Champion vs. Coalition team

CompUSA FLORIDA CITRUS BOWL -- The SEC and the Big Ten co-champion or runner-up will meet. The SEC team will be selected from the following:

1. SEC Championship Game runner-up, or
2. Conference team that has an equal or better record, or
3. Conference team ranked in the USA Today/CNN Coaches' Poll within five places of either team participating in the SEC Championship Game as of the first Monday after the regular season ends.

Date:	Saturday, January 1	Stadium:	Citrus Bowl (72,000)
Time:	1:30 PM (EST)	TV:	ABC
Site:	Orlando, FL	Teams:	SEC 2 vs. Big Ten 2

OUTBACK STEAKHOUSE GATOR BOWL -- The SEC will provide a top team to play a member of the Bowl Coalition Two.

Date:	Friday, December 31	Stadium:	Gator Bowl (80,128)
Time:	7:00 PM (EST)	TV:	TBS
Site:	Jacksonville, FL	Teams:	SEC 3 vs. Coalition

PEACH BOWL -- Will select the fourth SEC bowl team.

Date:	Friday, December 31	Stadium:	Georgia Dome (71,000)
Time:	6:00 PM (EST)	TV:	ESPN
Site:	Atlanta, GA	Teams:	SEC 4 vs. ACC 3

SUNSHINE FOOTBALL CLASSIC (formerly Blockbuster Bowl) -- Will match one of the top three teams in the Big East Football Conference with the fifth place SEC team.

Date:	Saturday, January 1	Stadum:	Joe Robbie Stadium (75,000)
Time:	1:30 PM (EST)	TV:	CBS
Site:	Ft. Lauderdale, FL	Teams:	SEC 5 vs. Big East 3

BOWL COALITIONS

Coalition One: Sugar, Cotton and Orange Bowls will select in order of the rank of their host teams, from a pool of five teams: Notre Dame, ACC Champion, Big East Champion, and two at-large teams (ACC, Big East, Big Eight, PAC-10 and SWC). Fiesta Bowl will choose from the remaining pool of teams.

Coalition Two: The Gator Bowl will select one team and the Hancock Bowl will select two teams from the remaining three teams.

SEC BOWL REVENUE DISTRIBUTION

(A) For bowl games providing receipts which result in a balance of less than $2,000,000 (two million), the participating institution shall retain the first $500,000 plus 20 percent of the balance. The remainder shall be remitted to the Commissioner and will be divided into 13 equal shares with two shares to the Conference and one share to each of the other 11 institutions. (Participating institution does not share in the distribution of shares.)

(B) For bowl games providing receipts which result in a balance of more than $2,000,000 (two million), the participating institution shall retain the first $700,000 plus 20 percent of the balance. The remainder shall be remitted to the Commissioner and will be divided into 13 equal shares with two shares to the Conference and one share to each of the other 11 institutions. (Participating institution does not share in the distribution of shares.)

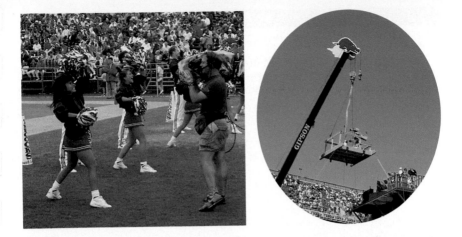

SEC GAMES' TELECAST

The SEC has a contract with Jefferson Pilot Sports extending through the 1995 season to telecast 12 or 13 games annually to a nine state area in the Southeast. The telecasts are syndicated to stations within the SEC area and offered, through cable or over-the-air distribution, to an even larger geographic area.

The Southeastern Conference and its member schools are part of the College Football Association (CFA) and, as such, are bound by contracts with ABC and ESPN television networks to the following extent. Games will be selected 12 days in advance after September and will be broadcast in the early Saturday afternoon time slot (12:40 PM Eastern).

The SEC has a three year contract with ABC Sports to televise the Championship Game from Birmingham. Air time is 2:30 PM CST.

The SEC has produced more than its share of outstanding football players over the years. Many of them have been recognized by prestigious organizations as the best in their class. Some of those honored and the awards they garnered include:

SEC Heisman Trophy Winners:
(Presented by the Downtown Athletic Club of New York to the Outstanding College Football Player in America)

1942	Frank Sinkwich	Georgia Halfback
1959	Billy Cannon	LSU Halfback
1966	Steve Spurrier	Florida Quarterback
1971	Pat Sullivan	Auburn Quarterback
1982	Herschel Walker	Georgia Tailback
1985	Bo Jackson	Auburn Tailback

SEC Outland Trophy Winners:
(Presented by the Football Writers Association of America to the Outstanding Interior Lineman in America)

1950	Bob Gain	Kentucky Tackle
1958	Zeke Smith	Auburn Guard
1964	Steve DeLong	Tennessee Tackle
1968	Bill Stanfill	Georgia Tackle
1988	Tracy Rocker	Auburn Defensive Tackle

SEC Vince Lombardi Award Winners:
(Presented by the Rotary Club of Houston to the Outstanding College Lineman of the Year)

| 1986 | Cornelius Bennett | Alabama Linebacker |
| 1988 | Tracy Rocker | Auburn Defensive Tackle |

SEC Butkus Award Winners:
(Presented by the Downtown Athletic Club of Orlando to the Top Collegiate Linebacker)

| 1988 | Derrick Thomas | Alabama Linebacker |

SEC Maxwell Award Winners:
(Presented by the Maxwell Football Club of Philadelphia to the Nation's Outstanding Football Player)

| 1946 | Charley Trippi | Georgia Halfback |
| 1982 | Herschel Walker | Georgia Tailback |

SOUTHEASTERN CONFERENCE
INDIVIDUAL RECORDS

TOTAL OFFENSE

PLAYS

Game   78 - Whit Taylor, Vanderbilt vs Georgia
20 Rushes, 58 Passes 1982

Season   559 - Whit Taylor, Vanderbilt
153 Rushes, 406 Passes 1982

Career   1,397 - Shane Matthews, Florida 1989-92

YARDS GAINED

Game   540 - Archie Manning, Ole Miss vs Alabama
104 Rushing, 436 Passing 1969

Season   3,159 - Shane Matthews, Florida
10 Rushing, 3, 130 Passing, 19 Receiving 1991

Career   9,241 - Shane Matthews, FLorida (35 Games) 1989-92

YARDS PER GAME

Season   285.6 - Pat Sullivan, Auburn
270 Rushing, 2,586 Passing, 10 Games 1970

Career   264.0 - Shane Matthews, Florida
9,241 Yards in 35 Games 1989-92

YARDS PER PLAY

Game   (Min. 10 Plays) 21.4 - Eagle Day
Ole Miss vs. Villanova (10 for 214) 1954

Game   (Min. 20 Plays) 12.8 - Pat Sullivan
Auburn vs. Florida (30 for 384) 1970

Game   (Min. 40 Plays) 8.6 - Eric Jones
Vanderbilt vs. Rutgers (43 for 368) 1987

Game   (Min. 50 Plays) 8.14 - Whit Taylor
Vanderbilt vs. Tennessee (64 for 521) 1981

Season   (Min. 300 Plays) 8.57 - Pat Sullivan, Auburn
(333 for 2,856) 1970

Career   (Min. 900 Plays) 7.03 - Pat Sullivan, Auburn
(974 for 6,844) 1969-71

TOUCHDOWN RESPONSIBILITY

Game   7 - Showboat Boykin, Ole Miss vs. Miss. State (All Rushing) 1951

Season   30 - Shane Matthews, Florida
(1 Rushing, 28 Passing, 1 Receiving) 1991

Career   82 - Shane Matthews, Florida
(7 Rushing, 74 Passing, 1 Receiving) 1989-92

RUSHING

MOST RUSHES
Game   47 - Herschel Walker, Georgia vs. Florida (192 Yards) 1981
Season 385 - Herschel Walker, Georgia (1,891 Yards) 1981
*Career 994 - Herschel Walker, Georgia (5,259 Yards) 1980-82

RUSHES PER GAME
Season 35.0 - Herschel Walker, Georgia (385 in 11 Games) 1981
Career 30.1 Herschel Walker, Georgia (994 in 33 Games) 1980-82

YARDS GAINED
Game   321 - Frank Mordica, Vanderbilt vs. Air Force (22 Rushes) 1978
Season 1,891 - Herschel Walker, Georgia (385 Rushes) 1981
*Career 5,259 - Herschel Walker, Georgia (33 Games) 1980-82

YARDS PER GAME
Season 171.9 - Herschel Walker, Georgia (1,891 in 11 Games) 1981
Career 159.4 - Herschel Walker, Georgia (5,259 in 33 Games) 1980-82

YARDS PER RUSH
Game   (Min. 40 Rushes) 6.5 - Herschel Walker
        Georgia vs. Ole Miss (265 on 41) 1981
Game   (Min. 30 Rushes) 10.2 - Emmitt Smith
        Florida vs. New Mexico (316 on 31) 1989
Game   (Min. 20 Rushes) 14.6 - Frank Mordica
        Vanderbilt vs. Air Force (321 on 22) 1978
Game   (Min. 10 Rushes) 19.6 - Harvey Williams
        LSU vs. Rice (196 on 10) 1987
Season (Min. 200 Rushes) 6.8 - Garrison Hearst, Georgia
        (228 for 1,547) 1992
Season (Min. 100 Rushes) 8.3 - Brent Fullwood, Auburn   (1,391 on 167) 1986
Career (Min. 400 Rushes) 6.6 - Bo Jackson, Auburn   (4,303 on 650) 1982-85

TOUCHDOWNS RUSHING
Season   18 - Herschel Walker, Georgia 1981
Career   49 - Herschel Walker, Georgia 1980-82
LONG TOUCHDOWN PLAYS (Rushing)
Game   99 - Kelsey Finch, Tennessee vs. Florida 1977
ALL-PURPOSE YARDS
Season   180.7 - Herschel Walker, Georgia
        (1,891 Rushing, 84 Receiving, 92 KOR in 11 Games) 1981
Career   5,749 - Herschel Walker, Georgia
        (5,249 Rushing, 243 Receiving, 247 KOR) 1980-82

PASSING

PASSING ATTEMPTS
Game   66 - John Reaves
        Florida vs. Auburn (33 Comp., 369 Yards) 1969
Season   493 - Kurt Page, Vanderbilt (286 Comp., 3,178 Yards) 1983
Career   1,202 - Shane Matthews, Florida
        (722 Comp., 9,287 Yards) 1989-92
COMPLETIONS
Game   37 - Kent Austin, Ole Miss vs. Tennessee (50 Attempts, 381 Yards) ... 1982
Season   286 - Kurt Page, Vanderbilt (493 Attempts, 3,178 Yards) 1983
Career   722 - Shane Matthews, Florida (1,202 Attempts, 9,287 Yards) 1989-92
CONSECUTIVE COMPLETIONS
20 - Kent Austin, Ole Miss (5 vs. Tulane, 15 vs. Tennessee) 1982
COMPLETION PERCENTAGE
Game   (Min. 10 Completions)
        94.7 - Kent Austin, Ole Miss vs. Tulane (18 of 19) 1982
Game   (Min. 20 Completions)
        80.8 - Alan Risher, LSU vs. Ole Miss (21 of 26) 1981
Game   (Min. 30 Completions)
        74.0 - Kent Austin, Ole Miss vs. Tennessee (37 of 50) 1982
Season   (Min. 100 Completions)
        70.7 - Wayne Peace, Florida (174 of 246) 1982
Season   (Min. 200 Completions)
        63.2 - Andy Kelly, Tennessee (228 of 361) 1991
Career   (Min. 300 Completions)
        61.98 - Jeff Francis, Tennessee (476 of 768) 1985-88
YARDS GAINED
Game   484 - Scott Hunter, Alabama vs. Auburn (30 of 55) 1969
Season   3,205 - Shane Matthews, Florida (275 of 463) 1992
Career   9,287 - Shane Matthews, Florida (722 of 1,202) 1989-92
TOUCHDOWN PASSES
Game   5 - (Record Shared by 7 Individuals)
        Babe Parilli, Kentucky - Twice 1950
        John Reaves, Florida - Twice 1969
        Most Recent: Shane Matthews, Florida vs. San Jose State 1991
Season   28 - Shane Matthews, Florida 1991
Career   74 - Shane Matthews, Florida 1989-92
INTERCEPTIONS
Game   9 - John Reaves, Florida vs. Auburn (66 Attempts) 1969
Season   29 - Zeke Bratkowski, Georgia (248 Attempts) 1951
        29 - Kurt Page, Vanderbilt (493 Attempts) 1983
Career   68 - Zeke Bratkowski, Georgia (734 Attempts) 1951-53
CONSECUTIVE ATTEMPTS WITHOUT AN INTERCEPTION
        137 - Alan Risher, LSU 1982

LOWEST PERCENTAGE OF INTERCEPTIONS

Season   (Min. 100 Attempts)
0.76 - Daryl Dickey, Tennessee (1 in 131) 1985

Season   (Min. 200 Attempts)
1.39 - Eric Zeier, Georgia (4 in 286) 1991

Season   (Min. 300 Attempts)
2.57 - Kurt Page, Vanderbilt (9 in 350) 1984

Career   (Min. 200 Attempts)
1.67 - Randy Campbell, Auburn (5 in 300)1982-83

Career   (Min. 400 Attempts) 2.95 - Condredge Holloway
Tennessee (12 in 407) 1972-74

Career   (Min. 600 Attempts) 3.38 - Jeff Francis
Tennessee (26 in 768) 1985-88

LONGEST TOUCHDOWN PASS

Game   99 - Chris Collinsworth to Derrick Gaffney, Florida vs. Rice 1977

RECEIVING

CATCHES
Game	17 - Keith Edwards, Vanderbilt vs. Georgia (141 Yards) 1983
Season	97 - Keith Edwards, Vanderbilt (909 Yards) 1983
Career	200 - Keith Edwards, Vanderbilt (1,757 Yards) 1980, 1982-84

YARDS GAINED
Game	263 - Alexander Wright, Auburn vs. Pacific (5 Catches) 1989
Season	1,329 - Carlos Alvarez, Florida (88 Catches) 1969
Career	2.964 - Boo Mitchell, Vanderbilt (188 Catches) 1985-88

YARDS PER GAME
Season	132.9 - Carlos Alvarez, Florida (1,329 in 10 Games) 1969
Career	83.9 - Terry Beasley, Auburn (2,507 in 30 Games) 1969-71

YARDS PER CATCH
Game	(Min. 5 Catches) 52.6 - Alexander Wright Auburn vs. Pacific (5 for 263) 1989
Game	(Min. 10 Catches) 20.2 - Buck Martin Georgia Tech vs. Auburn (10 for 202) 1951
Game	(Min. 15 Catches) 15.8 - Carlos Alvarez, Florida vs. Miami (15 for 237) 1969
Season	(Min. 25 Catches) 29.3 - Bucky Curtis, Vanderbilt (27 for 791) 1950
Season	(Min. 50 Catches) 20.5 - Eric Martin, LSU (52 for 1,064) 1983
Season	(Min. 75 Catches) 15.6 - Wendell Davis, LSU (80 for 1,244) 1986
Career	(Min. 50 Catches) 24.5 - Bucky Curtis Vanderbilt (61 for 1,496) 1947-50
Career	(Min. 100 Catches) 20.3 - Ozzie Newsome Alabama (102 for 2,070) 1974-77

TOUCHDOWN CATCHES
Game	5 - Carlos Carson, LSU vs. Rice 1977
Season	14 - Allama Matthews, Vanderbilt (11 Games) 1982
Career	29 - Terry Beasley, Auburn (30 Games) 1969-71

SCORING

MOST POINTS
   Game   42 - Showboat Boykin, Ole Miss vs. Miss. State (7 TD's) 1951
   Season 126 - Garrison Hearst, Georgia (21 TD's) 1992
   Career 353 - Kevin Butler, Georgia (122 PATs, 77 FGs, 44 Games) 1981-84

MOST TOUCHDOWNS
   Game   7 - Showboat Boykin, Ole Miss vs. Miss. State 1951
   Season 21 - Garrison Hearst (19 Rushing, 2 Receiving) 1992
   Career 52 - Herschel Walker, Georgia (33 Games) 1980-82

FIELD GOAL ATTEMPTS
   Game   7 - Al Del Greco, Auburn vs. Kentucky (Made 6) 1982
   Season 31 - Fuad Reveiz, Tennessee (Made 27) 1982
             31 - Philip Doyle, Alabama (Made 19) 1988
   Career 105 - Philip Doyle, Alabama (Made 78) 1987-90

FIELD GOALS MADE
   Game   6 - Al Del Greco, Auburn vs. Kentucky (7 Attempts) 1982
             6 - Bobby Raymond, Florida vs. Florida State (6 Attempts) 1983
             6 - Bobby Raymond, Florida vs. Kentucky (6 Attempts) 1984
             6 - Philip Doyle, Alabama vs. S.W. Louisiana (6 Attempts) 1990
   Season 27 - Fuad Reveiz, Tennessee (31 Attempts) 1982
   Career 78 - Philip Doyle, Alabama (105 Attempts) 1987-90

LONG FIELD GOALS
   Game   60 - Fuad Reveiz, Tennessee vs. Georgia Tech 1982
             60 - Kevin Butler, Georgia vs. Clemson 1984
             60 - Chris Perkins, Florida vs. Tulane 1984

CONSECUTIVE FIELD GOALS
             18 - Fuad Reveiz, Tennessee 1984

FIELD GOAL PERCENTAGE
   Season (Min. 10 Made) 100.0 - David Browndyke, LSU (14 of 14) 1989
   Season (Min. 20 Made) 88.4 - Bobby Raymond, Florida (23 of 26) 1984
   *Career (Min. 25 Made) 88.0 - Bobby Raymond, Florida (43 of 49) 1982-84

PAT KICKS ATTEMPTED
Game   13 - Red Lutz, Alabama vs. Delta State (Made 11) 1951
Season   58 - Hugh Morrow, Alabama (Made 46) 1945
Career   148 - Hugh Morrow, Alabama (Made 120) 1944-47

PAT KICKS MADE
Game   11 - Bill Davis, Alabama vs. Virginia Tech (11 Attempts) 1973
            11 - Red Lutz, Alabama vs. Delta State (13 Attempts) 1951
Season   51 - Bill Davis, Alabama (53 Attempts) 1973
Career   135 - Van Tiffin, Alabama (135 Attempts) 1983-86

PAT KICKS PERCENTAGE
Game   (Min. 10 Attempts)
            100 - Bill Davis, Alabama vs. Virginia Tech (11 of 11) 1973
            100 - Bob Gain, Kentucky vs. North Dakota (10 of 10) 1950
            100 - Bobby Morequ, LSU vs. Rice (10 of 10) 1977
Season   (Min. 30 Attempts) 100 - shared by 17 Players
            Most Recent: Greg Burke, Tennessee (50 of 50) 1990
Career   (Min. 100 Attempts)
            *100 - Van Tiffin, Alabama (135 of 135) 1983-86
            *100 - David Browndyke, LSU (109 of 109) 1986-89

CONSECUTIVE PAT KICKS MADE
            135 - Van Tiffin, Alabama 1983-86

TOTAL POINTS SCORED BY KICKING
Game   23 - Bobby Raymond
            Florida vs. Florida State (6 FG, 5 PATs) 1983
Season   107 - Greg Burke, Tennessee (19 FGs, 50 PATs) 1990
Career   353 - Kevin Butler, Georgia (77 FGs, 122 PATs) 1981-84

PUNTING

MOST PUNTS
Game   30 - Bert Johnson, Kentucky vs. Washington & Lee 1934
Season   101 - Ralph Kercheval, Kentucky (4,413 Yards for 43.5 Avg.) 1933
Career   277 - Jim Arnold, Vanderbilt (12,171 Yards for 43.9 Avg.) 1979-82

YARDS PUNTED
Game   1,155 - Bert Johnson
            Kentucky vs. Washington & Lee (30 for 38.5 Avg.) 1934
Season   4,413 - Ralph Kercheval (101 for 43.5 Avg.) 1933
Career   12,171 - Jim Arnold, Vanderbilt (277 for 43.9 Avg) 1979-82

PUNTING AVERAGE
Game   (Min. 2 Punts) 84.5 - Bill Smith
            Ole Miss vs. Southern Miss (2 for 169) 1984
Game   (Min. 7 Punts) 53.1 - Jim Arnold
            Vanderbilt vs. North Carolina (8 for 425) 1982
Game   (Min. 10 Punts) 52.0 - Ralph Kercheval
            Kentucky vs. Cincinnati (10 for 520) 1933
Game   (Min. 20 Punts) 43.0 - Hawk Cavette
            Georgia Tech vs. Florida (21 for 904) 1938
Season   (Min. 50 Punts) 48.2 - Ricky Anderson
            Vanderbilt (58 for 2,793) 1984
Season   (Min. 75 Punts) 45.3 - Bill Smith, Ole Miss (79 for 3,581) 1985
Season   (Min. 100 Punts) 43.5 - Ralph Kercheval
            Kentucky (101 for 4,394) 1933
Career   (Min. 100 Punts) 45.6 - Ricky Anderson
            Vanderbilt (111 for 5,067) 1983-84

MOST PUNTS, 50 YARDS OR MORE
*86 - Bill Smith, Ole Miss 1983-86
MOST CONSECUTIVE GAMES 1 PUNT OF 50 YARDS OR MORE
*32 - Bill Smith, Ole Miss 1983-86
MOST GAMES AVERAGING 40 OR MORE YARDS (Minimum 4)
*36 - Bill Smith, Ole Miss 1983-86
LONG PUNTS
Game   92 - Bill Smith, Ole Miss vs. Southern Miss 1984

PUNT RETURNS

MOST RETURNS
Game   17 - A. B. Stubbs, Mississippi State vs. TCU (122 Yards) 1936
Season   45 - Willie Shelby, Alabama (396 Yards) 1975
Career   125 - Greg Richardson, Alabama (1,011 Yards) 1983-86
YARDS RETURNED
Game   203 - Lee Nalley, Vanderbilt vs. Kentucky (6 returns) 1948
*Season 791 - Lee Nalley, Vanderbilt (43 Returns) 1948
*Season 1,695 - Lee Nalley, Vanderbilt (109 Returns) 1947-49
GAIN PER RETURN
Game   (Min. 3) 57.6 - Mike Fuller
            Auburn vs. Chattanooga (3 for 173) 1974
Season   (Min. 10) 26.7 - Hal Griffin, Florida (10 for 267) 1947
Season   (Min. 20) 19.1 - Mike Fuller, Auburn (20 for 381) 1973
Season   (Min. 40) 18.4 - Lee Nalley, Vanderbilt (43 for 791) 1948
Season   (Min. 50) 17.7 - Mike Fuller, Auburn (50 for 883) 1973-74
Career   (Min. 100) 15.6 - Lee Nalley, Vanderbilt (109 for 1,695) 1947-49
PUNT RETURN TOUCHDOWNS
Game   *2 - Tommy Casanova, LSU vs. Ole Miss 1970
            * 2 - Buzy Rosenberg, Georgia vs. Oregon State 1971
            *2 - David Langner, Auburn vs. Alabama 1972
            *2 - Mike Fuller, Auburn vs. Chattanooga 1974
LONG PUNT RETURNS
Game   100 - Bert Rechichar, Tennessee vs. Washington & Lee 1950
            100 - Jim Campagna, Georgia vs. Vanderbilt 1952

KICKOFF RETURNS

MOST RETURNS
Game   7 - Doug Matthews, Vanderbilt vs. Florida (168 Yards) 1969
            7 - Jeff Peeples, Vanderbilt vs. Ole Miss (138 Yards) 1970
            7 - Willie Gault, Tennessee vs. USC (123 Yards) 1981
Season   33 - Jeff Peeples, Vanderbilt (646 Yards) 1970
Career   107 - Mark Johnson, Vanderbilt (2,263 Yards) 1986-88, 1990
YARDS RETURNED
Game   197 - Kerry Goode, Alabama vs. Boston College (4 Returns) 1984
Season   669 - Gene Washington, Georgia (28 Returns) 1974
Career   2,263 - Mark Johnson, Vanderbilt (107 Returns) 1986-88, 1990
YARDS PER RETURN
Season   (Min. 20) 27.9 - Dan Bland, Mississippi State (20 for 558) 1964
Season   (Min. 30) 19.6 - Jeff Peeples, Vanderbilt (33 for 646) 1970
Career   (Min. 30) 27.1 - Calvin Bird, Kentucky (37 for 1,001) 1958-60
Career   (Min. 50) 25.4 - Robert Dow, LSU (70 for 1,780) 1973-76

KICKOFF RETURN TOUCHDOWNS
Season   3 - Willie Gault, Tennessee 1980
Career   4 - Willie Gault, Tennessee 1979-82
LONG KICKOFF RETURNS
Game   100 - Shared by 17 Individuals
              Most Recent: Kurt Johnson, Kentucky vs. Georgia 1989

TOTAL KICK RETURNS

MOST RETURNS
Season   66 - Thomas Bailey, Auburn (42 PR, 24 KOR) 1991
*Career   199 - Tony James, Mississippi State (123 PR, 76 KOR) 1989-92
MOST RETURN YARDS
Game   235 - Dicky Lyons, Kentucky vs. LSU (4/75 PR, 4/160 KOR) 1967
Season   1,119 - Thomas Bailey, Auburn (42/528 PR, 24/591 KOR) 1991
*Career   3,194 - Tony James, Mississippi State
              (1,332 PR, 1,862 KOR) 1989-92
YARDS PER RETURN
Game   50.0 - Mike Fuller
              Auburn vs. Chattanooga (200 Yards, 4 Returns) 1974
Season   (Min. 20) 24.8 - Calvin Bird
              Kentucky (10/169 PR, 14/426 KOR) 1959
Career   (Min. 100) 21.1 - Mark Johnson
              Vanderbilt (107/2,263 KOR) 1986-88,1990
KICK RETURN TOUCHDOWNS
Season   5 - Pinky Rohm, LSU (3 PR, 2 KOR) 1937
Career   6 - Lee Nalley, Vanderbilt (5 PR, 1 KOR) 1947-49

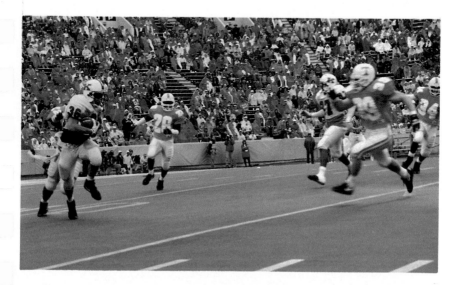

INTERCEPTIONS

MOST INTERCEPTIONS
Game   3 - Shared by 36 Individuals
           Most Recent: Will White, Florida vs. Alabama 1990
Season   12 - J. W. Sherrill, Tennessee (104 Yards) 1949
           12 - Terry Hoage, Georgia (51 Yards) 1982
Career   20 - Bobby Wilson, Ole Miss (379 Yards) 1946-49
           20 - Chris WIlliams, LSU (91 Yards) 1977-80

YARDS RETURNED
Game   162 - Joe Brodsky, Florida vs. Mississippi State (3 Int.) 1956
Season   244 - Joe Brodsky, Florida (5 Int.) 1956
Career   379 - Bobby Wilson, Ole Miss (20 Int.) 1946-49

YARDS PER INTERCEPTION
Game   (Min. 3) 54.0 - Joe Brodsky, Florida vs. Miss. State (3 for 162) 1956
Season   (Min. 5) 44.8 - Joe Brodsky, Florida (5 for 244) 1956
Season   (Min. 10) 17.7 - Bobby Majors, Tennessee (10 for 177) 1970
Career   (Min. 10) 28.2 - Wilbur Jamerson, Kentucky (11 for 310) 1947-50
Career   (Min. 15) 19.7 - Jake Scott, Georgia (16 for 315) 1967-68

INTERCEPTION TOUCHDOWNS
Game   *2 - Joe Brodsky, Florida vs. Mississippi State 1956
           *2 - Jake Scott, Georgia vs. Kentucky 1968
*Career   5 - Jackie Walker, Tennessee (32 Games) 1969-71

LONG INTERCEPTION RETURNS
Game   100 - Shared by 10 Individuals
           Most Recent: Greg Jackson, LSU vs. Mississippi State 1988

LONGEST TOUCHDOWN (Rushing)
99 - Kelsey Finch, Tennessee vs. Florida 1977

LONGEST TOUCHDOWN (Passing)
99 - Chris Collinsworth to Derrick Gaffney, Florida vs. Rice 1977

LONGEST KICKOFF RETURN
100 - Shared by 21 Individuals
Most Recent: Kurt Johnson, Kentucky vs. Georgia 1989

LONGEST PUNT
92 - Bill Smith, Ole Miss vs. Southern Miss 1984

LONGEST PUNT RETURN
100 - Bert Rechichar, Tennessee vs. Washington & Lee 1950
100 - Jim Campagna, Georgia vs. Vanderbilt 1952

LONGEST INTERCEPTION RETURN
100 - Shared by 11 Individuals
Most Recent: Greg Jackson, LSU vs. Mississippi State 1988

LONGEST FUMBLE-IN-AIR RETURN
100 - Dextar Stanphill, Sewanee vs. Florida 1936
100 - Ken Kavanaugh, LSU vs. Rice 1937

LONGEST FIELD GOAL
60 - Fuad Reveiz, Tennessee Vs. Georgia Tech 1982
60 - Chris Perkins, Florida vs. Tulane 1984
60 - Kevin Butler, Georgia vs. Clemson 1984

RUSHING

MOST RUSHES
Game   89 - Georgia vs. Kentucky 1967
Season   763 - Alabama (3,792 Yards in 11 Games) 1979

YARDS GAINED
Game   748 - Alabama vs. Virginia Tech (73 Rushes) 1973
Season   4,027 - Alabama (664 Rushes in 11 Games) 1973

YARDS PER GAME
366.1 - Alabama (4,027) 1973

YARDS PER RUSH
Game   10.7 - Tennessee vs. Tennessee Tech (44 for 469) 1951
Season   6.8 - LSU (306 for 2,632) 1945

PASSING

MOST ATTEMPTS
Game   66 - Florida vs. Auburn (33 Completions) 1969
Season   519 - Vanderbilt (296 Completions) 1983

COMPLETIONS
Game   37 - Ole Miss vs. Tennessee (50 Attempts) 1982
Season   296 - Vanderbilt (519 Attenpts) 1983

COMPLETION PERCENTAGE
Game   (Min. 20 Attempts) 95.0 - Ole Miss vs. Tulane (19 of 20) 1982
Game   (Min. 30 Attempts) 77.8 - Florida vs. Vanderbilt (28 of 36) 1982
*Season   (Min. 100 Attempts) 68.8 Florida (203 of 295) 1982
Season   (Min. 300 Attempts) 63.3 - Florida (193 of 305) 1983

YARDS GAINED
Game   484 - Alabama vs. Auburn (30 of 55) 1969
Season   3,393 - Florida (235 of 390) 1991

YARDS PER GAME
308.5 - Florida (3,393 in 11 Games) 1991

YARDS PER ATTEMPT
*Season   13.4 - Alabama (94 for 1,261) 1973

TOUCHDOWNS
Game   8 - Kentucky vs. North Dakota 1950
Season   32 - Florida (11 Games) 1991

INTERCEPTIONS
Game   9 - Florida vs. Auburn 1969
Season   35 - Georgia (356 Attempts, 180 Completions) 1982

FEWEST INTERCEPTIONS
Game   (Min. 30 Attempts) 0 - Shared by 40 SEC Squads over the years
Most Recent: Kentucky vs. Mississippi State (19-32-0; 1 TD) 1992
*Season   (Min. 100 Attempts) 0.96% - Alabama (1 in 104) 1980
*Season   (Min. 150 Attempts) 1.13% - Georgia (4 in 355 1991
Also: Record for Season (Min. 200 Attempts)

TOTAL OFFENSE

MOST PLAYS

    Game   105 - Georgia vs. Kentucky 1967

    Season   911 - Auburn (4,923 yards) 1984

YARDS GAINED

    Game   833 - Alabama vs. Virginia Tech (748 rushing, 85 passing) 1973

    Season   5,288 - Alabama (4,027 rushing, 1,261 passing, 11 games) 1973

YARDS PER GAME

                485.0 - Auburn (4,850 in 10 Games) 1970

YARDS PER PLAY

    Game   11.9 - Alabama vs. Virginia Tech (70 for 833) 1973

    Season   7.09 - Auburn (4,850 in 648) 1970

FIRST DOWNS

MOST RUSHING

    Game   28 - Auburn vs. Ole Miss 1985

    Season   213 - Alabama 1979

MOST PASSING

    Game   21 - LSU vs. Tennessee 1989

    Season   158 - Vanderbilt 1983

TOTAL

    Game   40 - Vanderbilt vs. Davidson 1969

    Season   273 - Florida 1990

PUNTING

MOST PUNTS

    Game   36 - Kentucky vs. Washington & Lee 1934

    *Season 139 - Tennessee 1937

YARDS PUNTING

    Game   1,386 - Kentucky vs. Washington & Lee (36 Punts) 1934

    Season   5,620 - Tennessee (139 Punts) 1937

PUNTING AVERAGE

    Game   (Min. 10) 52.0 - Kentucky vs. Cincinnati (10 for 520) 1944

    Game   (Min. 20) 43.0 - Georgia Tech vs. Florida 1938

    Season   47.6 - Vanderbilt (59 for 2,810) 1984

PUNT RETURNS

MOST RETURNS

    Game   20 - Mississippi State vs. TCU (128 Yards) 1936

    Season   71 - Alabama (783 Yards) 1946

YARDS RETURNED

    Game   225 - Mississippi State vs. Chattanooga (8 Returns) 1946

    Season   974 - Tennessee (68 Returns) 1940

YARDS PER RETURN

    Game   40.8 - Alabama vs. LSU (5 for 204) 1991

    Season   20.8 - Mississippi State (25 for 521) 1971

KICKOFF RETURNS

MOST RETURNS
Game   11 - Ole Miss vs. Alabama 1989
Season   58 - Vanderbilt 1990
YARDS RETURNED
Game   259 - Alabama vs. Auburn (8 Returns) 1969
Season   1,194 - Vanderbilt (56 Returns) 1987
YARDS PER RETURN
Game   (Min. 3) 66.7 - Kentucky vs. Vanderbilt (3 for 200) 1945
Season   28.8 - Mississippi State (19 for 547) 1940

SCORING

MOST POINTS
Game   93 - LSU vs. Southwestern Louisiana 1936
Season   454 - Alabama (11 Games) 1973
MOST POINTS TWO TEAMS
        97 - Georgia (62) vs. Vanderbilt (35) 1984
POINTS PER GAME
        44.0 - Alabama (396 in 9) 1945
MOST TOUCHDOWNS
Game   14 - Ole Miss vs. West Tennessee Teachers 1935
Season   61 - Alabama (11 Games) 1973

MOST FIELD GOALS

MOST PAT KICKS

CONSECUTIVE PAT KICKS

MOST POINTS IN A TIE GAME

SOUTHEASTERN CONFERENCE
TEAM DEFENSE RECORDS

RUSHING DEFENSE

FEWEST RUSHES ALLOWED
Game   13 - Florida vs. Vanderbilt 1983
Season   231 - Tennessee (9 Games) 1945
FEWEST YARDS ALLOWED
Game   Minus 93 - Kentucky vs. Kansas State 1970
Season   305 - Alabama (9 Games) 1938
FEWEST YARDS PER GAME
      33.9 - Alabama (305 Yards in 9 Games) 1938
FEWEST YARDS PER RUSH
Game   Minus 3.95 - Kentucky vs. Kansas State
      (-91 Yards in 23 Rushes) 1970
Season   0.95 - Alabama (305 Yards in 321 Rushes) 1938

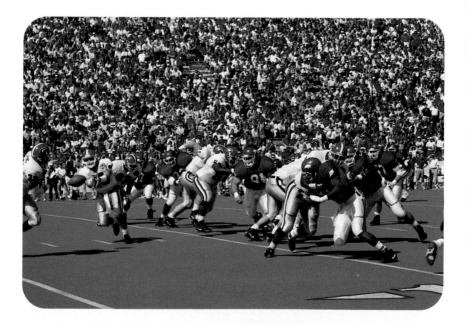

PASSING DEFENSE

FEWEST PASSES

    Game   0 - Kentucky vs. Tennessee 1952

                0 - Tennessee vs. Georgia Tech 1977

    Season   73 - Georgia Tech (10 Games) 1957

FEWEST COMPLETIONS

    Game   0 - Several Teams

                Most Recent: Ole Miss vs. Alabama 1988

    Season   31 - Alabama (9 Games) 1938

                31 - Georgia Tech (10 Games) 1957

LOWEST COMPLETION PERCENTAGE

    Game   0 - Several Teams

                Most Recent: Ole Miss vs. Alabama 1988

    Season   27.1 - Auburn (36 of 133) 1950

FEWEST YARDS

    Game   Minus 10 - Auburn vs. Alabama (1 Completion) 1952

    Season   291 - Alabama (9 Games) 1945

FEWEST TOUCHDOWNS

    *Season 0 - Tennessee (10 Games) 1939

INTERCEPTIONS

    Game   9 - Georgia vs. Presbyterian (42 Passes) 1943

                9 - Auburn vs. Florida (66 Passes) 1969

    Season   36 - Tennessee 1970

INTERCEPTION RETURN YARDS

    *Game   240 - Kentucky vs. Ole Miss (6 Interceptions) 1949

    *Season 782 - Tennessee (25 Interceptions) 1971

INTERCEPTION RETURN TOUCHDOWNS

    *Season 7 - Tennessee 1971

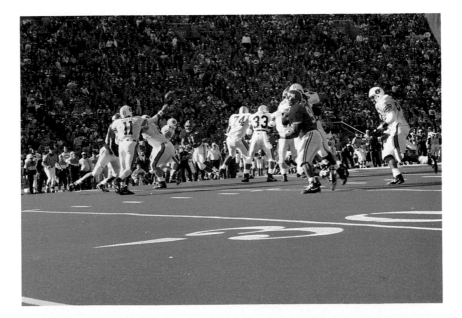

SCORING DEFENSE

FEWEST POINTS
*Season   0 - Tennessee (10) Games) 1939

FIRST DOWNS

FEWEST RUSHING
    Game   0 - Several Teams
             Most Recent: Ole Miss vs. South Carolina 1972
    Season   24 - Alabama (9 Games) 1938
FEWEST PASSING
    Game   0 - Several Teams
             Most Recent: Florida vs. Auburn   1989
    Season   11 - Alabama (9 Games) 1938
FEWEST TOTAL
    Game   0 - Auburn vs. Tennessee 1958
    Season   35 - Alabama (9 Games) 1938

TOTAL DEFENSE

FEWEST PLAYS
    Game   24 - Ole Miss vs. South Carolina 1947
    Season 368 - Tennessee 1945
FEWEST YARDS
    Game   Minus 30 - Auburn vs. Tennessee 1958
    Season 596 - Alabama (9 Games) 1938
FEWEST YARDS PER GAME
    Season 77.9 - Alabama (701 Yards in 9 Games) 1938

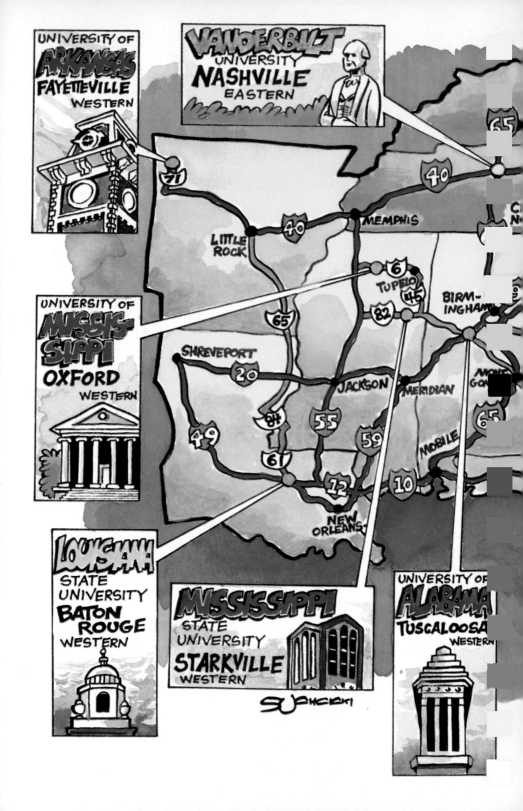

Denny Chimes has been a symbol of "The Capstone,"
the University of Alabama, since 1929.

A
L
A
B
A
M
A

*Clark Hall, housing part of the Arts & Sciences program,
adds beauty and architectural interest to the University of Alabama campus.*

The University of Alabama was founded in 1831, becoming the state's first university. Only 12 years had elapsed since Alabama's admission to the Union. At the time of the school's founding its host city, Tuscaloosa, was the capital and a bright future for both the University and the town seemed assured.

In 1846, the capital was suddenly moved eastward to Montgomery. During the Civil War, both the town and the school were burned by Union troops. For many years both entities languished. Just prior to World War I, however, the University began to grow and another growth spurt occurred after the Second World War. The trend continues today with student numbers approaching 20,000.

The University of Alabama is proud of its many outstanding and widely recognized schools and departments. These include the Business School rated among the top three in the Southeast; the Japanese studies program which ranks as the finest in the South; one of the nation's five oldest engineering colleges, founded in 1837; the country's sixth largest communications college; and of course the outstanding School of Law. The latter has produced many politicians, jurists and statesmen.

The heart of the Alabama campus is the Quadrangle, a large park-like central core around which are arranged a number of permanent buildings such as the Library, The Gorgas House, and the President's mansion. Denny Chimes is located on the edge of the "Quad." This area is often the scene of football-related activity whether it be picnicking, a pep rally, a pick-up game, or just walking across the Quad before or after the Tide plays.

In recent years the University has helped to stimulate growth in the Tuscaloosa area. Located in the West Central part of Alabama, Tuscaloosa County has a population approaching 150,000. The Black Warrior River flows through the city and brings barge traffic to the area. The name Tuscaloosa comes from two Choctaw Indian words: tusho, meaning "warrior" and loosa, meaning "black." The city's nickname, "The Druid City," may be traced to ancient times in England and France when a group of Celts practiced Druidism. One of the symbols of that religion was the mighty oak tree which happens to flourish in great numbers around Tuscaloosa: hence, "The Druid City."

The University has a nickname also: "The Capstone." That term was popularized by the late Chancellor, George H. Denny, who as president, called UA "The Capstone of Public Education in Alabama." With over 100,000 living graduates, Alabama has established a proven track record of excellence in achievement among its alumni, and service to the people of Alabama and the world!

The classic President's Mansion lends an air of serenity, stability and timelessness to the heart of the Alabama campus.

In his 1953 book, <u>History of the University of Alabama</u>, Professor James B. Sellers relates how the colors "crimson and white" were chosen to symbolize the school. It seems that as early as 1885 the colors were used in a drill competition by a university cadet company in New Orleans.

The Bama cheerleading squad performs their trademark "rolling bow," paying tribute to yet another Tide touchdown.

Upon learning that the cadets' uniforms were black, gray and white. The young lady who was the unit's sponsor objected, saying that the colors were "funereal" and too "neutral." She proposed crimson, white and gray.

By the time Alabama fielded its first football team, some seven years later, the team and the student body had apparently settled on crimson and white (minus the gray) as the school's colors. In 1892 Alabama's team sported white jerseys and pants with crimson stockings. Some white sweaters had a crimson "UA" on them, while other sweaters were crimson with a white "A." The student newspaper, in reporting on a spring dance in 1893, proclaimed,

Almost an infinite amount of crimson and white, the University colors of which we are all so proud, was draped from one end of the hall to the other.

Bama fans remain proud to this day of their "crimson" and white. The PMS Color of Alabama's red is # 200.

There are at least two stories about how Alabama came to be called the "Crimson Tide." You can choose your favorite.

FIRST STORY: When football began at the University in 1892, the team had no official nickname. Students seemed to favor the term "Varsity." That name and the "Crimson White" were used in early newspaper stories about Alabama football. "Crimson White" of course derived from the school's colors.

Around the turn of the century the nickname "The Thin Red Line" seems to have become predominant. It was used repeatedly in sports stories about the team and was popular with students and fans in general.

According to the 1992 University of Alabama Media Guide, the first time the nickname "Crimson Tide" was used was in 1907 following the Auburn game. It seems that the Birmingham field where the game was held had been turned into a quagmire of red mud by heavy rains. Alabama, a decided underdog, played its heart out and emerged with a 6-6 tie, equivalent to victory considering the circumstances. In writing about the game, Hugh Roberts, a writer for the Birmingham Age-Herald, used the term "Crimson Tide" playing on the school's color, crimson, the red mud, and the final outcome. Subsequently the moniker gained favor, especially after being promoted extensively by Zipp Newman, former sports editor of the Birmingham News.

SECOND STORY: Zipp Newman (the same) was said to have coined the nickname "Crimson Tide" in 1919 when he returned home from the service. It seems he got the inspiration by watching waves (the tide) pound a shore relentlessly. Apparently, this action reminded him of Alabama's "never give up" style of play. He used the nickname "Crimson Tide" in a headline and the rest is history!

A Bama cheerleader exhorts the "crimson-clad"
during last year's clash with Auburn at Birmingham's Legion Field.

Big Al represents a mascot tradition at Alabama which began 63 years ago. In 1930 the Crimson Tide, under Coach Wallace Wade, had assembled a very talented team. This was to be Coach Wade's last year at Alabama as he had already announced his resignation prior to the start of the season, planning to coach at Duke in the coming year. Perhaps he had something to prove to himself or others. In any event, the 1930 Bama squad showed no mercy, shutting out eight of ten opponents including Rose Bowl foe, Washington State, and staking a claim on the national championship.

On October 8 of that year the Tide met the Ole Miss team in Tuscaloosa. Everett Strupper, an Atlanta based journalist, was in attendance and could not believe his eyes. After watching the Tide score an initial touchdown and then battle Ole Miss on even terms for most of the period, Strupper wrote, "At the end of the quarter, the earth started to tremble, there was a distant rumble that continued to grow. Some excited fan in the stands bellowed, 'Hold your horses, the elephants are coming,' and out stamped this Alabama varsity." Coach Wade had once again started his second string. Strupper was shocked when he saw the size of the starting eleven. In subsequent writings he and others often referred to the Bama players as the "Red Elephants."

Although the image stuck and a mascot was created, it has been reported that Coach Wade detested the moniker, believing that elephants were slow and dumb. The current elephant mascot at Alabama, Big Al, also received a less than enthusiastic welcome from another Bama coach, namely "Bear" Bryant.

When representatives from the student body approached the great mentor with their desire to have a costumed mascot on the field, Coach Bryant at first objected, but he relented with the understanding that the mascot would not get in the way and distract fans from the game, and that children would like him. Named "Big Al" by a vote of the student body, the new mascot made his debut at the 1980 Sugar Bowl. Coach Bryant would be proud! Big Al has become a favorite with children of all ages.

Usually, two or three students rotate playing the role of Big Al. In the 1992 season the first female student took a turn "playing the heavy."

"Big Al -- two tons of fun -- a pal to fans of all ages.

Alabama's "Million Dollar Band" thrills the home crowd in Tuscaloosa.

Alabama's "Million Dollar Band" has been exciting collegiate football fans nationally for decades. The band's history dates back to 1913 when a group of Bama students organized a football band and collected money from everyone in the school and community to equip their musical aggregation.

For over twenty years the bands at Alabama had only volunteer or part-time directors. Then in 1935 Colonel Carlton K. Butler assumed the directorship. Over a career which spanned thirty-three years, Colonel Butler led the band to national prominence. Following Colonel Butler's retirement in 1968, the band was directed in succession by Earl Dunn (1968-70) and Dr. James Ferguson (1971-83). In 1984, the baton was passed to the current director, Kathryn Scott Mann. Ms. Mann was the first woman in America to direct a university marching band.

Over the years the 340 member band has represented the University in more consecutive bowl appearances than any other college band. Fans at the Sugar, Orange, Astro-Bluebonnet, Liberty, Gator, Hall of Fame and Block-buster bowls have all been treated to their money's worth as the band lived up to its name.

Oh, about that name---the "Million Dollar Band"---although stories exist about the origin, no one knows for sure who coined it!

ALABAMA'S FIGHT SONG
"Yea Alabama"

Yea Alabama! Drown 'em Tide
Ev'ry bama man's behind you:
Hit your stride!
Go teach the Bulldogs to behave,
Send those Yellow Jackets to a
    watery grave,
And if a man starts to weaken,
That's his shame!!
For Bama's pluck and grit have
Writ her name in Crimson flame,
Fight on! Fight on! Fight on! Men!
Remember the Rose Bowl,
    we'll win then.
Go! Roll to victory! Hit your stride!
You're Dixie's football pride,
Crimson Tide!

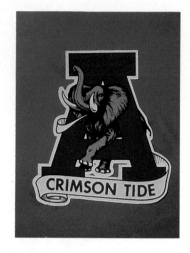

UNIVERSITY OF ALABAMA
"Alma Mater"

Alabama, listen mother, to our vows of love
To thyself and to each other, faithful friends we'll prove.
Faithful, loyal, firm and true, heart bound to heart will beat;
Year by year, the ages through, until in heav'n we meet.
College days are swiftly fleeting;
Soon we'll leave thy halls.
Ne'er to join another meeting;
'Neath thy hallowed walls.

Faithful, loyal, firm and true, heart bound to heart will beat;
Year by year, the ages through, until in heav'n we meet.
So, farewell, dear Alma Mater, may thy name, we pray.
Be reverenced ever, pure and stainless,
As it is today.

Faithful, loyal, firm and true, heart bound to heart will beat;
Year by year, the ages through, until in heav'n we meet.

Words: Helen Vickers, 1908
Music: Amici

The ever-present and never camera-shy "Tide Twins" display their handiwork and their sentiments: "Roll Tide!"

When interviewed for this book, Alabama fans overwhelming said their favorite tradition was "winning" and that a "winning tradition" is what makes them unique in the SEC. Eugene Willingham of Decatur, Alabama, said "No one in the history of the SEC has a record like Alabama," and like it or not, he is right! Alabama is the only school which every other school sees as their rival and perhaps that's because they are often the "team to beat." Statistics bear out the fact that Alabama is the only SEC team with a winning record against ALL other SEC teams. They are also the only SEC team to have won over 600 games, and as you know, Bama fans are mighty proud of their record!

That record makes Alabama "the school you love or love to hate!" That's what we discovered in our interviews. More fans from the other schools listed Alabama as their rival than any other school. Yet, even their rivals respected Bama's tradition, program, band and mascot. Although each school has some wonderful tradition and historic significance, Alabama seems to hold the lion's share. For example, the legend of Bear Bryant is so strong that you almost expect to see his spirit hovering over Legion Field or Bryant-Denny Stadium. It is the stuff of which dreams are made and it does add to the excitement of any game with Alabama. Some fields are prettier, in my estimation, but you have to respect the tradition of winning and the legacy of one such as the "Bear"

Other traditions at Alabama are not so legendary, but nevertheless, just as important to Tide fans. For example, their fight song "Yea Alabama" is quite beloved, but according to Bama graduate and long-time fan, Kirk Flowers of Birmingham, they also enjoy what is called the "Rammer Jammer" cheer. Fans say it started in the Johnny Vaught era at Ole Miss when that rivalry was very strong. Although it's known as the "Mississippi Cheer," it is used to excite the Tide fans against any opponent! It goes like this:

Rammer jammer, Yellow hammer
Give 'em hell, Alabama!

Other fun traditions for Bama fans are tailgating, homecoming and the pre-game player walk around the field, dressed in coats and ties. It is quite stirring, as though they are quietly taking the field.

Alabama fans also enjoy their rivalries with other SEC teams. They eagerly look forward to the 3rd Saturday in October (with Tennessee) and to their final game of each season with Auburn. It's no surprise, however, that Auburn is the school with which Alabama shares the most intense rivalry! They battle each year in what has been called the "Iron Bowl," because it was played in Birmingham, not for a trophy, but for something more important---bragging rights for a year. However, as any Alabama or Auburn fan knows, those rights are not truly granted, they are just shared more equally by the winning team!

Hot dogs seem to be the gameday food "of choice." Perhaps that's because Bama fans are very serious and many take time only for a hot dog at the game! Or maybe it's because Bama fans, like Kelly Tibbs of South Fulton, Tennessee, support their sponsors as strongly as their teams. Her favorite gameday foods were "Golden Flake potato chips, hot dogs {Lykes, of course} and Classic Coke!"

However, other fans, just as serious, seem to find time for some serious partying. Tailgating is very important whether from the trunk of their cars, the bed of their truck or with 15 or 20 friends in a motor home or fully-equipped travel bus! Bar-b-que, ribs, and chicken were favorites of both those who tailgate and those enjoy local restaurant fare. Every Alabama fan knows about Dreamland Bar-B-Q and, of course, it was their "favorite" restaurant. Other suggestions they made for visiting fans to try are Cypress Inn, Wings, The Landing, Solomon's, City Cafe and Johnny Ray's.

Bama fans are devoted. Though all SEC schools pride themselves in their hard-core fans, it does seem that Alabama fans do follow their team in greater numbers than the other schools. Our "Fan Scan" bore this out! If your team is playing Alabama you have to be careful or they will take over the stadium. Just ask Arkansas, whose fans found themselves without hotel rooms this year because of the influx of Bama fans!

The University of Alabama and its football program has a mystique all its own, for fan and foe alike. Long-time fan, Faye Brown of Gonzales, Florida, heard about this book from her family physicians (a husband and wife team who also happen to be Bama fans--Faye won't use a doctor who isn't!). She called and gladly gave us an interview. Her dad had hunted with Bear Bryant, so she grew up knowing and respecting him and likewise the University of Alabama. Like many fans, Faye is a member of the Century Club and does NOT miss a game, home or away. She also travels wherever they are for exhibition games or bowls. She told us what we have also heard expressed by many other Bama fans: Coach Stallings is very much respected and loved. Though Bear set the standard for Alabama football, it seems that Coach Stallings has definitely earned the right to bear that standard and gain that same reverence and respect.

Perhaps the secret of the Alabama legend was expressed best by Tammy Flowers of Homewood, Alabama, when asked what she most enjoyed about attending Alabama football games: "Getting caught up in the spirit of the winning tradition. You go <u>expecting</u> to win."

Bryant-Denny Stadium . . . "The House of Champions."

Head Coach:

Gene Stallings (Texas A&M, 1957)
Texas A&M Student Assistant, 1957;
Alabama Assistant, 1958-64;
Texas A&M Head Coach, 1965-71;
Dallas Assistant (NFL), 1972-85;

Birthday:	**March 2, 1935**
Hometown:	**Paris TX**

St. Louis Head Coach (NFL), 1986-87;
Phoenix Head Coach (NFL), 1988-89;
Alabama Head Coach, 1990-present

Assistant Coaches

Mike Dubose (Alabama, 1975)	Defensive Line
Jim Fuller (Alabama, 1967)	Centers/Guards
Ellis Johnson (The Citadel, 1975)	Outside Linebackers
Larry Kirksey (Eastern Kentucky, 1973)	Running Backs
Woody McCorvey (Alabama State, 1972)	Receivers
Mal Moore (Alabama, 1963)	Assistant Head Coach/ Quarterbacks
Bill Oliver (Alabama, 1963)	Secondary
Danny Pearman (Clemson, 1987)	Offensive Tackles/Kicking
Jeff Rouzie (Alabama, 1974)	Inside Linebackers

Viewed from "The Quad," the upper deck of Bryant-Denny Stadium, with its unique awning upraised, dominates the skyline.

Alabama is one of two schools in the SEC (the other being Arkansas) to regularly divide its home games between two stadiums. The on-campus facility in Tuscaloosa is Bryant-Denny Stadium. Bama's "home away from home" is Birmingham's Legion Field.

The Crimson Tide "owns" its home field in Tuscaloosa. Since 1929, Red Elephants have hammered out an unbelievable 161-17-3 (.898) record at Bryant-Denny Stadium, their on-campus facility.

When the field was dedicated on October 4, 1929, it didn't take Alabama long to inaugurate their winning tradition at home. In that first game the Tide defeated Ole Miss 22-7. The new stadium was named in honor of longtime University president, Dr. George Denny, who was in the 18th year of his near quarter century tenure. Dr. Denny was a great supporter of the Crimson Tide, so the tribute was fitting. 1929 was a good year for the president. Not only was the stadium named for him that year, Denny Chimes was also completed and named in his honor.

When first constructed, stadium capacity stood at 12,000. Seven years later, an additional 6,000 seats were added on the east side followed soon by an equal number on the west side. For several years the stadium's capacity remained at 24,000. After the Second World War, end zone bleachers were added to both ends of the facility lifting the capacity to 31,000.

Not until 1961 and the arrival of Coach Paul "Bear" Bryant did the stands grow again. In that year 12,000 seats, a new press box and a press elevator were added. Five years later, further expansion upped the total number of seats to 60,000. The stadium assumed its present configuration in 1988 when the west side upper deck with its unique awning was added, raising seating capacity to 70,123. The first game in the newly renovated stadium was played September 24, 1988, and saw Alabama defeat Vanderbilt 44-10. Since the expansion, 16 consecutive capacity crowds have witnessed Alabama home games in Tuscaloosa.

In 1991, the artificial surface was replaced by Prescription Athletic Turf and for the first time since October 12, 1968, Alabama played a home game on natural grass.

Denny Stadium was rededicated on April 10, 1976, at the Spring A-Day game. Following a resolution passed by the state legislature in 1975, the facility received an expanded name to honor then active coach, Paul William Bryant. Bryant-Denny Stadium is probably the only facility to have been named after two active university staff members: Denny in 1929 and Bryant in 1975.

Stadium Stats

Number of games:	181
Stadium record:	161-17-3 (.898)
First game:	October 4, 1929; Alabama 22, Ole Miss 7
Largest crowd:	70,123 (16 times)
Longest winning streak:	57 games (1963-82)
Playing surface:	Natural grass

Legion Field

With Alabama's phenomenal record at Bryant-Denny Stadium, it's a wonder they would even consider playing home games anywhere else. Actually though, Bama played in Birmingham's Legion Field even before there WAS a Bryant-Denny Stadium. The Tide's relationship with the friendly confines of Legion Field dates back to 1927. Through last year's Conference Championship Game, Alabama had completed a 141-48-11 record (.733) at the Birmingham stadium. By the end of the 1992 season, Alabama had played an even 200 games at the facility.

Over the years many renovations and expansions have taken place at Legion Field. The latest, completed in 1991, saw a new press box completed, new scoreboards installed, 14 skyboxes built and additional seating added. The present capacity is 83,091. With these improvements and the frequent use of the stadium by teams of all ability levels from high school to pro, Legion Field will continue to claim its title of "Football Capital of the South."

Stadium Stats

Capacity:	83,091
Largest crowd:	86,293; October 19, 1991; Alabama 24, Tennessee 19
Playing surface:	Artificial turf

Alabama's Bryant-Denny Stadium

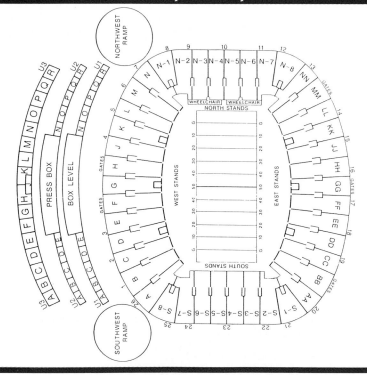

Legion Field in Birmingham

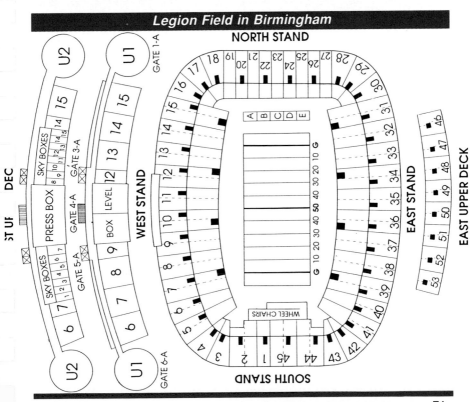

Eli Gold	-	Play-By-Play Announcer
Doug Layton	-	Color Analyst
Jerry Duncan	-	On-The-Field Announcer

ALABAMA FOOTBALL RADIO NETWORK
AM Stations   **FM Stations**

CITY	STATE	STATION	FREQUENCY	CITY	STATE	STATION	FREQUENCY
Albertville	AL	WAVU	630	Alexander City	AL	WZLM	97.3
Alexander City	AL	WDLK	1450	Arab	AL	WCRQ	92.7
Andalusia	AL	WTXQ	1400	Athens	AL	WZYP	104.3
Atmore	AL	WASG	550	Birmingham	AL	WZRR	99.5
Birmingham	AL	WJOX	690	Brewton	AL	WKNU	106.3
Bridgeport	AL	WBTS	1480	Butler	AL	WQGL	93.5
Butler	AL	WPRN	1330	Cullman	AL	WMFH	101.1
Centre	AL	WAGC	1560	Dothan	AL	WJJN	101.3
Centreville	AL	WBIB	1110	Enterprise	AL	WKMX	106.7
Columbus	GA	WPNX	1460	Erwin	TN	WEMB	103.9
Cullman	AL	WMFH	1460	Eufaula	AL	WULA	92.7
Decatur	AL	WAVD	1400	Jasper	AL	WFFN	92.9
Fayette	AL	WLDX	990	Linden	AL	WINL	98.5
Gadsden	AL	WGAD	1350	Mobile	AL	WKSJ	94.9
Haleyville	AL	WJBB	1230	Monroeville	AL	WMFC	99.3
Huntsville	AL	WTKI	1450	Montgomery	AL	WBAM	98.9
Jackson	MS	WPBQ	1240	Moulton	AL	WXKI	103.1
Jacksonville	FL	WZNZ	1460	Nashville	TN	WWTN	99.7
Jasper	AL	WARF	1240	Niceville	FL	WLGH	103.1
Memphis	TN	WHBQ	560	Oneonta	AL	WKLD	97.7
Mobile	AL	WKSJ	1270	Opelika	AL	WMXA	96.7
Montgomery	AL	WACV	1170	Opp	AL	WAMI	102.3
Oneonta	AL	WCRL	1570	Scottsboro	AL	WKEA	98.3
Opp	AL	WAMI	860	Talladega	AL	WEYY	92.7
Panama City	FL	WGNE	590	Tuscaloosa	AL	WFFX	95.7
Red Bay	AL	WRMG	1430	Tuscumbia	AL	WVNA	100.3
Robertsdale	AL	WXWY	1000	Valley	AL	WRLD	98.1
Sylacauga	AL	WFEB	1340	West Point	GA	WCJM	100.9
Tampa	FL	WQBN	1300	Winfield	AL	WKXM	105.9
Thomasville	AL	WJDB	630				
Tuscaloosa	AL	WTNW	1230				
Tuscumbia	AL	WVNA	1590				
West Point	GA	WPLV	1310				
Winfield	AL	WKXM	1300				

*Ticket Information

Ticket Office: (205) 348-6111

When people have extra tickets at Alabama games in Tuscaloosa or Birmingham, they generally offer them for sale in the immediate vicinity of the stadiums. **Ticket scalpers** have to be licensed in the State of Alabama, but rarely are the credentials of anyone selling tickets above face value checked by the authorities. Therefore, it is not uncommon to find Alabama tickets going for 200% or more of their face value.

At **Bryant-Denny Stadium** the "Million Dollar Band" sits near the students in the lower part of section MM and NN. The visiting band sits in the lower parts of sections BB and CC. Visiting fans sit in the lower half of sections CC and BB, sections AA, S1, S2 and the upper part of S4.

*Parking

Parking at **Bryant-Denny Stadium** is available around the stadium in several lots. First National Bank, First Alabama Bank and the Boy Scouts operate lots within 3 to 5 blocks of the facility. Many individuals and groups offer parking from $5 to $8 in yards, driveways and businesses. Free on-campus parking is available 4 to 5 blocks away at the Coliseum lot and at Ten Hoor Hall.

The key to finding good parking around Bryant-Denny Stadium is to come early. Fans arriving later than two hours before a game will find all of the good and/or free parking spaces claimed by "early birds" who know from experience that allowing extra time for enjoying pre-game campus atmosphere pays dividends in finding a better place to park.

RV parking is available beginning on Wednesdays at Coleman Coliseum and after 2:00 PM on Friday's behind Ten Hoor Hall. Parking is free, but space is limited

Legion Field has long been ranked as one of the worst facilities from a parking standpoint, but the Birmingham stadium is attempting to improve. Located in a largely residential section, Legion Field fans are often forced to park in individual's yards and driveways because there just aren't any lots to speak of. For the most part it still is that way---"you pays your money and you takes your chances."

Fees for parking range from $5 to $10. No guarantee of easy egress or vehicle safety is made, and when fans return after the game they often find their vehicles blocked in by others who arrived later. The best plan is to come early and park in one of the few city operated and attended lots around the stadium for a $5.00 fee. An alternate idea is to park downtown and take the shuttle for $4.00 per person (round trip).

RV operators may park in a lot behind the stadium's west side. Come early!

About 40 **handicapped parking spaces** are available at gate 10 on a first-come, first-served basis. Another 40 are located at the north end of the stadium but require a pass from the Athletic Department for entrance.

*ALL INFORMATION IS SUBJECT TO CHANGE

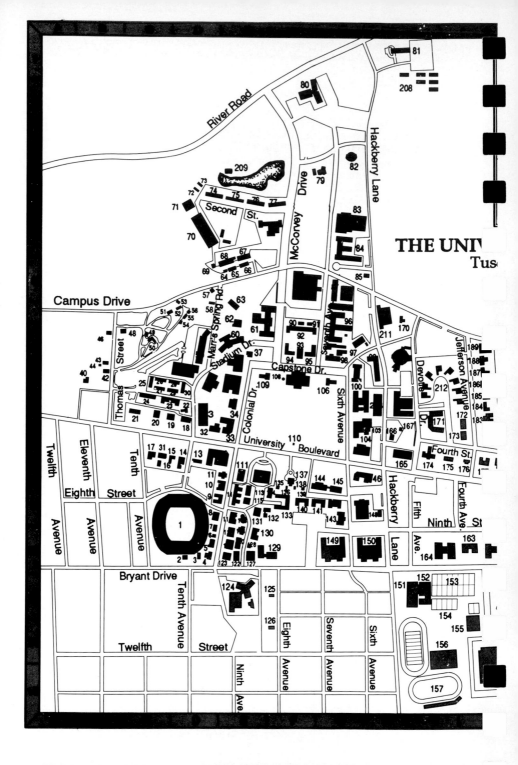

THE UNIV
Tus

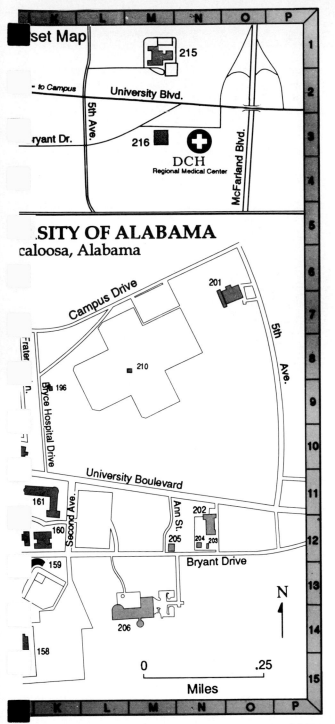

Inset Map

215

University Blvd.

5th Ave.

— to Campus

Bryant Dr.

216

DCH
Regional Medical Center

McFarland Blvd.

SITY OF ALABAMA
caloosa, Alabama

Campus Drive

201

5th Ave.

Frater

Bryce Hospital Drive

196

210

University Boulevard

Second Ave.

Ann St.

161

160

159

202

205

204 203

Bryant Drive

206

158

N

0   .25

Miles

The **Alabama Museum of Natural History** in Smith Hall, features several mounted specimens of large animals, a geological museum with fossils and dinosaurs and the Hodges meteorite (the only one ever to strike a person). Open Monday-Friday 8 AM-4:30 PM, Saturday 10 AM-4 PM, Sunday 2-4 PM. Free. (205) 348-7550.

Denny Chimes, built in 1929, ring every quarter hour and sometimes play an afternoon concert. The surrounding sidewalks have handprints and footprints of former great Alabama footballers. Located at the heart of the Campus on the Quadrangle, the Chimes have long been a symbol of the University of Alabama.

Father and son at Denny Chimes...and the tradition continues. But that blue hat has to go!

Built in 1828, the **Gorgas House** was one of the first buildings erected on campus and was used as a dining hall for students. It was one of four buildings to survive the burning of the campus during the Civil War. Located on the Quadrangle. Open Mon--Sat 10 AM-Noon and 2-5 PM; Sunday 3-5 PM. Free. (205) 348-5906.

The Garland Hall Art Gallery houses a permanent collection plus several temporary exhibits per year. Open Mon. - Fri., 8:00 AM-4:45 PM. (205) 348-5967.

Bryant-Denny Stadium. Home of the Alabama Crimson Tide. The old stadium has been expanded and modernized. Scene of great football tradition.

Bryant Museum. Located across Bryant Drive from Coleman Coliseum, the collection includes memorabilia from 100 years of Alabama football. A special section updates the current season. Open Monday-Saturday 9 AM-4 PM. Admission: $2.00 adults, $1.00 children. Active alumni, faculty, staff and UA students admitted free. 300 Paul W. Bryant Drive. (205) 348-4668.

- **Greenetrack.** Greyhound racing and dining. Entire track climate controlled. Handicapped accessible. Located 25 miles west of Tuscaloosa on I-59 at Exit 45. (205) 758-2709.

- **Mound State Monument.** Site of the most important prehistoric Indian settlement and ceremonial center in the South. Archaeological museum, a reconstructed Indian village, a restored temple, nature trails & picnic area. Located about 20 miles south of Tuscaloosa off State Road 69.(205) 371-2572.

- **The Old Tavern.** Built in 1827, was relocated to its present site where it serves as a museum. 2800 University Boulevard. (205) 758-2738.

- **Tannehill State Park.** Is built around the ruins of the pre-Civil War Tannehill Iron Works. Spreading over 1,500 scenic acres, the park includes many historic trails, pioneer homes and a working mill where corn meal is ground. *Tannehill Trade Days* are held the third weekend of each month from March through December. Exit 100 off I-59 East of Tuscaloosa. (205) 477-5711.

- **The Battle-Friedman House**, built in 1835, has18" brick walls Furnished with pieces from the early 1800's. 1010 Greensboro Ave. (205) 758-2238.

- **Gulf States Paper Corporation National Headquarters** on River Road features dramatic Oriental architecture and an outstanding collection of art, including historic Americana, primitive sculpture from Africa and Oceania, Oriental masterpieces and classical and modern paintings. Call about free tours. (205) 553-6200.

- **The Mildred Warner House** at the corner of 20th Avenue and Eighth Street was built in two stages. The one-story wing dates from 1820; the four-story Georgian section from 1832. Furnishings date back to the mid-1700's. Many artists are featured throughout the house including Mary Cassatt and James Whistler. Free. (205) 345-4062.

- **The Kentuck Festival**, held each October, is one of the South's major arts and crafts festivals and features over 200 artists and craftspersons. (205) 333-1252.

For complete information about events in the area, including a dining guide and hotel/motel guide, contact:

West Alabama Chamber of Commerce
2200 University Boulevard
P. O. Box 020410
Tuscaloosa, AL 35402
Phone: (205) 758-7588 or 1-800-330-2025

Where to Eat and Sleep in the Tuscaloosa Area

Tuscaloosa is proud of its growing list of accommodations and eating establishments. However, because of the crowd on game weekends you may have to stay in Northport which is an adjoining city. Birmingham, about an hour's drive to the northeast, also helps take up the excess on football weekends.

The restaurants of Tuscaloosa feature American cuisine from hamburgers, chicken and steak, to home cooking and bar-b-que. Mexican and Italian dominate the limited ethnic offerings.

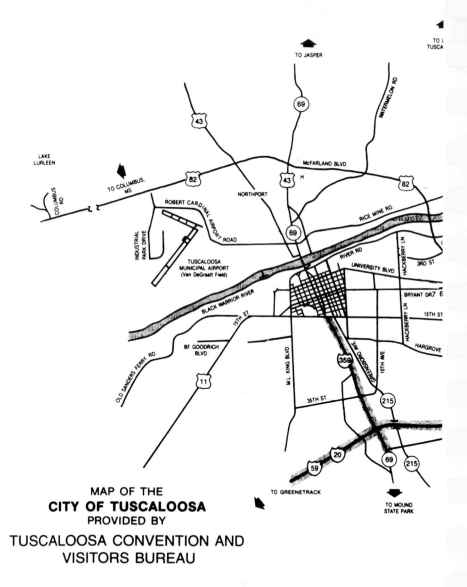

MAP OF THE
CITY OF TUSCALOOSA
PROVIDED BY

TUSCALOOSA CONVENTION AND
VISITORS BUREAU

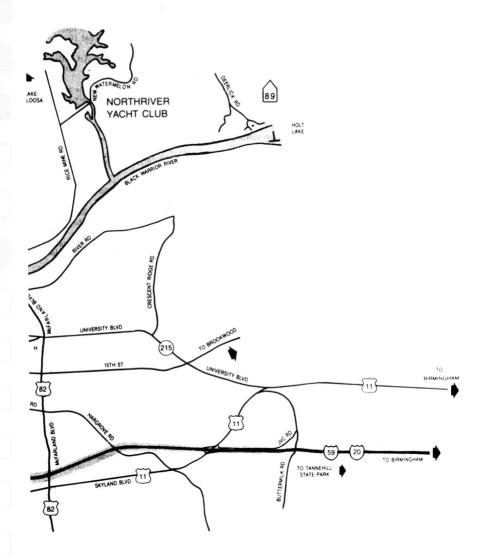

BIRMINGHAM ATTRACTIONS

1. Birmingham Museum of Art (D)
2. Birmingham / Jefferson Civic Center (D)
   Alabama Sports Hall of Fame (D)
3. Birmingham Public Library (D)
4. Sloss Furances (D, M)
5. Five Points South / Cobb Lane (D, M)
6. Vulcan (M)
7. UAB / Alabama Museum of The Health Sciences / Reynolds Historical Library / Visitors' Information Center (D, M)
8. Alabama Theatre (D)
9. Arlington Antebellum Home (M)
10. Tannehill State Park (M)
11. Meyer Planetarium (M)
12. Legion Field (M)
13. Downtown (D)
14. Birmingham Race Course (M)
15. Birmingham Municipal Airport / Visitors Information Center (M)
16. Southern Museum of Flight (M)
17. The Birmingham Zoo (M)
18. Birmingham Botanical Gardens (M)
19. Red Mountain Museum (D)
20. The Discovery Place (D)
21. Riverchase Galleria (M)
22. Oak Mountain State Park / Oak Mountain Ampitheater (M)
23. Civil Rights District (D)
24. Ruffner Mountain Nature Center (M)
25. Hoover Metropolitan Stadium (M)
26. Alabama State Fairgrounds (M)
27. Boutwell Auditorium (D)

D   - Downtown Map
M   - Metropolitan Area Map
D, M - Both Maps

METROPOLITAN BIRMINGHAM

Map courtesy of Birmingham Historical Society

~**Alabama Sports Hall of Fame**. Sports memorabilia from many of Alabama's sports greats from Joe Lewis and Willie Mays to Bear Bryant. Monday-Saturday 10 AM - 5 PM, Sunday 1 - 5 PM. Adults $1.50, students $.75, under 5 free; Family rate $4.00. Downtown at 1 Civic Center Plaza. (205) 333-6665.

~**The Birmingham Zoo** is home to almost 1,000 different species including mammals, birds and reptiles. Big cats and Spider Monkeys are featured. Zoo train. Open daily 9:30 AM - 5 PM. Adults $3.00, senior citizens and ages 2-17 $1.50. Located in Lane Park off U.S. Highway 280. (205) 879-0408.

~**The Birmingham Botanical Gardens** presents 67 acres of flowers and foliage from around the world. The clear glass conservatory is the largest in the Southeast. Nationally famous Bonsai tree collection. Open daily from dawn to dusk. Free. 2612 Lane Park Road. (205) 879-1227.

~**The Birmingham Museum of Art** is an up-and-coming gallery which has already grown into the largest municipally-supported museum in the South! It features Italian Renaissance art, 17th century Dutch and Flemish works, 18th century British and 19th century French art. Free. Located at 2000 - 8th Avenue North. (205) 254-2565.

~**The Discovery Place** is a hands-on museum just for kids and their parents. Enjoy investigating anatomy, occupations and communications. Open Tuesday through Friday 9 AM - 3 PM, Saturday-Sunday 1 PM - 4 PM. Closed during September. (205) 939-1176.

~**Sloss Furnace National Historic Landmark,** at 1st Avenue North and 32nd Street, allows visitors to gain a better understanding of what made Birmingham the "Magic City" and led to its rapid growth---its steel industry. The historic furnace operated for 89 years before closing in 1971 and is now a community gathering place offering art, blacksmiths, etc. Free. (205) 324-1911.

~**Vulcan**, the largest iron statue ever cast, honors the mythical god of metal working. From his perch atop Red Mountain, Vulcan watches over Birmingham. Visible for miles, his up-raised torch burns green when traffic flows smoothly; red when a traffic fatality has occurred in Birmingham within the last 24 hours. Cast in 1904, the statue was displayed at the St. Louis World's Fair. Open daily 1:30 AM-10:30PM. Admission $1.00, under 6 free. On U.S. 31. (205) 328-2863.

For complete information about Birmingham including a dining and hotel/motel guide, contact:

> **Birmingham Area Chamber of Commerce**
> **P. O. Box 10127**
> **Birmingham AL 35202**
> **Phone: (205) 323-5461**

Where to Eat and Sleep in the Birmingham Area

Birmingham isn't a small, Southern city anymore! The commercial, medical and educational communities have attracted people in large numbers from all over, with different tastes and expectations. The impact has been that Birmingham's businesses offering food and accommodations have experienced similar growth in numbers and variety. Accommodations should be available even on "big game" weekends.

NOTES

*Old Main, symbol of the University of Arkansas,
is a treasure brought back to vitality
through loving restoration.*

ARKANSAS

A Razorback fan's pride is reflected in his license plate.
Longtime SEC fans are proud to claim Arkansas, too!

The 14,500 students at the University of Arkansas main campus in Fayetteville must surely realize how fortunate they are to live and study where they do. The combination of Arkansas' premier institution of higher learning and what has been recognized as one of the most progressive and livable small cities in the nation, create a near ideal college environment.

Founded in 1871, the university has long enjoyed a symbiotic relationship with its host city, Fayetteville. The town actively pursued locating the school in this northwest corner of the state over the objections of many. Some claimed that the distance from other parts of Arkansas would work a hardship on students. Others, perhaps for personal or political reasons, fought the Fayetteville site. Today it only takes a drive through the campus, around downtown and up to one of many lofty vantage points around the city to see how well the school and community go together.

With its core of academic and business leaders fostered by the university, Fayetteville has become the cultural and financial hub of the region. With over 45,000 residents, the town is large enough to provide a wide range of activities for students and faculty, but small enough to have a "small town" spirit of friendliness. An example of how the two communities influence one another is the new Walton Arts Center which is arguably the finest facility of its kind for many miles in any direction.

Other examples of the special relationship the University of Arkansas has with the people of the state are Senior Walk, which displays the engraved names of the over 100,00 graduates of the institution, and the restorative work performed on Old Main. The love, money and talents of the people involved in bringing the venerable structure back to its vitality are repaid when one gazes over the city from the hills and sees the twin spires of Old Main rising atop the prominence of the campus near the city's literal and spiritual hearts.

The University of Arkansas cheerleaders spell excitement
whenever they perform at Razorback athletic contests.

In 1895, when the University was 23 years old and athletic competition was just beginning the student body held a contest to choose a school color. They voted to adopt "cardinal," a deep red color between scarlet and crimson, as the shade of red to represent Arkansas teams. The color that lost the contest? Heliotrope: a reddish-purple!

Arkansas' official red is PMS Color #200C. White is Arkansas' other color.

*The "Fighting Razorback" -- rowdy and rambunctious -- is
a real crowd pleaser!*

University of Arkansas athletic teams were nicknamed "Cardinals", for the school colors from 1895 through 1909. At a rally following that season, Arkansas coach Hugo Bezdek excitedly described his undefeated team as a "wild bunch of razorbacks."

The nickname quickly gained favor and by the 1920's, the now famous "Whooo, Pig! Sooie!" yell was added.

Big Red, the Arkansas Razorback, "roots" for his team
from the shade of his motorized pig pen.

The first live mascot to represent the University of Arkansas did not arrive on the scene until the mid-1960's and he wasn't even a razorback! His name was Big Red I. He and his successor, Big Red II, were actually Duroc hogs. Both were victims of heart attacks.

Big Red III, arriving in 1975, was the first wild boar to serve as mascot. Unfortunately, after escaping from an animal exhibit in 1977, he was shot and killed by a farmer while attempting to break into an animal pen.

The next mascot, named "Ragnar," was the first native Arkansas razorback to occupy that post. Captured in the wild in South Arkansas, he served only during the 1977 season, dying mysteriously in early 1978.

The current mascot is Big Red X. He makes appearances before home football games, circling the field in his custom red trailer. Sometimes he parks it near the visitors' stands, no doubt causing some ticket purchasers to inquire not only about row and section, but about wind direction as well!

The University of Arkansas Razorback Marching Band can always be counted on to make the crowd "go hog wild!" The band, numbering in excess of 200 members, is led by third year director, Mr. Dale Warren.

Band members report for rehearsals the week before classes start and practice nine hours a day for six days. From that point the band puts in hundreds of hours in practice and performance proudly representing the "Cardinal and White."

UNIVERSITY OF ARKANSAS
"Fight Song"

Hit that line, Hit that line, Keep on going,
Take that ball right down the field.
Give a cheer. Rah! Rah!
Never fear. Rah! Rah!
Arkansas will never yield.
On your toes Razorbacks to the finish.
Carry on with all your might.
For it's A-A-A-R-K-A-N-S-A-S for Arkansas,
Fight, Fight, Fi-i-ight, Fight, Fight.
GO HOGS GO !!!

Finishing with a flourish, the Razorback Marching Band
prepares to exit left in the traditional "GO HOGS" formation.

UNIVERSITY*of*ARKANSAS

≡ 1871 ≡

UNIVERSITY OF ARKANSAS
"Alma Mater"

Pure as the dawn on the brow of thy beauty
Watches thy soul from the mountains of God
Over the Fates of thy children departed
Far from the land where their footsteps have trod.
Beacon of Hope in the ways dreary lighted;
Pride of our hearts that are loyal and true;
From those who adore unto one who adores us---
Mother of Mothers, we sing unto you.

We, with our faces turned high to the Eastward
Proud of our place in the vanguard of Truth,
Will sing unto thee a new song of thanksgiving---
Honor to God and the Springtime of Youth.
Shout for the victory or tear for the vanquished;
Sunshine or tempest thy heart is e'er true;
Pride of the hills and the white-laden Lowlands---
Mother of Mothers, we kneel unto you.

Ever the Legions of Sin will assail us,
Even the Battle in Cities afar;
Still in the depth will thy Spirit eternal
Beckon us on like a piloting Star.
Down the dim years do thy dead children call thee,
Wafted to sleep while the Springtime was new;
We, of the Present, thy Hope of the Future---
Mother of Mothers, we pray unto you.

Words by Mr. Brodie Payne, '06 of Hot Springs, Arkansas
Music by Professor H. D. Tovey, Director of the Conservatory of Music and Art

The "new kid on the western block" of the SEC is the University of Arkansas and it's clear that the Razorbacks will bring the thrill of the "west" to the Southeast. During their first game with conference rival, Georgia, the whole pressbox shook from the roar of the crowd.

Arkansas' fans seem very happy to have joined the SEC. Being the only non-Texas team in the Southwest Conference was not bad, but the Razorbacks like the challenge and variety of their new conference opponents. Joe and Ruth Skaggs of Rogers, Arkansas, expressed the concern that "everyone wants to beat up the new kid on the block." However, it became apparent this new kid could certainly return the punches and "give the old boys some new competition," as Razorback fan Dickey Cleveland of Fayetteville predicted.

When interviewed about who they thought would be their biggest rival many picked Alabama, but others chose Tennessee and Georgia. However, Christine Williams of Helena, Arkansas and Gerald Tatum of Little Rock both confirmed there was a long-standing rivalry with Ole Miss, perhaps even more passionate than the one with Alabama! LSU should also prove to be a natural rival because of proximity.

Whoever their rival *du jour*, Arkansas fans are true "fanatics." For example, Dale Mather of Bentonville, Arkansas, responded this way to our question about who has the best band in the SEC: "Is this a trick question? Who cares?" Football!!" Well, some of us fanatics really enjoy the band performances, and the Razorback Marching Band in particular; but his remark

1992 -- Arkansas' first SEC football homecoming.
A frat house displays the season's theme, "It's A Whole New Ballgame!"

Razorback fans really know how to enjoy gameday!

does tell us that the Razorbacks do intend to play hard. Many others echoed his sentiment that the football game itself is very important. Dewey Logan of Malvern, Arkansas, has driven hundreds of miles roundtrip to every Arkansas game since 1946. Razorback fans are very ardent!

They are also avid tailgaters. It's a tradition for many to travel to all games in their motorhomes. This should provide the opportunity for some great experiences when visiting the hogs in Arkansas or when they visit you.

A unique tradition associated with Razorback football is their "hog call." "Whoo, Pig Soieee!" is proudly used to "call the hogs" before, during and after the game. As Lisa Nickel with the Alumni Association says, "seeing friends, calling the hogs and catching the spirit" is all part of the great football tradition in Arkansas.

Arkansas' fans recommend Hermann's Ribs and AQ Chicken if you're looking for some good food. We found no shortage of restaurants. Many of the fans we interviewed told us that, whether tailgating or eating out, barbecue is their favorite gameday food . . . beef, of course!

Razorback Stadium is a beautiful place to watch a game. The bright green of the turf along with the red and white of Arkansas' colors make the game even more enjoyable. Although we found a great home crowd when we visited Fayetteville, Paul Torchiniky of Fayetteville says there has been some low attendance and "it's embarrassing" when games are not sold out. However, we suspect the heated rivalries between the SEC schools should help that problem.

No doubt about it, it's a long trip from other conference cities to Little Rock, and even further to Fayetteville. However, it was worth every hour of driving. We can hardly wait to go again and again! A trip to Arkansas will allow you to see some most beautiful scenery. Be sure to allow some time to enjoy the view.

When you arrive, you will find Razorback fans warm, friendly and eager to meet their new brothers and sisters in the conference. John and Mary Haley of North Little Rock pointed out that Arkansas is the only SEC school "west of the Mississippi," so what better reason to "go west" for some adventure! You will find it easy to "catch the spirit" when playing the Razorbacks in their neck of the woods . . . so don't miss it!

The Razorbacks take the field in their first ever SEC game in Fayetteville!

Head Coach:

Danny Ford (Alabama, 1970)
Alabama Graduate Assistant, 1970-71;
Alabama Assistant 1972-73;
Virginia Tech Assistant, 1974-76;
Clemson Assistant, 1977;
Clemson Head Coach, 1978-89;
Arkansas Head Coach, 1993-present

Birthday:	**April 2, 1948**
Hometown:	**Gadsden AL**

Assistant Coaches

Louis Campbell (Arkansas, 1973)	Secondary
Greg Davis (McNeese State, 1973)	Quarterbacks
Rockey Felker (Mississippi State, 1975)	Running Backs
Fitz Hill (Ouachita Baptist, 1987)	Receivers
Buddy King (Clemson, 1973)	Offensive Line
Joe Kines (Jacksonville State, 1966)	Assistant Head Coach/ Defensive Coordinator
Joe Pate (Alabama, 1968)	Defensive Line
Scott Smith (Baylor, 1981)	Linebackers
Larry Van Der Hayden (Iowa State, 1964)	Offensive Line
Harold Horton (Arkansas, 1962)	Recruiting Coordinator

*Razorback Stadium, offering sharp contrasts of cardinal and green,
is one of the most colorful places to watch SEC football.*

Arkansas is one of two SEC schools which typical divide their "home" schedule evenly between two stadiums. In Fayetteville, games are played in Razorback Stadium, while in the capital city of Little Rock, War Memorial Stadium serves as the "Hogs" home away from home.

Razorback Stadium

Razorback Stadium was constructed as a WPA project during the Great Depression and opened in the 1938 season with an original capacity of 13,500. Through several expansion projects and upgrades (see chart below) the stadium now seats 51,000 and compares favorably with other SEC arenas in all aspects. With its bright green artificial turf and thousands of Hog fans decked out in Arkansas cardinal, Razorback Stadium is one of the most colorful places football is played in the conference.

Before the construction of Razorback Stadium, Arkansas football was played on a field located where the present-day University Library and Fine Arts Center are found. The "stadium," built in 1901, seated 300 fans and was surrounded by a fence.

Growth of Razorback Stadium

1938   Original stadium built; Capacity 13,500
1947   2,500 seats added to north end of each side

Growth of Razorback Stadium (continued)

1950	New press box constructed along with 5,200 seats on west side
1957	5,200 seat expansion completed on east side
1965-69	Capacity increased to 42,678
1969	Astro-Turf placed on playing surface
1975	Broyles Athletic Complex completed
1985	10,000 seats, sky boxes and covered areas added

Stadium Stats - Razorback Stadium

Stadium record:	(1938-1992) W - 114 L - 53 T - 2 (Pct. .680)
October 8, 1938	Razorback Stadium dedicated
October 8, 1938	First game; Baylor 9, Arkansas 6
September 17, 1969	First game played on artificial turf; Arkansas 55, Tulsa 0
November 11, 1989	First night game; Arkansas 19, Baylor 10
November 2, 1991	Last Southwest Conference game; Baylor 9, Arkansas 5
October 3, 1992	First Southeast Conference game; Georgia 27, Arkansas 3
Capacity:	51,000
Playing surface:	Artificial Turf

Arkansas Attendance Records

Single Game Attendance record:
- Razorback Stadium ....53,818, vs. Texas A & M (1986)
- War Memorial Stadium ....55,912, vs. Alabama (1992)

Season record:
- Razorback Stadium ....(4 games) 191,880 (1986)
- War Memorial Stadium ....(4 games) 221,686 (1979)

Home season record:
- Both stadiums ....(8 games), 381,221 (1971)

Highest season average:
- Razorback Stadium 52,122 (1989)
- War Memorial Stadium 54,570 (1981)

Highest season average:
- Both stadiums 51,138 (1989)

Largest crowds ever to see Arkansas play:
- 95,902 ....at Tennessee, October 10, 1992
- 82,910 ....at Sugar Bowl vs. Alabama, January 1, 1962
- 82,910 ....at Sugar Bowl vs. Ole Miss, January 1, 1963

Most fans to see Arkansas in a single season:
- Regular season ....(11 games) 566,264 (1978)
- Regular season and bowl ......(12 games) 621,466 (1977)

War Memorial Stadium

War Memorial Stadium was completed in 1948. Its original capacity was 31,000. Three expansions have increased the size of the facility to its present capacity of 53,727. As in Fayetteville, Astro-Turf was added in 1969. Also, a complete lighting system was installed that same year. In 1974, the press box was voted best in the nation by the Football Writers' Association.

Stadium Stats

September 18, 1948:	Stadium dedicated
September 18, 1948:	First game; Arkansas 40, Abilene Christian 6
September 20, 1970:	First game on Astro-Turf; Stanford 34, Arkansas 28
November 23, 1991:	Last Southwest Conference game; Arkansas 20, Rice 0
September 19, 1992:	First Southeastern Conference game; Alabama 38, Arkansas 11
Playing Surface:	Artificial turf

Arkansas' Razorback Stadium

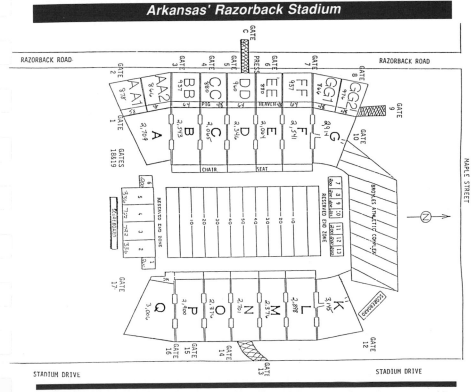

War Memorial Stadium in Little Rock

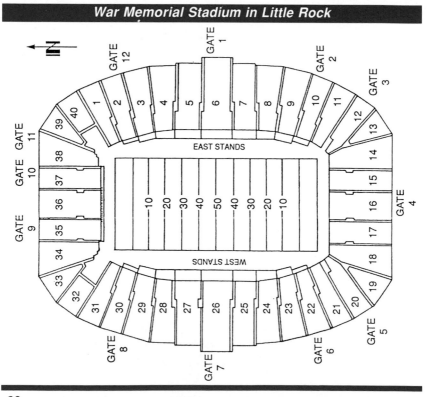

University of Arkansas - Sports Network

Paul Eells - Play-By-Play
Rick Schaeffer - Color Analyst

RAZORBACK RADIO NETWORK

AM Stations

CITY	STATE	STATION	FREQUENCY
Bald Knob	AR	KAPZ	710
Batesville	AR	KBTA	1340
Bellefonte	AR	KNWA	
Benton	AR	KEWI	
Blytheville	AR	KLCN	910
Corning	AR	KCCB	1260
Crossett	AR	KAGH	800
Dequeen	AR	KDQN	1390
Dumas	AR	KDDA	1560
Farmington	AR	KFAY	1030
Forrest City	AR	KXJK	
Fort Smith	AR	KFPW	1230
Heber Springs	AR	KAWW	1370
Helena	AR	KFFA	
Hot Springs	AR	KXOW	1420
Jonesboro	AR	KBTM	
Malvern	AR	KBOK	
Mena	AR	KENA	1450
Morrilton	AR	KVOM	
Newport	AR	KNBY	
Osceola	AR	KOSE	860
Ozark	AR	KDYN	
Pocahontas	AR	KPOC	1420
Prescott	AR	KTPA	1370
Searcy	AR	KWCK	
Shreveport	LA	KFLO	1300
Siloam Springs	AR	KUOA	1290
Stuttgart	AR	KWAK	1240
Tulsa	OK	KTRT	1270
Warren	AR	KWRF	
West Memphis	AR	KSUD	730
Wynne	AR	KWYN	1400

FM Stations

CITY	STATE	STATION	FREQUENCY
Ashdown	AR	KARQ	92.1
Bald Knob	AR	KKSY	107.1
Batesville	AR	KZLE	93.1
Batesville	AR	KWOZ	
Beebe	AR	KPIK	
Bentonville	AR	KESE	93.3
Blytheville	AR	KHLS	96.3
Brinkley	AR	KQMC	102.3
Camden	AR	KCXY	95.3
Clarksville	AR	KXIO	
Crossett	AR	KAGH	104.9
Dequeen	AR	KDQN	92.7
El Dorado	AR	KLBQ	99.3
El Dorado	AR	KIXB	
Fayetteville	AR	KKEG	92.1
Fayetteville	AR	KEZA	107.9
Fordyce	AR	KQEW	101.7
Forrest City	AR	KBFC	93.5
Fort Smith	AR	KBBQ	100.7
Fort Smith	AR	KEZU	
Glenwood	AR	KWXE	
Greenville	MS	WDMS	100.7
Gurdon	AR	KYXK	
Harrison	AR	KCWD	96.7
Harrison	AR	KHOZ	
Heber Springs	AR	KAWW	96.7
Helena	AR	KCRI	103.1
Hope	AR	KHPA	104.9
Hot Springs	AR	KLAZ	105.9
Joplin	MO	KKLL	97.9
Lake Village	AR	KUUZ	95.9
Little Rock	AR	KSSN	95.7
Magnolia	AR	KZHE	100.1
Malvern	AR	KBOK	93.3
Mammoth Spring	AR	KAMS	95.1
Mena	AR	KENA	101.7
Morrilton	AR	KVOM	
Mountain Home	AR	KPFM	105.5
Mountain Home	AR	KTLO	98.3
Nashville	AR	KNAS	105.5
Newport	AR	KOKR	
Ozark	AR	KDYN	
Paragould	AR	KDXY	104.9
Pine Bluff	AR	KPBQ	
Pocahontas	AR	KPOC	
Russellville	AR	KWKK	
Walnut Ridge	AR	KRLW	
Warren	AR	KWRF	
Wynne	AR	KWYN	92.7

*Ticket Information

Ticket Office: (501) 575-HOGS
In Arkansas it is illegal to sell tickets for more than face value. Arrests are made at times by campus and/or city police.
In **Fayetteville seating** for the Razorback Marching Band is in Section "O". Visiting band have a choice between Sections "L" and "K". Visiting fans sit in Sections "M," "K," and "GG" if needed.
In **Little Rock** the home band is seated in Section 3 while the visiting band may choose from Sections 11, 12, 14 or 15. Visiting fans are seated in the lower part of Sections 9-16.

*Stadium Policies

In **Razorback Stadium,** as in all SEC schools, no artificial noise makers are allowed . Fans are to keep off the playing field at all times and may be ejected for throwing objects in the stadium or being disruptive. Still cameras are allowed in the stadium but video cameras are prohibited. No banners may be hung without written permission by the Arkansas Athletic Department (501-575-7404).
Passes out are allowed only for emergencies and re-entry passes are available by presenting your ticket stub at Gates 5, 9 and 10 on the west, Gate 12 on the east, and south end zone Gate 18.
At War Memorial Stadium the same rules apply. Emergency passes out may be obtained at Gates 1, 3, 7 and 9 by presenting your ticket stub.

*Fayetteville Parking Information

The area around Razorback Stadium is restricted to permitted vehicles on gamedays. All other campus lots are unrestricted on Saturdays but they fill up quickly. Many fans may choose to park their vehicles at the Baldwin Piano lot at the intersection of 6th and Beechwood. There is a free **shuttle** which runs three hours before gametime and one hour afterward.
A van for the **handicapped** shuttles fans from the Baldwin lot to the stadium.
RV operators may park in a general lot four blocks south of the stadium. Parking is free and available after 5:00 PM on Friday. RV's may stay over until Sunday.

*Little Rock Parking Information

In Little Rock, stadium parking is controlled by the Razorback Foundation. Parking is available in the park which surround the stadium although this may involve walking a distance.
They issue **handicapped parking permits** (drop-offs are allowed) and rent spaces for those with special needs. For additional information call **War Memorial Stadium at (501) 663-6385.**

*ALL INFORMATION IS SUBJECT TO CHANGE

Resembling Grand Central Station on gameday,
the wonderful, multi-level Arkansas student union leads down to the stadium

~**Old Main.** To appreciate the history, traditions, growth and change the university has experienced, a tour of this venerable building is a must. Completed in 1875 when the school was only four years old, this grand structure, which over the years has been home to virtually every department of the University, has been beautifully restored. Open on game days.

~**Senior Walk.** Beginning at the front steps of Old Main, the sidewalks on the campus bear the names of all the graduates since 1876.

~**Chi Omega Greek Theatre.** Constructed in 1930, this interesting outdoor amphitheater hosts a variety of events including pep rallies.

~**Barnhill Arena.** Former home of Razorback basketball.

~**Arkansas Union.** A most interesting modern structure built into the sometimes steep terrain of the university's campus. Houses restrooms and bookstore. Open gamedays.

~**Spoofer's Stone.** "Love on the rocks." Traditional meeting place for couples in love. Front lawn of Old Main.

--**The Bud Walton Arena.** Marvelous new home of Razorback basketball.

UNIVERSITY OF ARKANSAS

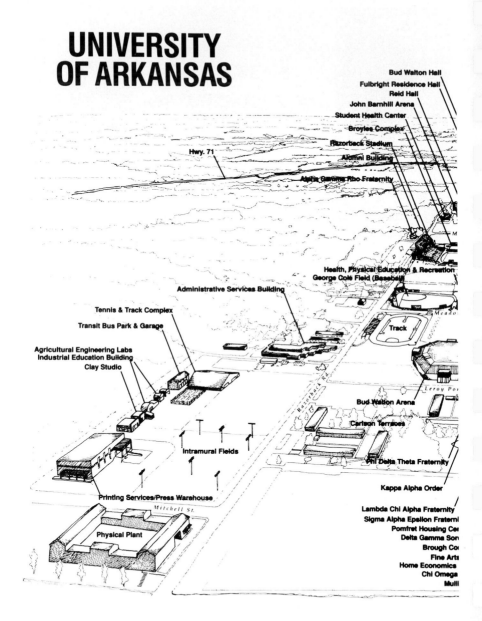

Bud Walton Hall
Fulbright Residence Hall
Reid Hall
John Barnhill Arena
Student Health Center
Broyles Complex
Razorback Stadium
Alumni Building
Alpha Gamma Rho Fraternity

Hwy. 71

Health, Physical Education & Recreation
George Cole Field (Baseball)

Administrative Services Building

Tennis & Track Complex

Transit Bus Park & Garage

Agricultural Engineering Labs
Industrial Education Building
Clay Studio

Track

Bud Walton Arena

Carlson Terraces

Phi Delta Theta Fraternity

Intramural Fields

Kappa Alpha Order

Printing Services/Press Warehouse

Mitchell St.

Lambda Chi Alpha Fraternity
Sigma Alpha Epsilon Fraterni
Pomfret Housing Ce
Delta Gamma Sor
Brough Co
Fine Art
Home Economics
Chi Omega
Multi

Physical Plant

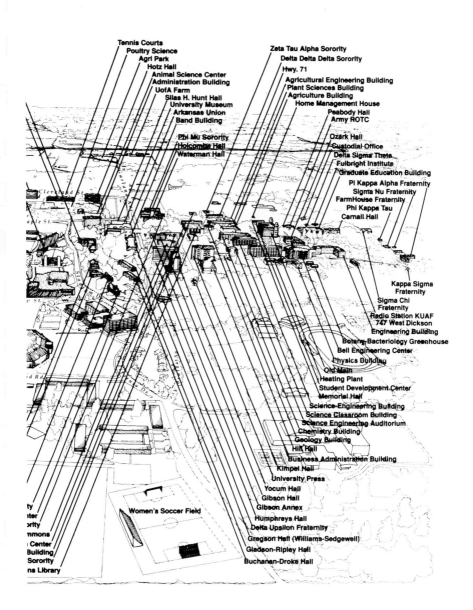

Tennis Courts
Poultry Science
Agri Park
Hotz Hall
Animal Science Center
Administration Building
UofA Farm
Silas H. Hunt Hall
University Museum
Arkansas Union
Band Building

Phi Mu Sorority
Holcombe Hall
Waterman Hall

Zeta Tau Alpha Sorority
Delta Delta Delta Sorority
Hwy. 71
Agricultural Engineering Building
Plant Sciences Building
Agriculture Building
Home Management House
Peabody Hall
Army ROTC

Ozark Hall
Custodial Office
Delta Sigma Theta
Fulbright Institute
Graduate Education Building
Pi Kappa Alpha Fraternity
Sigma Nu Fraternity
FarmHouse Fraternity
Phi Kappa Tau
Carnall Hall

Kappa Sigma
Fraternity
Sigma Chi
Fraternity
Radio Station KUAF
747 West Dickson
Engineering Building
Botany-Bacteriology Greenhouse
Bell Engineering Center
Physics Building
Old Main
Heating Plant
Student Development Center
Memorial Hall
Science-Engineering Building
Science Classroom Building
Science Engineering Auditorium
Chemistry Building
Geology Building
Hill Hall
Business Administration Building
Kimpel Hall
University Press
Yocum Hall
Gibson Hall
Gibson Annex
Humphreys Hall
Delta Upsilon Fraternity
Gregson Hall (Williams-Sedgewell)
Gladson-Ripley Hall
Buchanan-Droke Hall

Women's Soccer Field

ty
ter
ority
mmons
Center
Building
Sorority
ns Library

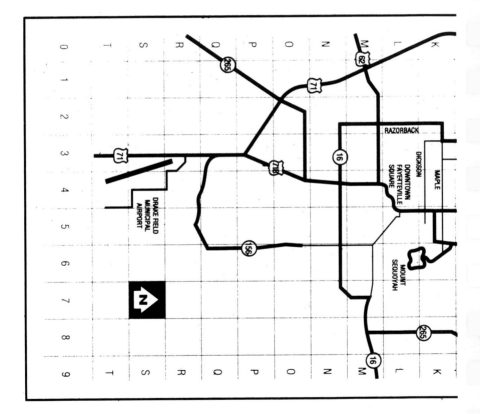

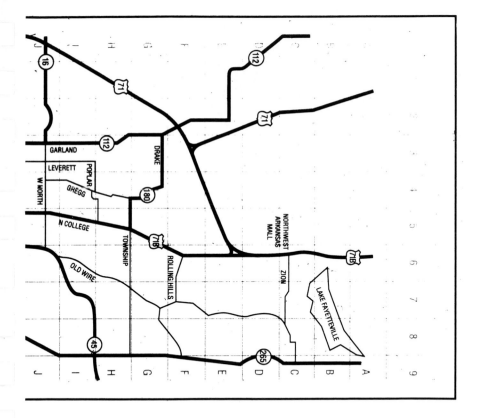

This handsome Bank building on Fayetteville's thriving square, serves as the exterior of Blue's Cafe on the TV series, "Evening Shade."

~**The Town Square.** Home to a variety of attractively renovated shops and restaurants including a building which serves as the exterior of Blue's Cafe on the *Evening Shade* TV series. Bordered by Block and East Avenues and Center and Mountain Streets.

~**All Seasons Trail.** Scenic drive through Fayetteville, includes many city landmarks. Maps available at the Chamber of Commerce office on 123 West Mountain Street. (501) 521-1710.

~**The Great Passion Play.** World's largest outdoor drama depicting Christ's last days. Eureka Springs. Highway 62. (501) 253-9200.

~**Terra Studio.** Known for redbirds, bluebirds and other beautiful glassware items. South of Fayetteville off Highway 16. (501) 643-3185.

~**Pea Ridge Park.** A 4,300 acre national park on the site of the largest Civil War battle west of the Mississippi River. North of Fayetteville on Highway 62. (501) 451-8122.

~**Eureka Springs.** You will find this picturesque mountain village northeast of Fayetteville. It features gingerbread Victorian houses and countless arts and crafts shops. Truly unique! Highway 62. (501) 253-8737.

~**Rogers and Bentonville**. Two small towns north of Fayetteville. Rogers is home of the world's first Wal-Mart store (1962) and Bentonville is Corporate Headquarters of Wal-Mart and home of the Wal-Mart Visitor Center located at 105 North Main. (501) 237-1329.

~**Branson, Missouri.** A few hours to the Northeast of Fayetteville. Country Music's new home in the Ozarks.

ANNUAL EVENTS

Autumnfest - Fayetteville celebrates the beauty and bounty of Fall. Three days of special events. (501) 521-1710.

Arkansas Apple Festival - Town of Lincoln (SW of Fayetteville) hosts a 3 day fair in praise of apples, the area's main cash crop. (501) 824-3232.

War Eagle Mill Arts and Crafts Fair - Largest and oldest fair of its kind in Arkansas. Held on the beautiful War Eagle River east of Fayetteville. (501) 789-5398.

This is merely a representative sampling of interesting places and activities in and around Fayetteville. For more information call or write:

Fayetteville Chamber of Commerce   (501) 521-1710
123 West Mountain
P.O. Box 4216
Fayetteville, AR 72702-4216

Where to Eat and Sleep in Fayetteville

Fayetteville has over 110 restaurants ranging from fast food to limited ethnic, including steak, barbecue, homecooking and variety. A complete listing which includes types of cuisine, phone numbers, street addresses and a map, may be obtained from the Chamber of Commerce (see above). With this variety you should not have any trouble finding a good place to eat. We certainly didn't! Local favorites include Hermann's Ribs, AQ Chicken (YUM!), B & B Barbecue and Rufino's Mexican.

There can be a shortage of accommodations in Fayetteville on football weekends but don't let that discourage you from traveling to Arkansas for a game. Without advance reservations, you may have to stay in one of the surrounding towns like Springdale, Alma or Fort Smith. Springdale is only a few minutes drive away and has many nice hotels/motels.

However, if you must stay in Alma or Fort Smith and travel to Fayetteville on game day, you will need to allow extra time since many of the roads are two lanes and pass through hilly or even mountainous terrain. Also, there are recreational vehicles on the roads throughout the resort region which further slow the pace of traffic.

Advance planning will help you enjoy not only the excitement of the game when you arrive, but also the beautiful drive to Fayetteville through Northwest Arkansas.

P.S.   Don't forget that Hot Springs, Arkansas and Branson, Missouri, are only a couple of the great side trips you can make when traveling to Fayetteville or Little Rock for a football game (see "What to See and Do" for more ideas).

Little Rock, located in the central part of the "Land of Opportunity," is the state's largest city as well as its capital. It was named *La Petite Rocke*, "Little Rock," by Bernard de La Harpe in 1722. After a period of slow growth prior to the Civil War, the town grew rapidly, especially in the late 1800's and early part of this century. At present the city claims about 190,000 residents with slightly over half a million in the metro area.

Little Rock is the "home away from home" for Razorback football. War Memorial Stadium is located in War Memorial Park west of the downtown district. The stadium may be reached by taking the Fair Park Boulevard exit north off of Interstate 630. In addition to football, the park encompasses tennis, baseball and golf facilities, an amusement park and also serves as home to the Little Rock Zoo.

The Little Rock area is promoted aggressively by several agencies that will eagerly provide helpful and interesting materials about the region's attractions and tourist related businesses, as well as a calendar of events. We encourage fans planning a trip to Central Arkansas to contact one or all of the following to make their trip more enjoyable:

Little Rock Convention and Visitors Bureau
Statehouse Plaza, P.O. Box 3232
Little Rock, AR 72203
Phone: (501) 376-4781 or 1-800-844-4781

North Little Rock Advertising and Promotion Commission
P.O. Box 5511
North Little Rock, AR 72119
Phone: (501) 758-1424 or 1-800-643-4690

Heart of Arkansas Travel Association
P.O. Box 3232
Little Rock, AR 72203

Arkansas Department of Parks and Tourism
One Capitol Mall
Little Rock, AR 72201
Phone: (501) 682-7777 or 1-800-NATURAL

TELEFUN (24 hours) 501-372-3399

What to See and Do in the Little Rock Area

~Arkansas Arts Center. A nationally recognized collection of 6,000 art objects including works by Old Masters. Free. Open 10 AM - 5 PM, M-F, 12 PM - 5 PM Sundays & holidays. MacArthur Park. (501) 372-4000.

~Central High School. The campus was a focal point in the Civil Rights movement of the late 1950's. Bordered by Jones, Park, 14th and 16th Streets.

~Quapaw Quarter District. Named for the Quapaw Indians, early residents of the Central Arkansas area, this 9 square mile district contains most of the historic buildings in Little Rock. A self-guided driving tour book is available for purchase. Walking tour brochures are available free at 1315 Scott Street. 9:00 AM - 5:00 PM, Monday through Friday. (501) 371-0075.

~Little Rock Zoo. Over 500 species, most in natural settings. Open 9:30 AM to 4:30 PM. Admission charged. #1 Jonesboro Drive in War Memorial Park. (501) 663-4733.

~Arkansas Riverboat Company. Excursions are available on the paddle wheel riverboat the "Spirit." Riverboat Park, No. Little Rock. (501) 376-4150.

~State Capitol Building. A 3/4 replica of the U.S. Capitol. Gift Shop. Woodlum & Capitol. (501) 371-1010 (ask for Tour Director).

~Old State House. Arkansas' original state capitol now houses a museum and Granny's Attic, a hands-on gallery that is fun and interesting for all ages. Admission by voluntary donation. 300 W. Markham St. Monday thru Saturday, 9AM - 5PM, Sunday 1 - 5PM. (501) 324-9685.

~Villa Marre. A restored Victorian house which serves as a period museum. The 1881 beauty is used for exterior scenes on the TV series *Designing Women*. Admission charged. Open 9 AM - 1 PM, Monday - Friday; Sunday 1 - 5 PM; Saturdays, advance booking only. 1321 South Scott Street. (501) 374-9979.

Where to Eat and Sleep in Little Rock

There are approximately 300 places to eat in the Little Rock/North Little Rock area! A current listing of restaurants, cuisines, addresses and phone numbers may be obtained from the Little Rock Convention and Visitors Bureau. Ask for the pamphlet, ***"Places to Go, People to See, Things to Do."***

You may also call **TELEFUN**, at **(501) 372-3399**, for 24 hour information on what is happening in Little Rock, including concerts, plays, festivals and other events which might be of interest to you.

Approximately 60 motels/hotels are listed by the Visitors Bureau in the Little Rock area. However, even with a large number of rooms available, it is possible that during weekends of big games accommodations may be hard to come by. Advance planning and reservations are a must in these instances.

Little Rock Area

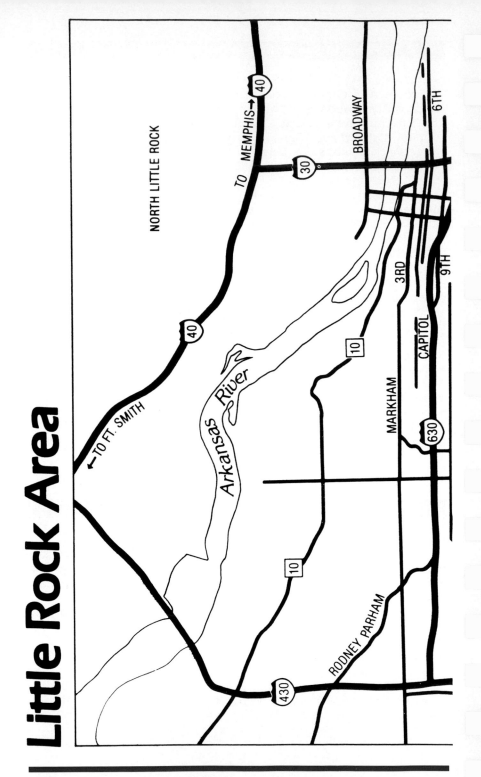

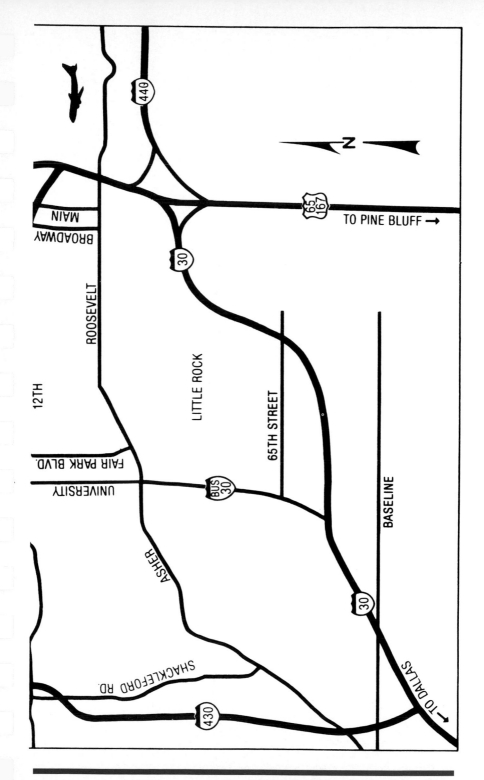

Samford Hall, symbol of Auburn University since 1888, houses the President's office.

U
B
U
R
N*

Haley Center, a huge classroom building,
towers even over Jordan-Hare Stadium, its next door neighbor

Auburn University had its beginnings in 1856 when the East Alabama Male College, a liberal arts school supported by the Methodist Church, was founded. The first eighty students arrived on site in October, 1859. Forty years later the name was changed to Alabama Polytechnic Institute (A.P.I.). The school had long since become a state supported institution. Six decades later, in 1960, the college's name was changed once again, this time to Auburn University. The school had been known informally as "Auburn" for many years prior to the official name change.

Auburn fans point with pride to the long tradition of academic excellence and public service which AU graduates have amassed. The schools of Veterinary Medicine, Pharmacy, Engineering, Architecture and Forestry, as well as others, have achieved international reputations for excellence. For example, at least five "Auburn astronauts" have flown in space and the formula for McDonald's "McLean" low-fat hamburger was developed in the foods lab at AU.

From humble beginnings Auburn has grown to be the largest university in Alabama with 21,537 students. In fact, the student body almost rivals the population of the host city of Auburn which stood at 33,830 in 1992. Nearby Opelika counted 24,500 residents. Both cities are in Lee County which is some 50 miles east of Montgomery in East Central Alabama. With the capital city so near and with Birmingham and Atlanta each 100 miles or less from the campus, Auburn appeals to the student who appreciates the friendly "hometown" spirit found in a small city, while enjoying the excitement and convenience of large metro areas.

The fact that Auburn athletic teams and fans today wear blue and orange may be due to the admiration George Petrie, founder of football at Auburn and the school's first football coach, had for his Alma Mater, the University of Virginia. When Petrie ordered team uniforms in December, 1891, the canvas jerseys and pants were of a neutral, off-white color. In place of helmets, rugby caps trimmed in blue and orange were sent. Perhaps Petrie had specified these colors since they also represented the colors of the University of Virginia.

Whatever, the colors stuck and the cries of "Go Big Blue" are heard at each Auburn football game a hundred years later! Officially, Auburn's colors are navy blue (PMS Color #289) and burnt orange (PMS Color # 172).

The Auburn cheerleaders rally the faithful with
a "War-r-r-r Eagle" cheer.

*Aubie, Auburn's tiger mascot, is a playful prankster
and symbol of that irrepressible Auburn spirit.*

Perhaps no team in America, college or professional, has as much confusion about its nickname as Auburn. For example, some people believe that Auburn's nickname is the "Tigers." Others maintain that they are the "War Eagles" and point to the sidelines where Auburn's golden eagle mascot, "Tiger" (yes, Tiger!), sits atop her perch. A third contingent cites numerous reference in the media to the "Plainsmen" of Auburn and concludes that AU's nickname must therefore be the "Plainsmen." Which group is correct? All have some basis for their claims, but only those who said "Tigers" are correct.

Actually, the nickname comes from a poem which also gave the town of Auburn its name. Poet Oliver Goldsmith penned the lines in England in 1770, never realizing the impact they would have two centuries later in a small American town. In his poem, "The Deserted Village," Goldsmith writes, "Sweet Auburn, loveliest village of the plain...." This inspired town founders to name their village, also located on a plain, Auburn, since they no doubt felt it was the loveliest village around.

It is only natural that men who live on a plain are called "plainsmen." Since newspaper writers are constantly looking for new and different ways to describe people, places and things, it should come as no surprise that Auburn football players have, from time to time, been referred to as "plainsmen." But in reality, it was another line in the same poem which provided Auburn teams with their nickname: "Where crouching tigers wait their hapless prey...."

As to the War Eagle business, please be informed that "War Eagle" is the battle cry of Auburn (see traditions) and is used in a similar way to the cries "Roll Tide" and "Sooie Pig" at the Universities of Alabama and Arkansas. Auburn fans may shout "War Eagle!" when watching something exciting on the football field, or simply say, "War Eagle" as a friendly greeting or farewell, but never should the term be used to refer to the team or fans as in "the War Eagles."

Now . . . ready for your final exam? The Auburn nickname is:

    A.   Tigers
    B.   Plainsmen
    C.   War Eagles
    D.   All of the above

Correct answer: "A."

"Tiger," alias War Eagle VI, watches as "Aubie,"
Auburn's other mascot, gives the number 1 sign.

Auburn has to be one of the few teams with two mascots of different species. Several teams in the SEC, such as Arkansas, Georgia, LSU and Mississippi State, have real, "live" animal, mascots present on the sidelines, as well as, humans dressed in razorback, bulldog or tiger suits. But only Auburn, in the conference, has two totally different mascots!

One is the gregarious and highly animated "Aubie" the tiger, who existed for many years only in cartoon form. He first appeared on the cover of the Auburn/Hardin-Simmons football program of October 3, 1959, as drawn by artist Phil Neel of the Birmingham Post-Herald. Thus began a tradition which was to continue for eighteen years. Over time, Aubie began to stand upright, wear clothes and, in general, become more like the Aubie seen cavorting today with people and props on the sidelines. Aubie's last regular appearance on a program cover was October 23, 1976. His only other appearance on a game-day program was on November 30, 1991, against Alabama, Auburn's last "home" game at Legion Field.

For three years, 1976-1979, Aubie dropped out of sight. He resurfaced "in the flesh" at the 1979 SEC Basketball Tournament after James Lloyd, Auburn Spirit Director for the SGA, with help from the Alumni Association, purchased a custom-designed "Aubie" suit from a company in New York which also provides costumes for Walt Disney. Aubie's surprise entrance at the basketball tournament spurred the ninth place tigers to the semifinal round of the championship!

Since then, Aubie has made countless appearances at athletic events, alumni functions and public service projects around the region. So busy is the lively mascot that a new $2000.00 suit (now made by Bienville Costumes in Mobile, Alabama) is needed each year due to wear and tear from almost constant use.

Each Spring a contest to choose a new Aubie is held. Open to all Auburn students, many vie for the honor. Three students are chosen. Two serve as alternates, but all three get to play the role of Aubie during the year. In 1990-91, Aubie was selected as the nation's number one college mascot by the Universal Cheerleader Association.

Auburn's second mascot has actually been around much longer than Aubie. "Tiger", also known as War Eagle VI, is Auburn's golden eagle. She is symbolic of the spirit of the first War Eagle (see traditions) and the sixth mascot to bear the name "War Eagle".

After the death of the first War Eagle in 1892, no live mascot resided at Auburn until 1932 when a group of fans bought an eagle from a farmer for ten dollars. During economic hard times during the Great Depression, the group could not afford to feed War Eagle II and had to give it away to a traveling carnival.

In 1960, the year after Aubie made his first appearance, War Eagle III arrived in the form of a wounded eagle donated by Dr. Dell Hill of Talladega, Alabama. Eventually the eagle came under the care of a student, Elwyn Hamer, a member of the Alpha Phi Omega fraternity. Ever since, the brothers of that organization have cared for Auburn's eagle mascots. The aviary where War Eagle VI lives is named in honor of Elwyn Hamer.

War Eagle III served as mascot for four years before meeting a tragic end. The week before the Alabama game in 1964, War Eagle III broke free and landed in a neaby yard. The owner of the property shot and killed him, claiming he was attacking his children. The next year Auburn was presented with a new mascot by the city of Birmingham. Arriving from the Jackson, Mississippi Zoo, War Eagle IV quickly settled in for a fifteen year reign, dying of natural causes a week before the 1980 Alabama game!

When Coach Pat Dye arrived on the Plains from the University of Wyoming in 1981, he was followed within a few weeks by War Eagle V who hailed from Casper, Wyoming. This coincidence was viewed by many as a good omen for Auburn football fortunes. War Eagle V died of internal injuries just before the 1986 season opener, but not before helping to lead the Tigers to their first conference championship since 1957!

After a search lasting several weeks, a new eagle, War Eagle VI, was found at Land Between the Lakes, Kentucky. She was introduced on November 15, 1986, at the Georgia game at Jordan-Hare Stadium. Now in her seventh year as mascot, Tiger weighs in at eleven pounds and has a wingspan of seven feet. When not inspiring the Tigers on the sideline, she may be seen in her aviary on Roosevelt Drive near the stadium.

*The Auburn University Marching Band awaits its cue
during halftime of the Alabama game in Birmingham.*

The Auburn University Marching Band has a history dating back almost a hundred years. The group has represented the school and the state of Alabama across the nation, and today, with membership totaling 330, enjoys a national reputation for excellence. Almost every college and major at the university are represented by the band's members, about 50 of which are music majors. The director of the marching band is Timothy Kelley.

Members of the band are proud of their campus facilities, Goodwin Hall, which houses the band, and Henton Field, one of the finest marching band rehearsal sites in the nation!

AUBURN UNIVERSITY "Alma Mater"

On the rolling plains of Dixie
Neath its sun-kissed sky,
Proudly stands, our Alma Mater
Banners high.

Hear thy student voices swelling,
Echoes strong and clear,
Adding laurels to thy fame
Enshrined so dear.

To thy name we'll sing thy praise,
From hearts that love so true,
And pledge to thee our
Loyalty the ages through.

From thy hallowed halls we'll part,
And bid thee sad adieu;
Thy sacred trust we'll bear with us
The ages through.

We hail thee, Auburn, and we vow
To work for thy just fame,
And hold in memory as we do now,
Thy cherished name.

We hail thee, Auburn, and we vow
To work for thy just fame,
And hold in memory as we do now
Thy cherished name.

AUBURN'S FIGHT SONG
"War Eagle"

War . . . Eagle, fly down the field,
Ever to conquer, never to yield.
War . . . Eagle fearless and true.
Fight on , you orange and blue.
Go! Go! Go!
On to vic'try, strike up the band,
Give 'em hell, give 'em hell.
Stand up and yell, Hey!
War . . . Eagle, win for Auburn,
Power of Dixie Land.

War Eagle VI strikes a majestic pose
at last year's Alabama game.

*Looking out Auburn's main gate at "Toomer's Corner,"
fittingly festooned after a Tiger victory!*

What do Auburn fans like best about their school? Linda Wood of Pensacola, Florida, sums up what many Tiger fans feel is important:
> "The atmosphere of Auburn. It is a large school that
> feels 'small' because of the friendliness of the Auburn
> people . . . truly a family."

Auburn fans are friendly and they take pride in being friendly. In our experience they would probably win the "friendliest school in the Conference award" and that's saying a lot because we found wonderful, friendly fans at every school. With the University of Alabama's dominance in the SEC it may be easy to forget that Auburn University IS the largest school in the state. Thus it is no mean feat to retain that "small town," friendly, family atmosphere of which the fans are so proud.

Andy Fuller of Huntsville, Alabama say that "people are important" at Auburn and though academics and athletics are both stressed he feels that Auburn University has found a way to keep the personal touch alive and well. In fact, many Tiger fans feel this is what caused the problem which plagues their athletic program now---not big payoffs---but the caring of the coaches for a student's need. Well . . . you may doubt it, but Auburn does have devoted fans who find something good about every bad situation . . . as any good fan would!

Despite their problems, Auburn football has some great history and tradition. Tiger fans believe they will be on top again, pointing to the fact that their school has more award-winning athletes and NFL athletes than many SEC schools.

Auburn's in-state rivalry with Alabama is quite heated. Tiger fans say Bama fans are "snooty" and "snobby" while Bama fans retort that AU is a "hick" school, referring to their agricultural and mechanical beginnings. Like Mississippi State, Auburn fans say they are proud of their beginnings and point to successful schools of Business, Architecture, Pharmacy, Engineering and Veterinary Medicine. Dorothy Fuller and Ruby Friend of Huntsville believe that academics are great at AU and say their sons are proof of it!

Another trait of Auburn "fanatics" is that they are "laid back" says Marvin Brown of Marietta, Georgia. These authors found that to be true. AU fans do enjoy the whole "gameday experience." They dress for comfort and a day of fun. However, like many schools, the students often dress-up for the games and that's not easy since student seating is crowded beyond words.

Auburn football has many great traditions and fans love to talk about their famous alumni and future possibilities. Gameday is an event and "just being there" says Wayne Howard of Foley, Alabama, is great! Sherry Lee, also of Foley, looks forward to the "Tiger Walk" to the stadium while students Lori Carneal and Matt Colwell like the school colors, "War Eagle" cheer and "Toomer's Corner" festivities, where fans gather after games with the cheerleaders and pick-up band to join in rolling the giant oaks at AU's entrance! Hick? Maybe. But it is great fun!

John B. White, III, of Irmo, South Carolina, reminds us that the real tradition at Auburn is "Bama, {Georgia} Bulldogs, and Vols!!!!" Auburn wants to be the best in the SEC and happily recalls the 50's Championship Team and glory days of Sullivan and Beasley. However, the Tigers don't live in the past and look forward to the future against their rivals . . . old and new!

Auburn fans enjoy another beautiful gameday experience!

*The Auburn offensive line pass protects
as their quarterback scans the Alabama defense during the '92 contest.*

Head Coach:

Terry Bowden (West Virginia, 1978)
Florida State Graduate Assistant, 1979-81;
Florida State Assistant, 1982;
Salem Head Coach, 1983-85;
Akron Assistant, 1986;
Samford Head Coach, 1987-92;
Auburn Head Coach, 1993-present

Birthday: February 24, 1956
Hometown: Birmingham AL

Assistant Coaches

Wayne Hall (Alabama, 1974)	Assistant Head Coach/ Defensive Coordinator
Tommy Bowden (West Virginia, 1977)	Wide Receivers
Jimbo Fisher (Salem College, 1988)	Quarterbacks
Rodney Allison (Texas Tech, 1978)	Running Backs
Rick Trickett (Glenville State, 1972)	Offensive Line
Joe Whitt (Alabama State, 1972)	Defensive Ends
Jack Hines, Jr. (West Virginia, 1972)	Defensive Backs
Rodney Garner (Auburn, 1990)	Tight Ends/Special Team
Kurt Crain (Auburn, 1988)	Defensive Tackles

Jordan-Hare Stadium, home of the Auburn Tigers, is imposing from any angle and one of the prettiest stadiums in the conference.

When the Auburn Tigers tangle with their football rivals several Saturdays each fall at Jordan-Hare (pronounced JURD-un HAIR) Stadium, the host city of Auburn, Alabama is dwarfed by the sea of fans. Over its fifty-four years, Jordan-Hare has grown from the original 7,440 seats in 1939 to a capacity of 85,214 in 1993, making it not only the nation's seventh largest on-campus football facility, but, when filled, the fifth largest "city" in the state of Alabama. The city of Auburn has only about 34,000 residents. When so many fans descend upon a small town, one can imagine the stresses and strains that result.

Parking, for example, is at a premium. Late arriving spectators often have to walk more than a mile to reach the stadium after parking alongside the road. The few motels and restaurants in the area fill to capacity quickly. Perhaps these conditions have led Auburn fans to become one of the biggest devotees of motor homes in the SEC! Whether at home or on the road, Auburn fans typically arrive earlier and in more motor homes than any other school. The small town environment found in Auburn caused some Alabama supporters to argue against moving the Alabama-Auburn game to Jordan-Hare in Auburn's home years.

Although the number of motels and eateries in the Auburn-Opelika (pronounced Opuh-LIKE-uh) area has grown, access to them is hampered by the fact that most of the development has taken place away from Interstate 85, making it difficult for visitors to locate them. Many visiting fans stay and dine in Montgomery, fifty miles away, or even Birmingham or Atlanta, each about 110 miles distant. Rival SEC fans consistently listed Auburn as one of the most difficult game sites to attend for all the above reasons. One Georgia fan summed up the collective frustration by saying, "You can't get there, and once you're there, you can't get out." Actually, since Auburn is located on an Interstate highway and near two U.S. highways, traveling there and back is NOT that difficult, with a little advance planning.

Fans who end up walking some distance to the stadium can count on being met by about one "War Eagle" greeting per hundred feet. This spirited Auburn "cry" comes with equal friendliness, whether issued as welcome to a friend or warning to a foe. It is truly a great tradition and a treasured part of SEC football.

When fans arrive at their seats they discover one of the "prettiest" stadiums anywhere. The stands are truly symmetrical with the east and west sides being covered by tremendous upper decks. Landscaping in the corners of the field, sideline hedges and the rich green of the natural turf remind fans that Auburn is a great agricultural school. The press box and executive sky boxes are built as an integral part into the west and east upper decks, respectively.

Because of the design of the stadium, there are some bad seats, for example, those on the lower rows and most especially those behind the players' benches. The upper decks, however, are all great, even those beyond the end zones. Because they are so high, a great view of the field is afforded. Binoculars are a must, however, for those who want to follow the play closely.

When first constructed in 1939, Auburn Stadium, as it was known then, consisted only of the bottom section of the lower west stands. The stadium was dedicated November 30 of that year at a Florida game; a contest which ended in a 7-7 tie.

Ten years later, in 1949, the facility was renamed to honor Cliff Hare, quarterback on Auburn's first team and later Dean of the Chemistry Department, President of the old Southern Conference and chairman of Auburn's Faculty Athletic Committee. By this time, the stadium had been expanded to 21,500 seats by adding the present lower east stands.

In the fifteen years after Ralph "Shug" Jordan became coach in 1951, the stadium grew by more than 40,000 seats under his and Athletic Director, Jeff Beard's, leadership. In recognition of Jordan's contribution to Auburn University, the stadium was given an expanded name in 1973, two years before his retirement. Jordan-Hare Stadium became the first arena in the country to be named after an active coach. By the time Jordan stepped down, Jordan-Hare's bowl had been completed by adding the top half of the lower west stands and the two end zones.

Exciting teams with big name players in the later 1970's necessitated further expansion. The west side upper deck was completed in 1980, upping capacity to 72,167. Once the teams of coach Pat Dye hit their stride in the mid-1980's, even more seats were needed! The east side upper deck was finished in 1987, achieving today's 85,214 seating level.

Stadium Stats

First game:	November 30, 1939; Auburn 7, Florida 7
Largest single game attendance:	85,319; Auburn 30, Alabama 20
Largest Home Season Attendance:	1989; 577,554 in 7 games; 82,508 average
Longest Home Winning Streak:	30 games, beginning with a 3-0 win over Clemson in 1952 and ending with a 14-12 loss to Kentucky in 1961
Stadium Record:	227 games, 1939-1992 (53 Seasons) W - 181 L - 40 T - 6 (Pct. .811)
Playing surface:	Natural grass

Auburn's Jordan-Hare Stadium

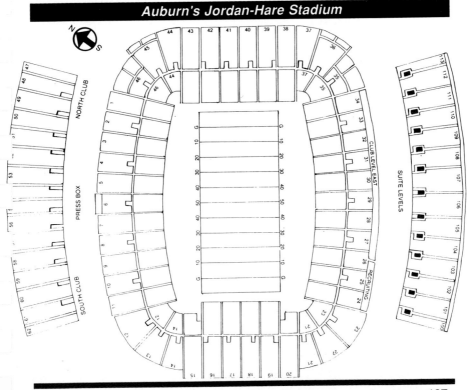

Auburn University - Sports Network

Jim Fyffe - Play-By-Play
Charlie Trotman - Color Analyst
Paul Ellen - Studio Host
Quentin Riggins - Sideline Reporter
Andy Burcham - Lockerroom Host

AUBURN RADIO NETWORK

AM Stations

CITY	STATE	STATION	FREQUENCY
Americus	GA	WISK	1390
Anniston/Oxford	AL	WOXR	1580
Ashland	AL	WZZX	780
Atlanta	GA	WGUN	1010
Athens	AL	WVNN	770
Bay Minette	AL	WBCA	1110
Birmingham	AL	WYDE	850
Centre	AL	WEIS	990
Centreville	AL	WBIB	1110
Chattanooga	TN	WFLI	1070
Clanton	AL	WKLF	980
Cullman	AL	WXXR	1340
Dalton	GA	WLSQ	1430
Decatur	AL	WHOS	800
Evergreen	AL	WIJK	1470
Florence	AL	WSBM	1340
Foley	AL	WHEP	1310
Ft. Payne	AL	WZOB	1250
Gainesville	GA	WDUN	550
Haleyville	AL	WJBB	1230
Huntsville	AL	WBHP	1230
Jasper	AL	WZPQ	1360
Lanett	AL	WRLD	1490
Macon	GA	WNEX	1400
Memphis	TN	WAVN	1240
Moulton	AL	WHIY	1190
Nashville	TN	WIZO	1380
Newnan	GA	WCOH	1400
Oneonta	AL	WCRL	1570
Roanoke	AL	WELR	1360
Scottsboro	AL	WZCT	1330
Selma	AL	WMRK	1340
Tallassee	AL	WACQ	1130
Thomasville	AL	WJDB	630
Troy	AL	WTBF	970

FM Stations

CITY	STATE	STATION	FREQUENCY
Alexander City	AL	WZLM	97.3
Americus	GA	WPUR	97.7
Andalusia	AL	WAAO	103.7
Anniston/Oxford	AL	WVOK	97.9
Ashland	AL	WASZ	95.3
Atmore	AL	WYDH	105.9
Auburn/Opelika	AL	WKKR	97.7
Birmingham	AL	WWIV	105.9
Carrollton	GA	WBTR	92.1
Citronelle	AL	WKQR	101.9
Clanton	AL	WEZZ	97.7
Columbus	GA	WVRK	102.9
Demopolis	AL	WZNJ	106.3
Destin	FL	WWAV	102.3
Dothan	AL	WDJR	96.9
Eufaula	AL	WDMT	97.9
Evergreen	AL	WPGG	93.3
Florence	AL	WQLT	107.3
Gadsden	AL	WKXX	102.9
Greenville	AL	WQZX	94.3
Guntersville	AL	WTWX	95.9
Haleyville	AL	WJBB	92.7
Mobile	AL	WZBA	104.9
Montgomery	AL	WLWI	92.3
Moulton	AL	WXKI	103.1
Oneonta	AL	WKLD	97.7
Roanoke	AL	WELR	102.3
Rome	GA	WQTU	102.3
Selma	AL	WALX	100.9
Stevenson	AL	WKZA	101.7
Sylacauga	AL	WAWV	98.3
Talladega	AL	WSSY	97.5
Tifton	GA	WJYF	95.3
Winfield	AL	WKXM	105.9

*Ticket Information

Ticket Office: (205) 844-4040.

Scalping of tickets is legal in Alabama if the seller possesses a state license. At Auburn tickets are sold in the vicinity of the stadium quite often at prices above face value. We have never witnessed anyone being checked for a license or otherwise being questioned about the practice.

Stadium Seating: The Auburn University Marching Band is usually seated in sections 21, 22 and 23. Visiting bands will be seated in section 34 and visiting fans in sections 34-38.

*Locating the Stadium

Jordan-Hare Stadium is located in the central part of the Auburn campus. There are several approaches to the area.

From Montgomery (I-85) you can take the Wire Road Exit, a two-lane county road, which leads to parking by the Intramural Fields not too far from the stadium. If you proceed further east on I-85, you can take the U.S. Highway 29 Exit north to Auburn.

In the city, Highway 29 becomes College Street. You may turn left on Shug Jordan Boulevard, if you are running late, and go around the southwest side of the stadium as far as time permits. If you are early, continue on Highway 29 (College Street) downtown to the campus which is on your left. Several streets lead to the campus core. You may find parking near the coliseum or if you are not feeling adventuresome, you may park downtown in an unattended business lot and take a stroll across the campus to the stadium.

From the South (U.S. 29), cross the I-85 interchange heading north, then same as the above.

From the East on I-85 (from Atlanta) take U.S. 29 Exit (Auburn). Turn right on Highway 29 which becomes College Street. Then same as the above.

From Birmingham via U.S. Highway 280 turn right (south) on U.S. 29 which becomes College Street in Auburn. You may continue south to the heart of Auburn and then turn right onto several streets which lead onto the campus. Or you may turn right onto Shug Jordan Boulevard which skirts the town on the west and intersects with Wire Road. Turn left to reach the stadium and parking.

*Parking Information

Parking at Auburn on gameday can be a challenge to those who do not arrive early. Many of the campus lots in close proximity to the stadium are restricted. There are no shuttles operating to serve fans who have to park some distance away.

To Auburn's credit, most on-campus parking is free. The University suggests that fans park at the intramural fields off Wire Road. There are uniformed police officers and game parkers to direct you to and from the nearest parking area as quickly as possible.

Parking for handicapped fans and special seating is available by contacting the Auburn Athletic Department.

*ALL INFORMATION IS SUBJECT TO CHANGE

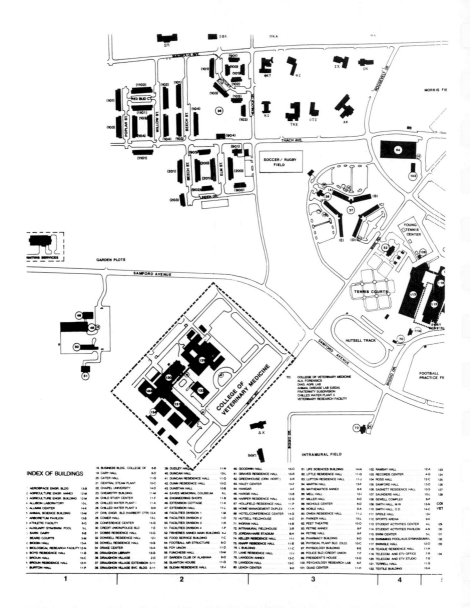

INDEX OF BUILDINGS

		18. BUSINESS BLDG, COLLEGE OF	8-B	39. DUDLEY HALL	11-N	60. GOODWIN HALL	10-O
		19. CARY HALL	8-D	40. DUNCAN HALL	13-L	61. GRAVES RESIDENCE HALL	10-R
		20. CATER HALL	11-G	41. DUNCAN RESIDENCE HALL	11-Q	62. GREENHOUSE (ORN. HORT.)	9-R
		21. CENTRAL STEAM PLANT	10-C	42. DUNN RESIDENCE HALL	11-Q	83. HALEY CENTER	10-F
AEROSPACE ENGR. BLDG	13-B	22. CHAPEL UNIVERSITY	14-D	43. DUNSTAN HALL	10-B	84. HANGAR	4-F
1 AGRICULTURE ENGR. ANNEX	12-M	23. CHEMISTRY BUILDING	11-M	44. EAVES MEMORIAL COLISEUM	9-L	85. HARGIS HALL	13-B
2 AGRICULTURE ENGR. BUILDING	12-M	24. CHILD STUDY CENTER	11-F	45. ENGINEERING SHOPS	11-B	86. HARPER RESIDENCE HALL	12-G
3 ALLISON LABORATORY	10-L	25. CHILLED WATER PLANT I	11-A	46. EXTENSION COTTAGE	11-K	87. HOLLIFIELD RESIDENCE HALL	11-P
4 ALUMNI CENTER	14-K	26. CHILLED WATER PLANT II	9-N	47. EXTENSION HALL	11-K	88. HOME MANAGEMENT DUPLEX	11-H
5 ANIMAL SCIENCE BUILDING	13-M	27. CIVIL ENGR. BLD (HARBERT CTR)	13-A	48. FACILITIES DIVISION 1	1-M	89. HOTEL/CONFERENCE CENTER	14-G
6 ARBORETUM PAVILION	13-B	28. COMER HALL	13-L	49. FACILITIES DIVISION 2	1-O	70. HUTSELL FIELDHOUSE	4-O
7 ATHLETIC FACILITY	8-O	29. CONFERENCE CENTER	14-G	50. FACILITIES DIVISION 3	1-N	71. INGRAM HALL	14-B
8 AUXILIARY GYM/SWIM POOL	5-L	30. CREDIT UNION/POLICE BLD	7-E	51. FACILITIES DIVISION 4	1-P	72. INTRAMURAL FIELDHOUSE	3-R
9 BARN DAIRY	5-B	31. DOBBS RESIDENCE HALL	10-Q	52. FISHERIES ANNEX MAIN BUILDING	4-J	73. JORDAN-HARE STADIUM	8-H
BEARD COURTS	5-M	32. DOWDELL RESIDENCE HALL	12-I	53. FOOD SERVICE BUILDING	7-C	74. KELLER RESIDENCE HALL	11-I
1 BROUN HALL	13-A	33. DOWELL RESIDENCE HALL	10-B	54. FOOTBALL AIR STRUCTURE	8-O	75. KNAPP RESIDENCE HALL	11-B
3 BIOLOGICAL RESEARCH FACILITY	12-N	34. DRAKE CENTER	10-A	55. FOY UNION	11-D	76. L BUILDING	11-C
5 BOYD RESIDENCE HALL	11-Q	35. DRAUGHON LIBRARY	13-G	56. FUNCHESS HALL	13-G	77. LANE RESIDENCE HALL	11-I
6 BROUN HALL	10-C	36. DRAUGHON VILLAGE	2-O	57. GARDEN CLUB OF ALABAMA	9-D	78. LANGDON ANNEX	13-C
6 BROUN RESIDENCE HALL	12-H	37. DRAUGHON VILLAGE EXTENSION	3-11	58. GLANTON HOUSE	11-G	79. LANGDON HALL	13-C
7 BURTON HALL	11-P	38. DRAUGHON VILLAGE SVC BLDG	3-11	59. GLENN RESIDENCE HALL	12-J	80. LEACH CENTER	9-O

81. LIFE SCIENCES BUILDING	14-N	102. RAMSAY HALL	12-A
82. LITTLE RESIDENCE HALL	11-G	103. RECORDS CENTER	4-G
83. LUPTON RESIDENCE HALL	11-J	104. ROSS HALL	12-C
84. MARTIN HALL	13-F	105. SAMFORD HALL	13-D
85. MATHEMATICS ANNEX	9-K	106. SASNETT RESIDENCE HALL	10-S
86. MELL HALL	12-I	107. SAUNDERS HALL	10-L
87. MILLER HALL	8-D	108. SEWELL COMPLEX	8-P
88. NICHOLS CENTER	8-D	109. SMITH HALL, M.W	13-N
89. NOBLE HALL	9-A	110. SMITH HALL, O.D.	14-C
90. OWEN RESIDENCE HALL	11-J	111. SPIDLE HALL	13-I
91. PARKER HALL	10-L	112. SPORTS ARENA	9-K
92. PEET THEATRE	10-O	113. STUDENT ACTIVITIES CENTER	4-L
93. PETRIE ANNEX	9-F	114. STUDENT ACTIVITIES PAVILION	4-N
94. PETRIE HALL	9-F	115. SWIM CENTER	5-L
95. PHARMACY BUILDING	9-D	116. SWIMMING POOL/AUX.GYMNASIUM	5-L
96. PHYSICAL PLANT BLD. (OLD)	10-C	117. SWINGLE HALL	12-O
97. PHYSIOLOGY BUILDING	8-E	118. TEAGUE RESIDENCE HALL	11-H
98. POLICE BLD./CREDIT UNION	7-F	119. TELECOM AND ETV OFFICE	7-B
99. PRESIDENT'S HOUSE	13-G	120. TELECOM AND ETV STUDIO	7-B
100. PSYCHOLOGY RESEARCH LAB	9-F	121. TERRELL HALL	11-S
101. QUAD CENTER	11-H	122. TEXTILE BUILDING	10-A

	123
	124
	125
	126
	127
	128
COL	
VET	
	129
	130
	131
	132
	134

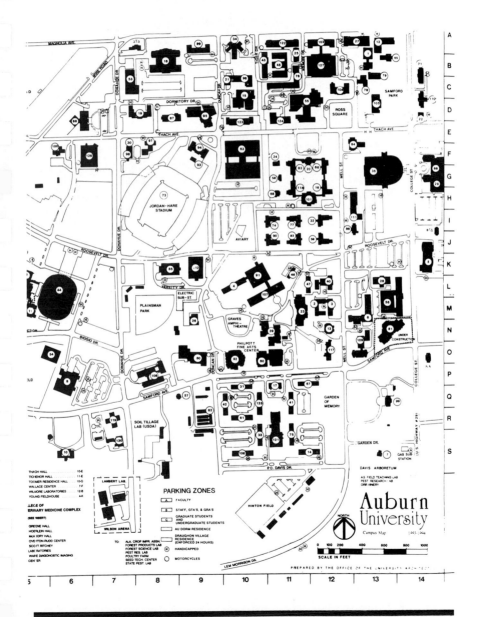

The Aviary, located in a natural setting, is a spacious and specially designed home for Tiger, the War Eagle.

~**Tours of Auburn University.** (205) 844-4080 or 844-1193.

~**Jordan-Hare Stadium.** Donahue Drive. Home of Auburn Tiger football.

~**Aviary.** Roosevelt Drive, south of Haley Center and east of Jordan-Hare Stadium. Home of Tiger, the "War Eagle," mascot of Auburn University.

~**Samford Hall.** South College Street. 1888 symbol of Auburn University. Houses the President's office.

~**Haley Center**. Adjacent to Jordan-Hare Stadium. High-rise classroom building. Houses bookstore, giftshop, restrooms. Open game days. Offers a great view of Auburn campus from its roof.

~**The Main Gate.** Corner of Magnolia and College Streets across from Toomer's Corner. At one time, freshmen students with their "beanie caps" were not allowed to enter the campus via this route. The brick gateposts date from 1917; the eagles from 1931.

What to See and Do in the Auburn Area

~**Old Main and Church Street District (Auburn).** Located on North College Street between Glenn Avenue and Sanders Street. Listed in the National Register, the site contains 52 significant structures dating from 1847 to 1927. A variety of architectural styles is represented. (205) 887-8747.

~Golf. Several Beautiful courses open to the public are located in the Auburn area. They include:

Auburn Links	(205) 821-5151
Grand National	(205) 749-9011
Indian Pines	(205) 826-8751
Pin Oaks	(205) 821-0893

~Chewacla State Park. Located four miles south of Auburn off U.S. Highway 29. Offers a 26 acre lake, rental cottages, picnicking, nature trails, swimming, beach, playgrounds, fishing and camping facilities. (205) 887-5621.

~Salem-Shotwell Covered Bridge. From I-85 take U.S. 280 South 7-1/2 miles, left on Lee County 83 for 1-1/2 miles; turn right on unpaved road; 1/4 mile to bridge. Dating from the early 1900's, this is one of the few covered bridges remaining in Alabama.

~Museum of East Alabama. Half block north of the Lee County Courthouse in Opelika on 9th Street. Hundreds of items focusing on the history of Alabama, the Southeast and the nation. FREE. (205) 749-2751.

~Tuskegee University. I-85 South, Exit 38. See the museum of George Washington Carver, the home of Booker T. Washington and the gravesites of both. (205) 727-8011.

~Victoryland. I-85 South, Exit 22. Nation's largest modern greyhound racing track. Open early January to late December. Racing nightly except Sunday, rain or shine. Post time 7:30 PM; Matinees Monday, Wednesday and Friday 3 PM. Saturday 1 PM. (205) 727-0540 / 1-800-OUT-2-WIN.

~Montgomery. First Capitol of the Confederacy, First White House of the Confederacy, Civil Rights Memorial designed by Maya Lin (Architect of the Viet Nam Memorial in Washington) ALL FREE. Shakespeare Festival Theatre. (205) 277-BARD.

Take a drive of less than two hours from Auburn and you can visit:

~Callaway Gardens
~Horseshoe Bend National Military Park
~Lake Martin
~Six Flags Over Georgia
~Talladega International Speedway and Motorsports Hall of Fame

Where to Eat and Sleep in the Auburn Area

If you are unable to get a motel room in Auburn or Opelika, you can usually find a room in Montgomery, Columbus, Georgia, or even Atlanta. All are close enough for you to travel to Auburn on gameday or to get to after an evening game.

For complete information about attractions or accommodations in the Auburn, area contact:

Auburn-Opelika Convention and Visitors Bureau
714 East Glenn Avenue
P. O. Box 2216
Auburn, AL 36831
(205) 887-8747   Fax (205) 821-5500

AUBURN

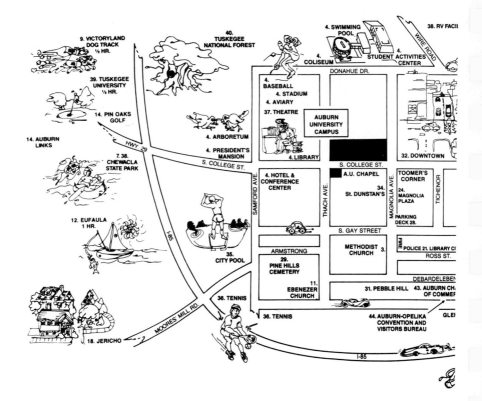

9. VICTORYLAND DOG TRACK ½ HR.

40. TUSKEGEE NATIONAL FOREST

4. SWIMMING POOL

38. RV FACII

39. TUSKEGEE UNIVERSITY ½ HR.

4. COLISEUM

4. STUDENT ACTIVITIES CENTER

WIRE ROAD

DONAHUE DR.

14. PIN OAKS GOLF

14. AUBURN LINKS

4. BASEBALL
4. STADIUM
4. AVIARY
37. THEATRE

AUBURN UNIVERSITY CAMPUS

HWY 29

4. ARBORETUM

4. LIBRARY

32. DOWNTOWN

7. 38. CHEWACLA STATE PARK

4. PRESIDENT'S MANSION

S. COLLEGE ST.

S. COLLEGE ST.

A.U. CHAPEL

TOOMER'S CORNER

SAMFORD AVE.

4. HOTEL & CONFERENCE CENTER

THACH AVE.

34. St. DUNSTAN'S

MAGNOLIA AVE.

24. MAGNOLIA PLAZA

TICHENOR

12. EUFAULA 1 HR.

I-85

S. GAY STREET

PARKING DECK 28.

35. CITY POOL

ARMSTRONG

METHODIST CHURCH 3.

FIRE

POLICE 21. LIBRARY CI
ROSS ST.

29. PINE HILLS CEMETERY

36. TENNIS

11. EBENEZER CHURCH

DEBARDELEBEN

31. PEBBLE HILL

43. AUBURN CHA OF COMMER

MOORES MILL RD.

36. TENNIS

44. AUBURN-OPELIKA CONVENTION AND VISITORS BUREAU

GLEI

18. JERICHO

I-85

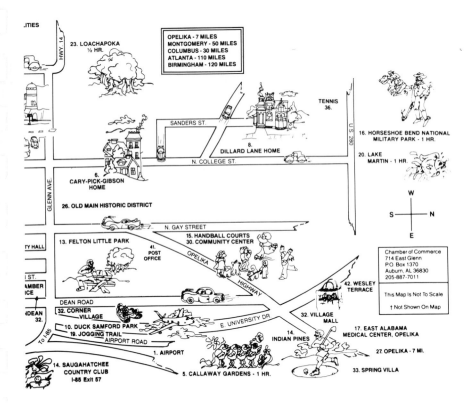

23. LOACHAPOKA
½ HR.

OPELIKA - 7 MILES
MONTGOMERY - 50 MILES
COLUMBUS - 30 MILES
ATLANTA - 110 MILES
BIRMINGHAM - 120 MILES

TENNIS
36.

SANDERS ST.

8.
DILLARD LANE HOME

N. COLLEGE ST.

6.
CARY-PICK-GIBSON
HOME

26. OLD MAIN HISTORIC DISTRICT

16. HORSESHOE BEND NATIONAL
MILITARY PARK - 1 HR.

20. LAKE
MARTIN - 1 HR.

W
S — N
E

N. GAY STREET

13. FELTON LITTLE PARK

41.
POST
OFFICE

15. HANDBALL COURTS
30. COMMUNITY CENTER

Chamber of Commerce
714 East Glenn
P.O. Box 1370
Auburn, AL 36830
205-887-7011

This Map Is Not To Scale

† Not Shown On Map

42. WESLEY
TERRACE

DEAN ROAD

32. CORNER
VILLAGE

10. DUCK SAMFORD PARK

19. JOGGING TRAIL

AIRPORT ROAD

1. AIRPORT

E. UNIVERSITY DR.

32. VILLAGE
MALL

14.
INDIAN PINES

17. EAST ALABAMA
MEDICAL CENTER, OPELIKA

27. OPELIKA - 7 MI.

14. SAUGAHATCHEE
COUNTRY CLUB
I-85 Exit 57

5. CALLAWAY GARDENS - 1 HR.

33. SPRING VILLA

GLENN AVE.

HWY. 14

US 280

OPELIKA HIGHWAY

To I-85

*Century Tower, symbol of the University of Florida,
commands the tree-shaded UF campus.*

Florida's tropical flora gives a distinctive look to the University campus.

The University of Florida is the largest school in the Southeastern Conference. With over 35,000 students, it has over four times as many students as the league's smallest school. Only two other universities in the U.S. offer as many academic programs on a single campus as Florida with its sixteen colleges and four schools. But quality doesn't get pushed to the side by quantity. Currently UF ranks 4th in the nation among public universities and 13th among all schools in the number of entering National Merit and Achievement Scholars in attendance.   In 1985, UF was admitted to the Association of American Universities (AAU), the most prestigious higher education organization in the nation. The AAU is made up of the top 58 universities in graduate and professional teaching and research.

The University of Florida's seal bears the date 1853. That was the year Kingsbury Academy in Ocala was taken over by the state-funded East Florida Seminary. Following the Civil War the seminary was moved to Gainesville. In 1906 it was consolidated with Florida Agricultural College and became the University of Florida. UF did not become a coed university until 1947. Prior to that time it was for men only. Florida State College for women in Tallahassee (now Florida State University) and Florida A & M were the only other state-supported institutions of higher learning in Florida.

Gainesville, UF's host city, is located in north central Florida on Interstate 75. With a resident population of 85,000, it affords a nice balance to the student numbers in the area. This coupled with the beauty of the region and the near ideal climate, makes Gainesville one of the most attractive campus environments.

Gator cheerleaders incite a capacity crowd at Florida Field.

The first few club football teams at Florida Agricultural College in Lake City selected blue and white for their colors. In 1906, the state legislature consolidated that school and Ocala's East Florida Seminary into the University of Florida and moved the new school to Gainesville. At that time, the football program began in earnest.

By the time the "gator" nickname and mascot made their debut in 1908, the colors "blue and orange" were already being used by students and fans to identify the "new" University.

Today, Florida's official colors are "orange" (PMS Color #172) and "blue" (PMS Color #286).

Albert, Florida's bull gator mascot, expresses his opinion about the "Fightin' Gators."

In the fall of 1907, just one year after the University of Florida fielded its first football team, the idea for the school's nickname was conceived. It seems that a Gainesville merchant, Phillip Miller, was visiting his son, Austin, in Charlottesville, Virginia. The younger Miller was a student at the university there. Since Florida students frequented Phillip Miller's combination drug store and stationery supply back in Gainesville, it was felt that items such as pennants and banners with school colors and logos would go over well if offered for sale there.

As luck would have it, there was a firm in Charlottesville that produced such products: the Michie Company. So father and son went to discuss designs with the folks there. When asked what the Florida nickname was they could only respond that there was none. In pondering the dilemma it was agreed that the alligator might be a good choice because it was an animal native to Florida and was not common like other school nicknames. Once the initial problem of choice was solved a second problem surfaced. The manager of the Michie Company had never seen an alligator and therefore could not do the artwork! Austin came to the rescue by tracking down a suitable picture in the University of Virginia Library.

The first items with the new emblem appeared in 1908 at Miller's store. A blue banner which measured six by three feet and depicted an orange alligator. Other smaller banners and pennants showed the alligator in various poses and moods.

As with most new ideas, the originators of the University's nickname could only guess how it would be received. Austin Miller himself expressed this concern when he said, "I had no idea it would stick, or even be popular with the student body." It's fun to imagine how Miller might react today if he could see the Florida faithful doing the gator chomp! Did the idea stick? Is a gator green?

(Based on an article in the *Florida Times-Union*, August 2, 1948)

The "Gator Chomp" . . . with visual aids!

Gator fans are quick to point out they have **two** mascots on the sidelines
. . . Albert and Alberta. Though some SEC schools have females "acting" as
the mascot, their identity is usually thought of as male. Florida is unique in
having both a female and male representative in uniform.

It's an interesting tradition, especially when you realize that the singing
of "We Are the Boys" is just as important to both male and female fans!   The
University of Florida seems to have done well to recognize and honor their past,
as an all-male school, while moving into the 21st century with it's female gator.
Thank you Alberta!

The "Pride of the Sunshine" is one of the nation's finest marching bands. With approximately 300 members, the group performs outstanding musical numbers and creative halftime shows. The "Fightin' Gator Marching Band," as the band is also called, is directed by Dr. D. A. Waybright.

FLORIDA'S FIGHT SONG
"The Orange and Blue"

On, brave old Flor - i - da, just keep on marching on your way!
On, brave old Flor - i - da, and we will cheer you on your play!
Rah! Rah! Rah!
And as you march a-long, we'll sing our victory song anew.
With all your might Go on and Fight Gators Fight for Dixie's rightly proud of you.

CHORUS: So give a Cheer for the Orange and Blue,
            Waving for-ev-er, forever.
            Pride of old Flor - i - da.
            May she droop nev-er.
            We'll sing a song for the flag to-day,
            Cheer for the team at play!
            On to the goal we'll fight our way for Flor - i - da.

Reflecting a tropical, laid-back attitude, the Florida Fightin' Gator Marching Band salutes Jimmy Buffet during a half-time show.

UNIVERSITY OF FLORIDA
"Alma Mater" (pregame)

Florida, our Alma Mater
Thy glorious name we praise
All thy loyal sons and daughters
A joyous song shall raise
Where palm and pine are blowing
Where southern seas are flowing
Shine forth thy noble;
Gothic walls . . .Thy lovely
vineclad halls
Neath the Orange and Blue victorious
our love shall never fail
There's no other name so glorious
all hail, Florida hail.

"We are the Boys"
(end of 3rd quarter)

We are the boys from old Florida,
F - L - O - R - I - D - A
Where the girls are the fairest,
the boys are the squarest
of any old state down our way.
We are all strong for old Florida
down where the old Gators play.
In all kinds of weather
we'll all stick together for
F - L - O - R - I - D - A

Thawing his mouthpiece at frigid Legion Field during the Championship Game,
a Florida sousaphone player may be thinking of the warmth of home.

The "Swamp Gang," a group of gator faithful having two things in common with one another: their passion for gator football, and their tailgating in this shady ravine at each Florida home game.

What makes the University of Florida unique in the Southeastern Conference? Many things, such as it's distance from the other schools and location in a "resort state," the hanging moss around the stadium and the terrible heat which plagues both teams and their loyal fans. However, Richard Elwell of Ft. Myers, Florida, summed it up this way: "It's not truly a 'southern' school--- Florida is a cosmopolitan state."

When you think about it, that's true! There are small towns and farmers in Florida, but most Florida residents are NOT native Floridians (the editors included!) and that does make for some interesting differences in the make up of the football fans. In the 1950's Florida ranked near the bottom of the population charts when compared with the 8 other SEC states, but today it is by far the most populous state in the Southeast, which means that Florida grew mighty fast!!

However, don't be misled by the "cosmopolitan" description of the University of Florida. Cosmopolitan or not, Gator fans take their football seriously, and in some ways, more seriously than the other SEC schools! For example,

Florida fans party, bring their families to the game, tailgate and enjoy having fun with "waves" and "gator chomps;" but many fans had little time to be interviewed by these authors or even complete a "Fan Scan" for fear of distraction! No other fans responded thusly. This did not deter us, we continued to seek out fans and met many who were just as eager to talk football and tradition as at the other schools, but it does describe an attitude which Edwin Durden of O'Brien, Florida, put into words, "It's always us against them!"

Perhaps it's the distance from the other schools, but we did find that many Florida fans considered themselves to be rivals of ALL other SEC fans. Of course their "rival of choice" is Georgia and both schools enjoy the tradition which has developed around their game. The Florida-Georgia game is always played in Jacksonville, not Athens or Gainesville, and is billed as "The Largest Outdoor Cocktail Party in the World." It is truly a great experience! That was the only game where we saw little stuffed versions of the mascot (bulldogs and gators) being dragged about and "abused" as symbols of the strong rivalry! Florida fans look forward all year to the "Gator Growl," a huge pep rally which helps them prepare for this important game.

Other favorite traditions are the "awesome slow-fast" wave (as student Charlene Batton called it), the "gator chomp" and Mr. 2 Bits, a long-time fan who decks himself in yellow (?) and moves about the stadium leading the fans in the cheer, with the complete support of the official cheerleaders! Another unheard-of tradition among colleges is the "beer run" at half-time. Florida is the only school where passes out are given so that fans can leave the stadium for a drink. Some fans gather around their vehicles, while others visit the nearby "Purple Porpoise," a favorite bar. So don't be alarmed if you are attending a game in Ben Hill Griffin Stadium at Florida Field when the hometown fans leave the stadium at half-time!

Florida is also the only SEC school with both a male and female version of their mascot! Though the fans still enjoy singing "We Are the Boys" at the end of the 3rd quarter, a song which reflects back to their beginnings as an all-male school, they are serious about including Alberta. Fans, Halie Nabi of Tallahassee and Judy Fessler of Gainesville, were quick to point out their favorite mascot "other than Albert" was Alberta!

Like most SEC fans, Gators enjoy chicken, bar-b-que, hot dogs and burgers on gameday. However, when you are in the area, Florida fans recommend you try Outback Steakhouse, Sonny's BBQ, the Brown Derby, Ashley's, Skeeter's, The Mill, Nero's, Bono's and Mr. Han's for food and fun!

Despite the heat and the distance which many fans have to travel to see their team play, Florida fans are devoted. One group we met gathers each year in a beautifully wooded ravine near the stadium. They meet only for the game, but celebrate their experiences with a new tablecloth each year (made by Edwin Roberts of Franklin, NC, who drives 500 miles one way to attend all the games!). This one used tombstones to show game scores---Gator fans expect to win!

So they come, bringing families, meeting friends . . . but always celebrating their common bond . . . a love of their team. As Veronica Zerrilla said when asked how long she had been a Gator fan: "'Gator' was my first word!"

Gator fans react to their team's success on the field.

Head Coach:

Birthday:	April 20, 1945
Hometown:	Johnson City TN

Steve Spurrier (Florida, 1967)
Florida Assistant, 1978;
Georgia Tech Assistant, 1979;
Duke Assistant, 1980-82;
Tampa Bay Head Coach (USFL), 1983-85;
Duke Head Coach, 1987-89;
Florida Head Coach, 1990-present

Assistant Coaches

Jerry Anderson (Florida, 1967)	Assistant Head Coach/Defensive Tackles
Jim Collins (Elon College, 1974)	Assistant Defensive Co-Coordinator/Inside Linebackers
Dwayne Dixon (Florida, 1985)	Wide Receivers
Carl Franks (Duke, 1982)	Tight Ends/Recruiting Coordinator
Jimmy Ray Stephens (Florida, 1977)	Offensive Line
Bob Sanders (Davidson, 1976)	Assistant Defensive Co-Coordinator/Banditback/Gatorback
Charlie Strong (Central Arkansas, 1982)	Defensive Ends
Ron Zook (Miami-Ohio, 1976)	Defensive Coordinator/Defensive Backs

Moss-draped oaks and palm trees provide a lovely setting
for Florida football at Ben Hill Griffin Stadium.

One of the most interesting stadiums in the SEC from a design standpoint is Ben Hill Griffin Stadium at Florida Field. The original part of the stadium, built in 1930, consisted of the lower half of the present facility, seating 21,769, and was constructed below ground level. To reach the playing field you must descend quite a distance down steps or ramps. The lowness of the gridiron coupled with the warm, moist air which seems to hang heavy at the bottom of the arena (much to the dismay of visiting northern teams), has given the stadium a nickname: "The Swamp." What could be more fitting for "the home of the Fightin' gators.?"

From a visual perspective, the various asymmetrical lines and angles show the growing pains the old stadium has experienced over the years and may, in some ways, seem more reminiscent of a baseball facility than football. Fans may rest assured however, that when it comes to watching football, there is not a bad seat in the house, from the shaded seats deep under the overhangs to the uppermost end zone seats!

When it comes to fan convenience, age notwithstanding, Ben Hill Griffin Stadium has no equal in the conference. Restrooms and concessions for food and souvenirs are more plentiful than anywhere in the SEC, although here, as with other stadium restroom facilities, the ladies must do a disproportionate share of standing in line. Concession areas offer, by far, the greatest variety of goodies found in any league stadium.

Known simply as Florida Field for the first fifty-nine of its sixty-three seasons, the stadium received a new name in 1989. Prior to that season the name was officially changed to "Ben Hill Griffin Stadium at Florida Field." Ben Hill Griffin, Jr., had been a life-long University of Florida supporter and benefactor.

Florida was the last of the present SEC member schools to begin football. The first team was not fielded until 1906, the year the University of Florida received its name. The first game in Gainesville was played on a field located immediately north of the present-day Ben Hill Griffin Stadium. From humble beginnings the university has built a fan following which ranked fifth in the nation in 1991 with an average attendance of 84,455 and which was voted "the most participative and supportive home crowd in collegiate athletics" in 1987 by the National Cheerleaders Association of America. Today Ben Hill Griffin Stadium is the eighth largest on-campus football facility in the nation with a capacity of 83,000.

The first stadium expansion project took place in 1950 when the facility was twenty years old. At that time over 11,000 seats were added to the west side stands and about 7,000 bleacher seats were placed on the east side. The capacity at the end of this phase stood at 40,116. During the decade of the 1950's, additional bleacher seats were constructed so that by 1960, 46,146 fans could watch games at Florida Field.

In 1965-66, ten thousand permanent seats were constructed on the east side and some of the bleacher seats were relocated to the south end zone. Total capacity stood at 62,800. In 1982 the South end zone was enclosed creating a horseshoe-shaped structure with seating for over 72,000. An athletic training center, luxury skyboxes and a new press box were added also.

Finally, in 1991, the north end zone project added more skyboxes, thousands of club and upper level chairback seats, concession stands, a gift shop and a new museum featuring UF athletics. This seventeen million dollar project rounded out seating capacity at 83,000 and was completed with no state funding!

Stadium Facts

First game:	November 8, 1930, Alabama 20, Florida 0
First victory:	1932; Florida 27, Citadel 7
Largest crowd:	85,461 - November 30, 1991; Florida vs Florida State
Stadium record:	1930-1992: W-200 L-80 T-13 (Pct. .703)
Playing surface:	Natural grass since 1990.
	The surface was artificial from 1971-1989

Florida's Ben Hill Griffin Stadium at Florida Field

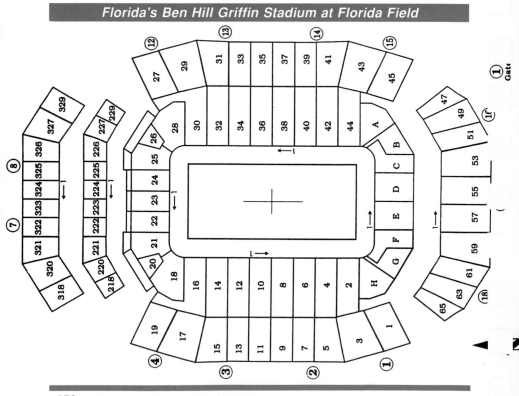

The Gator Bowl in Jacksonville

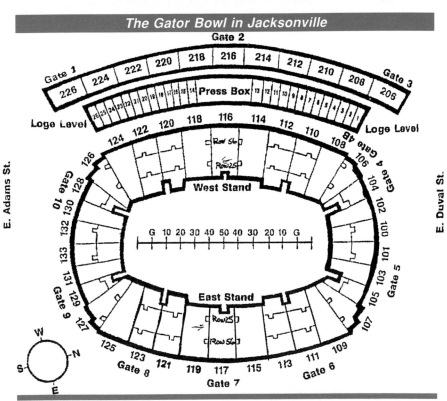

Mick Hubert	-	Play-By-Play/"Voice of the Gators"
Lee McGriff	-	Color Analyst
Steve Babik	-	Sideline Reporter/Host for "Steve Spurrier Post-Game Show"

GATOR RADIO NETWORK

AM Stations   **FM Stations**

CITY	STATE	STATION	FREQUENCY	CITY	STATE	STATION	FREQUENCY
Bartow	FL	WWBF	1130	Apalachicola	FL	WOYS	100.9
Blountstown	FL	WYBT	1000	Blountstown	FL	WPHK	102.3
Bradenton	FL	WBRD	1420	Chiefland	FL	WLQH	97.3
Brooksville	FL	WWJB	1450	Clewiston	FL	WAFC	106.3
Chipley	FL	WBGC	1240	Crestview	FL	WAAZ	104.9
Cocoa	FL	WWHL	1350	Crystal River	FL	WXCV	95.3
Crestview	FL	WJSB	1050	Gainesville	FL	WRUF	103.7
Dade City	FL	WDCF	1350	Lake City	FL	WNFB	94.3
Daytona Beach	FL	WNDB	1150	Macclenny	FL	WJXR	92.1
DeFuniak Springs	FL	WZEP	1460	Marianna	FL	WJAQ	100.9
Ft. Myers	FL	WMYR	1410	Monticello	FL	WJPH	101.9
Ft. Pierce	FL	WJNX	1330	Perry	FL	WNFK	105.5
Ft. Walton Beach	FL	WFTW	1260	Quincy	FL	WGWD	93.3
Gainesville	FL	WRUF	850	Sebring	FL	WCAC	105.5
Jacksonville	FL	WOKV	600	Starke	FL	WEAG	106.3
Key West	FL	WKIZ	1500	Venice	FL	WCTQ	92.1
Lake City	FL	WDSR	1340	Wauchula	FL	WZZS	106.9
Lakeland	FL	WLKF	1430				
Leesburg	FL	WLBE	790				
Live Oak	FL	WQHL	1250				
Marianna	FL	WTOT	980				
Miami	FL	WMRZ	790				
Monticello	FL	WMFL	1090				
Ocala	FL	WTMC	1290				
Orlando	FL	WWNZ	740				
Palatka	FL	WIYD	1260				
Panama City	FL	WLTG	1430				
Pensacola	FL	WCOA	1370				
Perry	FL	WPRY	1400				
St. Augustine	FL	WFOY	1240				
Sebring	FL	WITS	1340				
Starke	FL	WEAG	1490				
Tampa/St. Petersburg		WHMZ	570				
Titusville	FL	WAMT	1060				
Venice	FL	WAMR	1320				
Vero Beach	FL	WTTB	1490				
West Palm Beach	FL	WJNO	1230				
Winter Haven	FL	WHNR	1360				

*Ticket Information

Ticket office phone number is (904) 375-4683.

When calling this number, you will receive a short tape-recorded message that will instruct you how to reach the desired department with a touch-tone phone. You will be asked to push 1 and then the four digit extension number you desire:

Gator Gift Shoppe .... Ext. 6514

Gator Scoreline

Men .... Ext. 3020

Women .... Ext. 3030

Radio & Television Network Information .... Ext. 6600

Ticket Office .... Ext 6800/01/02/03

Although Florida has one of the best per game attendance averages based on percentage of capacity in the SEC, tickets are often available around the stadium. You need to be aware that **ticket scalping** (which in the state of Florida is defined as selling a ticket for more than $1.00 above its printed price) is illegal. Undercover police officers do make arrests at times and the University discourages such activity and tries to keep it away from the gates. Of course, it is not illegal to BUY a ticket for any price you are willing to pay.

SEATING: The Fightin' Gator Band is seated in sections 38 & 40 at Ben Hill Griffin Stadium at Florida Field. The visiting band is seated in sections 24 & 25. while visiting fans are seated in sections 38-42 (rows 1-10) and in sections 23-26, 47, 49 and 51. This information is subject to change.

*Stadium Policies

The University enforces a "No Smoking" policy in the stands but smoking is permitted in the concourse areas.

Unique in the SEC is Florida's **"Passes Out" policy** at Florida Field. Fans may receive a pass to leave the stadium and return at halftime. UF fans call this practice the "Beer Run."

Of course, the University of Florida adheres to all SEC policies.

*Locating the Stadium

Ben Hill Griffin Stadium may be approached from the west off I-75 by taking either **Exit 76** (State Road 26 also known as Newberry Road which becomes University Avenue as you get into town) or **Exit 75** (State Road 24 also known as Archer Road).

From the east, the stadium may be approached by the same two roads from U.S. Highway 441. Highway 441 is also known as 13th Street and borders the UF campus on the east side. On the west the University is bordered by 34th Street.

*Parking

When driving around the University/Downtown area of Gainesville before and after a football game, fans will notice that the traffic signals at all major intersections are turned off. Traffic is allowed to flow in its normal patterns since no streets are closed or restricted, but most intersections will be "manually controlled" by a uniformed law officer from one of the law enforcement agencies, campus, city or county, serving the area.

For those who plan and arrive early there are three **public parking garages** which open at 8:00 AM with a collective 1500 parking spaces. Two of these are about a 10 minute walk away from the stadium. One of these is located on North-South Drive just south of the Museum Drive at the intersection of Newell Drive, southeast of the stadium. The third garage is a 15-20 minute walk from Florida Field. It is located near the Health Science Center on Center Drive at the intersection of Archer Road.

If all of these lots are filled, the general public can park free at any **university parking space that is not reserved or restricted**. If no signs or attendants are present and no person's name appears on the space, fans may park there. Many Florida fans park in open parking lots near Shands Hospital off Archer Road, the Harn Museum at the intersection of Hull Road and Bledsoe Drive, and at the Law Center on SW 2nd Avenue off West University Avenue.

One area where close-in parking is available is the district on the north side of University Avenue across from Ben Hill Griffin Stadium. The going rate for **parking in someone's yard or drive** on game day is $5.00-$10.00. Be aware that there can be problems since in some cases these makeshift lots are not attended. Sometimes a person's vehicle can be blocked in resulting in a frustrating delay in getting away. Use common sense in sizing up each opportunity to park in this area. One great benefit of this area is its proximity to the stadium. Often only a five minute walk is necessary to arrive at the stadium. Do be aware that city police are especially active in this district citing all illegal parking. Vehicles blocking access may be fined, towed or both!

For the less adventuresome, the city of Gainesville and the University offer a **shuttle system** called **"Gator Park and Ride."** Fans may park at either Oaks Mall at the intersection of I-75 and University Avenue (Newberry Road) or at Downtown Plaza located 1 block east of the intersection of Main Street and University Avenue. Cost is $4.00 per person, round trip. Shuttles begin running three hours before game time and continue for three hours after the game's conclusion.

R.V. parking is located in the large commuter lot off North-South Drive. Signs direct traffic off Archer Road and University Avenue. The lot opens at 5 PM on Friday. Vehicles may stay overnight until Sunday morning. There is no charge.

Handicapped parking is available on a "first come, first served" basis at three lots on the northeast side of the stadium. Signs direct traffic. A state handicapped permit on your license plate is required for entrance. All other handicapped spaces on campus are available on game day as well.

*ALL INFORMATION IS SUBJECT TO CHANGE

Take a walking or driving tour of the lovely campus. The balance between the natural beauty of the moss-draped oaks, the palms and magnolias, and the man-made beauty of the many courtyards scattered around the 2,000 acre school will impress you as you move about. Secure a visitor's pass at UF's main entrance on S.W. 13th Street (U.S. 441) and S.W. 2nd Avenue.

~**Stephen C. O'Connell Center**. Home to Gator basketball, track, swimming, volleyball and gymnastics. Adjacent to Florida Field. (904) 392-5500.

~**Ben Hill Griffin Stadium at Florida Field**. Home of the "Fightin' Gators."

~The **Samuel P. Harn Museum of Art** features permanent and semi-permanent exhibits of American and Latin American paintings, Oceanic, African, and pre-Colombian collections, as well as contemporary works of art. Museum store. (904) 392-9826.

~The **Center for the Performing Arts** is a brand new 1800 seat facility which presents theatre, orchestral and dance events. Hull Road and S.W. 34th Street. (904) 374-4484.

~**Alligators.** See Albert and Alberta's real life cousins in their natural habitat at Lake Alice. Western end of Museum road.

~**UF Bookstores.** Located in the Reitz Student Union and the Hub, these stores offer Gator souvenirs and apparel. The Reitz Union store is open Monday through Friday, 9 AM-9 PM; the Hub store, Monday-Friday 8 AM-5:30 PM. Both are open 11AM-5 PM on Saturday.

~**University Memorial Auditorium and Century Tower.** The auditorium is listed on the National Register of Historic Places. The Tower has become a symbol of the University.

~The **Natural History Museum** is the Southeast's largest of its type. It offers a constantly changing variety of lectures and demonstrations on fascinating topics in addition to permanent and temporary exhibits and hundreds of natural science specimens, fossils, skeletons, computer games. Collectors Gift Shop. Free. Museum Road and Nowell Drive. (904) 392-1721.

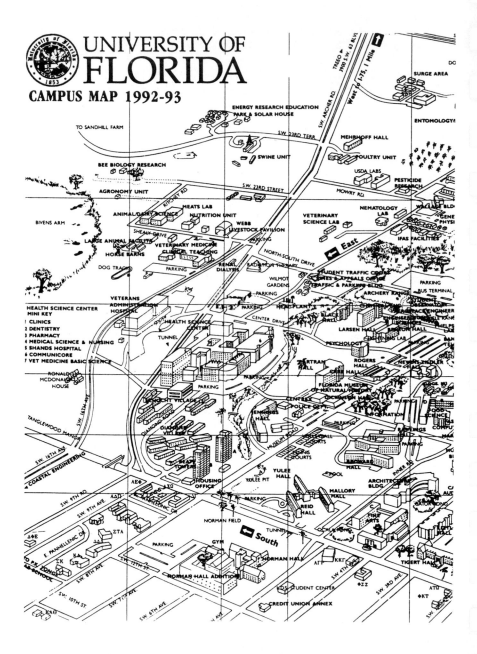

UNIVERSITY OF FLORIDA
CAMPUS MAP 1992-93

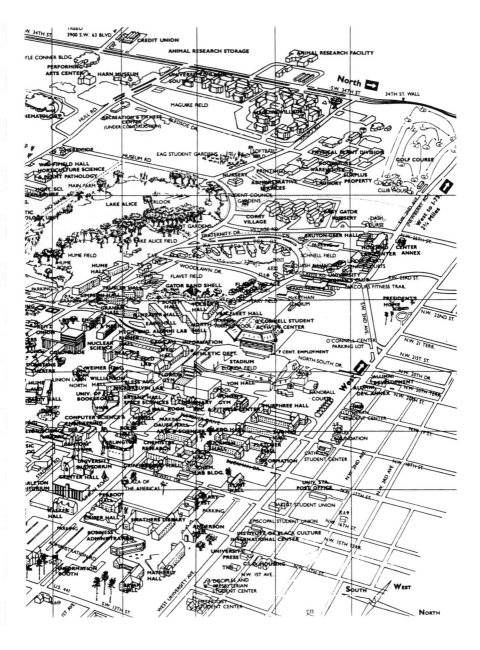

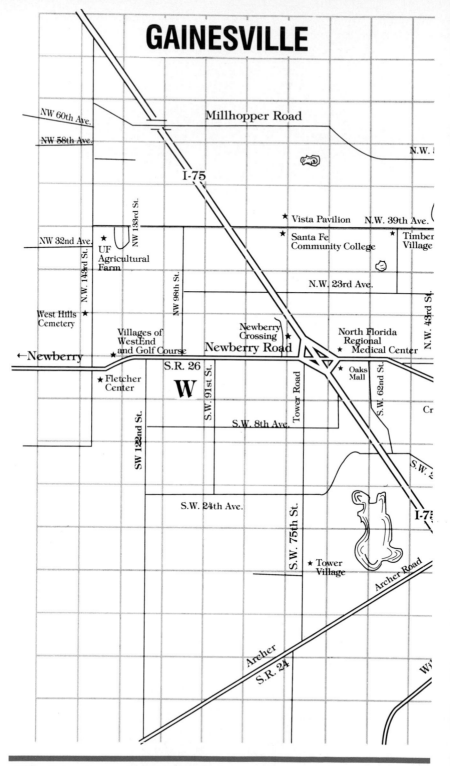

GAINESVILLE

NW 60th Ave.

NW 58th Ave.

Millhopper Road

N.W.

I-75

★ Vista Pavilion   N.W. 39th Ave.

NW 32nd Ave.   ★   ★ Santa Fe   ★ Timber
UF   Community College   Village
Agricultural
Farm

NW 183rd St.

N.W. 183rd St.

N.W. 143rd St.

NW 98th St.

N.W. 23rd Ave.

West Hills ★
Cemetery

Villages of   Newberry   North Florida
WestEnd   Crossing   Regional
and Golf Course   ★   ★ Medical Center
←Newberry   Newberry Road

S.R. 26

★ Fletcher   **W**
Center

N.W. 43rd St.

Tower Road

★ Oaks
Mall

S.W. 62nd St.

Cr

SW 122nd St.

S.W. 91st St.

S.W. 8th Ave.

S.W. 24th Ave.

S.W.

I-7

S.W. 75th St.

★ Tower
Village

Archer Road

Archer
S.R. 24

Wi

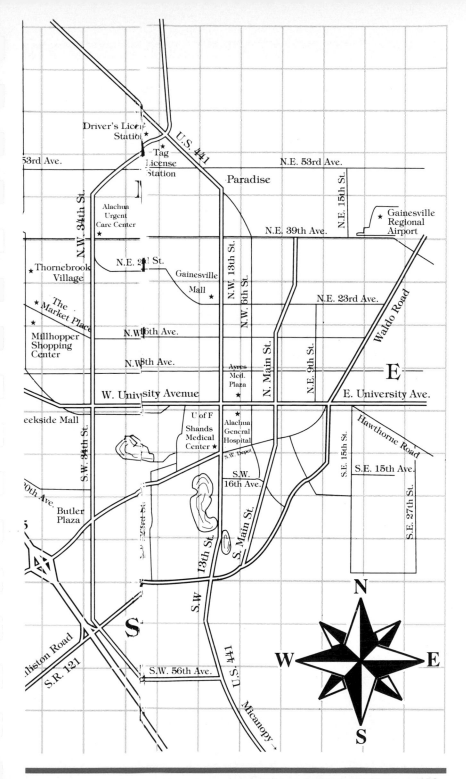

Driver's License Station

Tag License Station

U.S. 441

53rd Ave.

N.E. 53rd Ave.

Paradise

N.W. 34th St.

Alachua Urgent Care Center

Thornebrook Village

N.E. 2nd St.

Gainesville Mall

N.W. 13th St.

N.W. 6th St.

N.E. 39th Ave.

N.E. 15th St.

Gainesville Regional Airport

N.E. 23rd Ave.

Waldo Road

The Market Place

Millhopper Shopping Center

N.W. 16th Ave.

N.W. 8th Ave.

Ayres Med. Plaza

N. Main St.

N.E. 9th St.

E

W. University Avenue

E. University Ave.

eekside Mall

S.W. 34th St.

U of F Shands Medical Center

Alachua General Hospital

S.W. Depot

S.W. 16th Ave.

S.E. 15th St.

Hawthorne Road

S.E. 15th Ave.

20th Ave.

Butler Plaza

23rd St.

13th St.

S. Main St.

S.W.

S.E. 27th St.

5

S

illiston Road

S.R. 121

S.W. 56th Ave.

U.S. 441

Micanopy

N

W   E

S

~History buffs will enjoy strolling or driving through the **Northeast Historic District of Gainesville** to see how Floridians built their homes from the 1880's to the 1920's. Over 290 vintage homes are located in this 63 block area. Begin your tour at the **Clock Tower**.

~If Gainesville proper doesn't quench your thirst for history, venture out to the town of **Micanopy**, Florida's second oldest. Just 13 miles south on U.S. 441, Micanopy features antique, art, and curio shops. Most shops are open until 6:00 PM.

~For a picnic in a natural setting you might want to choose **Bivens Arm Nature Park**. Near the University, Bivens' Park features 57 acres of oak hammock and marsh which may be viewed from a 1200 foot walkway. Wildlife sanctuary, nature center, picnic tables. Free. 3650 S. Main Street. (904) 334.2056.

~**Devil's Millhopper State Geological Site**. An ancient sinkhole some 500 feet in diameter that allows visitors to descend 221 wooden steps to the bottom. On the way down, visitors can see a dozen small waterfalls, as well as many plant species rarely found in Florida. 4732 N.W. 53rd Avenue. (904) 336-2008.

~**Kanapoka Botanical Gardens** gives visitors a chance to slow down their pace while reflecting on the beauty of 62 acres of woodlands and meadows with a variety of gardens including rock and sunken. Lily pad pond, gazebos, picnic areas, gift shop. 4625 S.W. 63rd Boulevard. (904) 372-4981.

~The **Marjorie Kinnan Rawlings State Historic Site** at Cross Creek showcases the home of the Pulitzer Prize winning author of *The Yearling*. Restored just as it was when she was there, the site affords visitors the opportunity to learn about Florida cracker living. 21 miles southeast of Gainesville on County Road 325.

~The **Morningside Nature Center** is a favorite for visitors of all ages allowing them to experience life on a family farm in central Florida 100 years ago. The 278 acre Living History Farm includes barnyard animals, an 1840's cabin and a barn. There are over seven miles of trails and boardwalks from which to watch over 130 bird species, 223 wildflower species, mammals and reptiles. Free. 3540 E. University Avenue. (904) 334-2170.

~**Paynes Prairie State Preserve** affords visitors the chance to boat, camp, hike, bird watch, fish, swim and picnic all at one site---but what a site it is---over 18,000 acres of marsh and wet prairie vegetation with many migrating birds and many alligators! 10 miles south of Gainesville on U.S. 441. (904) 466-3397.

For more information contact:

Visitors and Convention Bureau   **(904) 374-5231**
10 S.W. 2nd Avenue, Suite 220
Gainesville, Florida 32601

Where to Eat and Sleep in the Gainesville Area

Like so many SEC towns, gameday at UF finds fans motoring in from all parts, some by design, and some because accommodations in town are unavailable. Fortunately, access to Gainesville and the University is very good via Interstate 75 and U.S. Highways 441 and 301.

Though rooms may not be available in Gainesville nearby towns such as Alachua, Lake City, Starke and Ocala are good bets for accommodations. Because of Florida's flat land and great interstate system, getting to the University from these towns.

Fans who are lucky enough, or brave enough, to attend the "Largest Cocktail Party in the World" (that is the game between Georgia and Florida) in Jacksonville will hardly have time for sight-seeing. However, in the event time is available, Jacksonville is the **only** place where SEC football is played with beaches nearby so take time to enjoy them!

~**The Beaches.** Twelve miles from Downtown via Atlantic Boulevard (State Road 10) or by J. Turner Butler Expressway.

~**Anheuser-Busch Brewery Tour.** See the beer-making process and sample the results (adults only). Closed Sunday. 111 Busch Drive. (904) 751-8116.

~**The Jacksonville Landing.** Downtown marketplace with festive atmosphere featuring over 19 restaurants and 40 specialty shops. (904) 353-1188.

~**Jacksonville Zoo.** Located at 8605 Zoo Road off Heckschere Drive at Exit 124 on I-95. Features over 800 animals. (904) 757-4463.

~**Mayport Naval Station.** One of the navy's largest carrier facilities. Open Saturdays and Sundays. Free. (904) 270-5226.

~**Riverwalk.** A one mile boardwalk along the south bank of the St. Johns River where several restaurants, hotels and shops are located.

~**The Water Taxi.** Provides transportation between the north and south banks of the St. Johns with a relaxing ride as a side benefit. (904) 730-8685.

~**Museums.** Several outstanding museums are located in Jacksonville featuring everything from the fine arts, history (including Civil War and Maritime) and science and technology. Interactive displays for children and families. (904) 78-9148

.~**Theodore Roosevelt Preserve.** A 600 acre wilderness lining the lower St. Johns River. Features several ecological communities with rare plants and animals. Hiking trails. Open daily during daylight hours. (904) 641-7155.

~**St. Augustine.** America's oldest city has Spanish-Colonial houses, quaint shops, beaches and history at every turn. Located a half-hour south of Jacksonville on U.S. Highway 1, I-95 or A-1A. (904)829-5681.

Where to Eat and Sleep in the Jacksonville Area

Jacksonville has many rooms available for this event, but make plans early or you may not be able to find accommodations in your price range or the area you desire. Hotels and motels in the area require a deposit and guarantee for rooms nearly two weeks in advance. There is at least a two night minimum and some require more.

The partying goes on for days before the game and sometimes the fans celebrate late into the evening, so sleep may not be a reality during this event! After-the-game partying can become rowdy, especially in and around the downtown area. But let the authors be quick to say their trip to Jacksonville was great! The fans were fun and the whole weekend was memorable because we were aware of and prepared for these eventualities.

For complete information contact:

Jacksonville and the Beaches Convention & Visitors Bureau
3 Independent Drive
Jacksonville, FL 32202   **Phone: (904) 798-9148**

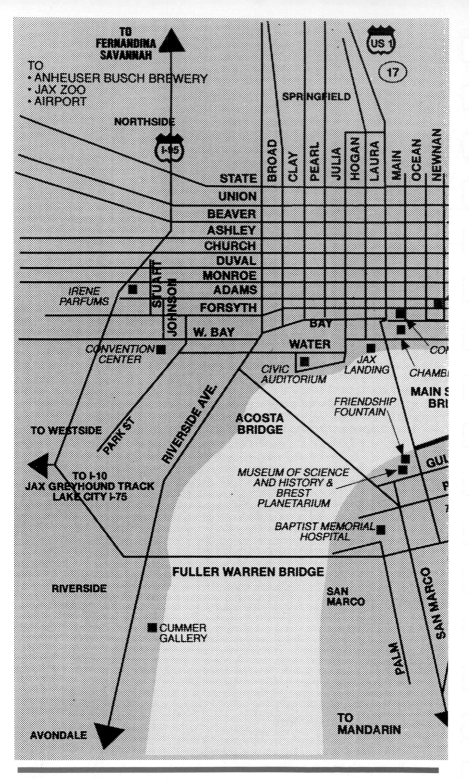

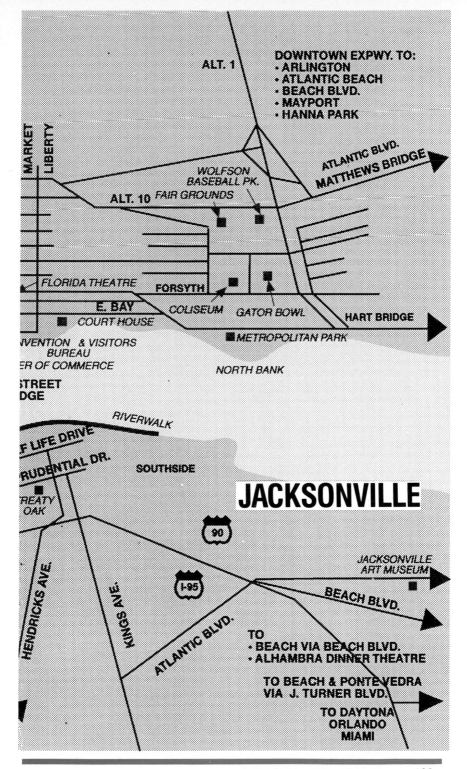

*Erected in 1864, the Arch, which marks the gateway
between downtown Athens and the UGA campus,
has come to symbolize the University.*

G
E
O
R
G
I
A

*The beautiful University of Georgia Chapel on the North Campus.
At its rear is the bell tower whose bell signals Georgia victories.*

Founded in 1785, the University of Georgia is the oldest state-supported institution in America. The school was situated on its campus even before the founding of its host city, Athens. Begun as a tiny settlement at Cedar Shoals in 1801, Athens was not incorporated until 1806.

Athens is located about sixty-five miles northeast of Atlanta in Clarke County. With a population of 42,500, it is the largest town in the northeastern part of the state. It can arguably be defined as the ideal college town for several reasons. It is large enough to offer the necessities of student life including a very large variety of music and dance hangouts. It has shopping and recreation areas and cultural offerings, and it is not so large that the individual student and the collective student body lose their identities. The special relationship between a host city and its university, which greatly adds to a student's college days, certainly exists in Athens. The expression "town and gown" is used locally to express the mutual respect and benefit Athens and the University of Georgia enjoy. At the same time, Atlanta is just a short trip down the road whenever a wider circle of experiences is desired. All things considered, it would be difficult to find a better college environment.

As students and graduates of the university began to move their families into the Athens area in the early eighteen hundreds, the city's size, as well as political and cultural influence grew. The Civil War dealt a devastating blow to both the town and the school. So much so, that at the turn of the century, UGA had fewer than 300 students. From that point the university has sustained steady growth to its present enrollment of some 28,000 students.

When the current campus of the University was established in 1801, it was due to the generosity of John Milledge, later Governor of Georgia, who presented the original 633 acres to the state. The view from one of the red clay hills on the site reminded him of the Acropolis in ancient Athens, Greece, the center of classical learning. From this inspiration, the city of Athens, Georgia, later took its name as well as its nickname, the "Classic City."

The first permanent structure on the campus, Old College, was not completed until 1806, two years after the first class graduated, but it still stands today. The part of the grounds where Old College and most of the older buildings are located is known as North Campus. The area below Sanford Stadium has been the scene of most campus construction since the 1940's and is known as South Campus or New Campus.

Today, the University of Georgia is ranked among the nation's top research institutions. It is widely recognized for its schools of Veterinary Medicine, Bio Sciences, Pharmacy, Business and Journalism. The school's library, with over three million volumes, is ranked 19th in the U. S. More than ever the University of Georgia is meeting the mission expressed in its motto: "Et docere et rerum Exquirere Causas" which means, "To teach and to inquire into the nature of things."

Since undergoing a revitalization, downtown Athens,
with its fashionable shops, businesses and outdoor eateries,
has moved even closer to becoming the ideal environment for a college community.

Right back at you, Razorbacks! Georgia's cheerleaders yell for the "Dawgs" in Fayetteville.

Georgia's school colors seem to have been "red and black" since the school began. In our survey, 100% of fans said they wear the school colors to the game, but there seems to be no written history about how they colors were chosen.

Though two years of research did not uncover the truth, we will continue to seek the answer and look forward to hearing from fans about how the colors were chosen.

The University of Georgia's "red" is PMS Color # 185.

Wearing his "game face," Hairy Dawg seems to be saying, "Put me in, Coach. I'm ready. Can I play? Huh, Coach? I promise I won't bite anybody this week."

There are two stories about how Georgia athletic teams first acquired the nickname "Bulldogs." One traces the name to Georgia's early ties to Yale University, also known as the Bulldogs. The first president of Georgia, Abraham Baldwin, was a Yalie and the first buildings on North Campus were copied from plans of buildings at the New Haven school. When Sanford Stadium was dedicated, the visiting team was Yale. So it was natural that admiration turned to emulation and the Southern "Bulldogs" have tried to surpass their Northern counterparts ever since!

The second story traces the nickname to an article which appeared on November 3, 1920, in the "Atlanta Journal." The writer of the piece, Morgan Blake, suggested the nickname when he wrote, "The Georgia Bulldogs would sound good because there is a certain dignity about a bulldog, as well as ferocity." Three days later reporter Cliff Wheatley, writing in the "Atlanta Constitution" about Georgia's 0-0 tie with Virginia, referred to the Georgia team five times as the "Bulldogs." The name caught on and has been used ever since.

Which story is correct? There is good reason to believe they both are!

Animal magnetism?
Our polls show it's true!
Georgia's UGA V
is one of the most
widely recognized
and popular of the
SEC mascots!

Georgia mascots have come a long way from that day in February of 1892 when at the Auburn game, the boys from Athens were represented by a goat! Although the goat did his best to win the job permanently, showing up for the game in a black coat with a red "U.G." on each side and wearing a hat with flowing ribbons, he just didn't project the type of image the university wanted. Two years later, in 1894, Georgia took a step in the direction of the modern mascot when the team was supported by a solid white female bull terrier who belonged to a Georgia student.

It is hard to believe that from these first attempts to find a fitting symbol for the university's athletic teams, Georgia would settle on a mascot that not only conveys the desired characteristics of dignity and ferocity, but would also become arguably the most famous and popular of all the collegiate mascots. As reported in the section on nicknames, the university's teams have been referred to as "bulldogs" since at least 1920.

Over the years several dogs have served as mascot; some official, some not. One of the earliest of note accompanied the team to the 1943 Rose Bowl.

He was also the grandfather of UGA I, the first in the present line of Bulldog mascots. Before UGA I began his reign in 1955, and with it, the present line of solid white English bulldogs, he was preceded by two official mascots who were both brindled, like "Bully", the Mississippi State bulldog. The first one, "Butch," served from 1947-1950. He got the job after being spotted at a Georgia Tech game in Athens in 1946. Butch was followed by "Mike" who served from 1951-1955.

In 1956, UGA I assumed the post. He served honorably until 1966 when he was succeeded by his son. He was the first mascot to be buried inside Sanford Stadium. Since then three other bulldog mascots have joined him in marble crypts built into the end of the South stands. Before each game, flowers are placed at the site and hundreds of fans visit to pay their respects. Each of the tombs has an inscription. UGA I's reads, "A real Georgia Bulldog - Damn Good Dog."

UGA II ruled from 1966 to 1972. His epitaph states, "Two SEC Championships, Five Bowl Teams - Not Bad for A Dog."

The third UGA had a long career, spanning nine seasons. His inscription says it all: "Georgia Mascot 1972-1981, Two SEC Championships, Six Bowl Teams, The undefeated, untied, undisputed and undenied National Champion of College Football 1980. How 'Bout This Dog." UGA III died only a few weeks after passing the torch to UGA IV.

UGA IV had the distinction of being the only mascot to attend a bowl game during every year of his service, making nine trips from 1981 to 1989. He also attended the Heisman Trophy Banquet in New York in 1982 and the NCAA Final Four in 1983. He was labeled "Dog of the Decade" by Vince Dooley and is so described on his tombstone. So great were UGA IV's accomplishments that he was awarded in 1991 the highest posthumous honor available to University of Georgia mascots--the Georgia varsity letter!

A touching story accompanies UGA V's path to becoming the official mascot. UGA V was the last pup sired by UGA IV who had passed away just a week before the birth of the litter. UGA V was the last pup born and the only solid white male. He was only six months old when he began his reign with the 1990 season.

In addition to the mascot mausoleum near the west end zone, there are at least three other reminders to the players and fans that Georgia is the "Home of the Bulldogs." In the east end zone there is a statue of a white bulldog which is strategically placed so that the players pass alongside it as they emerge onto the field from the dressing room. It has become a habit of Georgia players to pat or rub the stone mascot as they take the field. In the nearby Northeast corner near the cheerleaders' platform, sits UGA V's home, a permanent, air conditioned, red doghouse which the mascot dearly loves--especially on hot days--and from which he watches the two-legged Bulldogs do battle.

Wandering the sidelines and helping to lead cheers is another two-legged bulldog, "Hairy," the "hybrid" mascot with the head of a bulldog and the uniform of a football player. All these reminders of Georgia's mascot present in the stadium show how deeply the bulldog has been absorbed into the psyches of Georgia fans and athletes. Judging by this and the success of Georgia teams over the years, UGA isn't likely to lose his job to a goat any time soon!

Boasting 375 members, the University of Georgia's Redcoat Marching Band is an awesome sight as it takes the field in its bright uniforms. If the goal of the organization is to excite and inspire Georgia fans, the band succeeds admirably. Many consider the Redcoat Band to be the "heart" of the Bulldog spirit.

R. E. Haughey, the Band's first director, assumed the post in 1905, one of only six directors the band has had to date. Haughey was followed by Robert T. "Fess" Dottery, J. Harris Mitchell, Roger Dancz, Gary Teske and the current leader, Dwight Satterwhite. Roger Dancz continues to serve as Director of Bands.

The Redcoat Band is proud of the diversity and academic achievements of its members. Many band members maintain some of the highest GPA's at the University. Approximately 30 percent of the group's membership is made up of music majors. Almost every other academic major is represented in the band as well.

Piccolos on parade. The "Redcoat Marching Band," huge even by college standards, is a "class act," proudly representing UGA wherever they are seen.

GEORGIA'S FIGHT SONG "Glory to Georgia"

Hail to Georgia, down in Dixie!
A college honor'd fair, and true;
The Red and Black is her standard,
proudly it waves.
Streaming today and the ages through.
She's the fairest in the Southland
We'll pledge our love to her for aye;
To that college dear we'll ring a cheer,
All hail to dear old U-G-A!
Hail, our Varsity of Georgia!
Thy sons will e'er thy glory sing:
To thee we'll ever be faithful, loyal and true;
Ever and aye will thy praises ring.
Grand old time of ours at Georgia
The happiest days they'll be always;
Alma mater, fair beyond compare,
All hail to dear old U-G-A!

UNIVERSITY OF GEORGIA
"Alma Mater"

From the hills of Georgia's northland
Beams thy noble brow.
And the sons of Georgia rising
Pledge with sacred vow.

'Neath the pine trees' stately shadow
Spread thy riches rare.
And thy sons, dear Alma Mater,
Will thy treasure share.

And thy daughters proudly join thee,
Take their rightful place,
Side by side into the future,
Equal dreams embrace.

Through the ages, Alma Mater,
Men will look to thee;
Thou the fairest of the Southland
Georgia's Varsity.

CHORUS:
Alma Mater, thee we honor,
True and loyal be,
Ever crowned with praise and glory,
Georgia, hail to thee.

"GLORY"

Glory, glory to old Georgia!
Glory, glory to old Georgia!
Glory, glory to old Georgia!
G-E-O-R-G-I-A.
Glory, glory to old Georgia!
Glory, glory to old Georgia!
Glory, glory to old Georgia!
G-E-O-R-G-I-A.

When we think of the University of Georgia we think of "class and tradition." Being from the state of Alabama, now living in Florida, we interviewed Georgia fans with some prejudiced ideas; but we came away with a great appreciation for both the fans and the whole athletic program! They seem to exemplify the phrase "grace under pressure," getting the job done and making it look easy. This was especially true of the Sports Information Department. Though we received wonderful assistance "above and beyond the call of duty" from every SID office, Georgia was by far the most accommodating.

Right now the football team is in transition and even though the going is tough they too are showing grace under fire. They believe in their "tradition 'par excellence'" as one fan said, and remain faithful through good times and bad. No complaining and "belly-aching," just reserved confidence and tenacity, much like their lovable Bulldog mascot.

Speaking of which, UGA was chosen as the favorite mascot (other than their own, of course) by fans of most other schools, and Georgia fans are rightly proud of him. They believe in their Dawgs and honor them at every turn in Sanford Stadium. There are mini-mausoleums and statues for past mascots, an adorable red house for the current bulldog and the football players even touch a large bulldog statue as they come onto the field! The bulldog heritage at Georgia is more than skin deep!

Georgia fans were also some of the most knowledgeable we met. They loved to recite the lore about their own heritage and tradition, but also were very familiar with their rival SEC schools. They even knew which bands were good and were familiar with the other mascots. One of their favorite traditions is "Larry Munson" (play-by-play announcer) so perhaps their knowledge can be attributed to the good job he does in helping to keep them informed. Another reason may be that they are also well-traveled fans. While the majority of fans at some SEC schools attend only home games, Georgia fans follow their bulldogs anywhere! They could even tell us about parking problems at most of the schools!

We were surprised, however, to find that Georgia was the **only** school where 100% of the fans interviewed said they "wear school colors" (red and/or black) to ALL football games! This is a real irony because we have been unable to discover a story about how their colors were chosen. We are still trying and hope to hear from the fans!

Georgia fan Bill Smiley of Knoxville, Tennessee, (and many others) told us the dedication of "Georgia fans" is what makes their school unique in the SEC. Jean Allison of Marietta, calls it that "undying fan support." Many agreed with Georgianna K. Ingram of Conyers, Georgia, saying they would "travel to the ends of the earth," because "distance doesn't matter" when the Dawgs are playing, says William Dent of Alpharetta, Georgia! It never seems to be difficult to get 85,000 people "'tween the hedges" when the Dawgs are playing at home, but Georgia fans also follow their team in great numbers anywhere!

Most Georgia fans are like Terry Earnest of Jacksonville, Florida, who has "always" been a fan," but Thomas M. Nunn said, when asked how long he had been a Bulldog fan, "Since birth, no since conception. I'm a pro-lifer!" That's how devoted these Bulldog fans are!

Favorite traditions at Georgia are the "hedges" (which may have to be removed in preparation for the Olympics, though they will be kept safely for replanting afterwards), the "Redcoat Marching Band," tailgating and the GA-FL game in Jacksonville. Georgia fans enjoy their rivalries, perhaps with the exception of some hard feelings about Auburn, something about the water sprinklers?!

With that one exception, we found that

Georgia fans were some of the most devoted fans we met . . . just as this T-shirt describes!

Georgia fans don't dwell on the past and there's not a lot of talk about the "glory days." Jim Peacock of Atlanta said one of his favorite traditions associated with Georgia football was the "quality of the program," and Georgia fans believe in the end that's what is most important . . . the wins will follow. As an aside, we found out later that Jim was a member of the '68 Championship Team, but he did not tell us until we asked. Just another sign of that "class" of Georgia.

So, what foods do these "classy" Georgia fans enjoy? Well, Matt Daugherty of Valdosta, Georgia, said his favorite gameday food was "gator tail," but we found that chicken was by far the food of choice. Boiled peanuts were also mentioned often. Georgia fans recommend the Varsity, The Grill, Guthries, T-Bone's and Ronnie B's as their favorite places to eat in Athens. However, most Georgia fans enjoy tailgating.

Well, whether you travel to Georgia to see your favorite team, to try some boiled peanuts or eat great fried chicken, it's well worth the time and effort. Sanford Stadium is full of tradition that all SEC fans need to experience, but the Georgia fans will make it a day to remember . . . "How 'bout them Dawgs!"

Sanford Stadium surrounds it team with tradition.

Head Coach:

Ray Goff (Georgia, 1978)
Georgia Graduate Assistant, 1977;
South Carolina Head JV Coach, 1978-79;
South Carolina Assistant, 1980;
Georgia Recruiting Coordinator, 1981-82;
Georgia Assistant, 1983-88;
Georgia Head Coach, 1989-present.

Birthday:	**July 10, 1955**
Hometown:	**Moultrie GA**

Assistant Coaches

Wayne McDuffie (Florida State, 1968)	Assistant Head Coach/Tight Ends/ Offensive Coordinator/Offensive Line
Richard Bell (Arkansas, 1959)	Defensive Coordinator/Secondary
Steve Ensminger (LSU, 1980)	Passing Game Coordinator/ Quarterbacks
Dicky Clark (Georgia, 1977)	Force Unit Coordinator/ Outside Linebackers
Darryl Drake (Western Kentucky, 1980)	Wide Receivers
Steve Greer (Georgia, 1970)	Defensive Line
Willie McClendon (Valdosta State, 1987)	Running Backs
Mac McWhorter (Georgia, 1974)	Offensive Line/Tight Ends
Frank Orgel (Georgia, 1961)	Inside Linebackers

A view of the English privet hedge which surrounds Sanford Stadium and has made the expression "'Tween the hedges" part of America's football folklore.

Before Sanford Stadium became the home of Georgia football two other historic gridirons filled that role. The first game on the campus was played January 30, 1892, on a field named in honor of "The Father of Georgia Football," Dr. Charles Herty, who taught chemistry and brought the game back to Athens from Baltimore where he had become fascinated with it while a student at Johns Hopkins. Herty Field, as it was dubbed soon after Dr. Herty began his efforts to organize a team and prepare a playing surface, was located on North Campus near the Chapel. It was bordered by Moore College and New College. Today the site is, for the most part, a parking lot, but in 1992 to commemorate the centennial and significance of that first game, a historic marker was placed there. Less than a month after that inaugural Georgia football game was played at Herty Field (a 50-0 victory over Mercer College), Georgia met Auburn in a game at Atlanta's Piedmont Park. That February 20th encounter was the first contest in what is now the South's oldest intercollegiate rivalry!

In 1911, Sanford Field became home to the Bulldogs. A dual purpose park (football and baseball), Sanford Field was located a few hundred feet west of the present Sanford Stadium, past the Student Center where Stegeman Hall now sits. Sanford Field, like Sanford Stadium, was named to honor Dr.

Steadman V. Sanford, campus Physical Director, who later served as Dean, University President and University System Chancellor. Dr. Sanford was often referred to as "a friend of athletics." Sanford Field was succeeded by Sanford Stadium after 18 seasons.

One of the most pleasant stadiums anywhere in which to view a college football game has to be Sanford Stadium. Not only pleasing to the eye with the graceful symmetry of its bowed horseshoe, the arena is also rich in tradition and lore which enhances the experience of watching the Bulldogs play "between the hedges."

Located in the east central part of the campus , Sanford Stadium is built in a ravine making it important that fans plan the approach to their seats carefully lest they end up walking over and around some fairly challenging terrain. When the stadium was dedicated in 1929, it consisted of only the lower portion of the north and south stands and seated 30,000 spectators. Both end zones were open. The tops of the stands were just above street level. For the dedication game, the mighty Yale Bulldogs came south expecting to prove the prognosticators correct by whipping the Georgia boys. To their chagrin and to the delight of an overflow first game crowd that October 12th, the home team carried the day 15-0!

When Sanford Stadium hosted that game 64 years ago, the English privet hedges which have become so famous in Georgia tradition were only a foot high and had to be protected by a wooden fence. Since then, the hedges and the stadium have grown in size and fame. In 1940 night football came to Athens when field level lighting was installed. In 1949, twenty years after it opened, the stadium was expanded to 36,000 seats. In its thirty-fifth year, end zone seating was added, raising the capacity to 43,621. At the same time, the lights, which had not been used for a night game since 1951, were removed. Just three years later in 1967, 19,640 seats were constructed when the stadium was "double decked." Seating rose to the 59,000 level. At the beginning of the 1980's the east end zone was fully enclosed, maintaining the same sweep of lines found on the north and south stands. The 19,000 plus seats increased the stadium's size to 82,122. In 1982, lights were reinstalled, and in 1984 the Lettermen's Club was added to the east end providing dining and meeting space. The facility assumed its present capacity and configuration in 1991 when the west end zone was enclosed adding 4,205 totally new seats and excellent restroom and concession areas. Today, Sanford Stadium ranks as the sixth largest on-campus sports facility with seating for 85,434 fans.

Stadium Stats

Capacity:	85,434
Largest home crowd:	85,434; September 7, 1991, and various times since
First victory:	October 12, 1929; Georgia 15, Yale 0
First loss:	November 2, 1929; Tulane 21, Georgia 15
First night game:	October 26, 1940; Georgia 7, Kentucky 7
First night game with new lights:	September 6, 1982; Georgia 13, Clemson 7
Longest home streak:	24 wins (9/13/80 - 11/12/83)
Stadium record:	1929-1992 - W-226 L-71 T-10 (Pct. .752)
Playing surface:	Natural grass

Georgia's Sanford Stadium

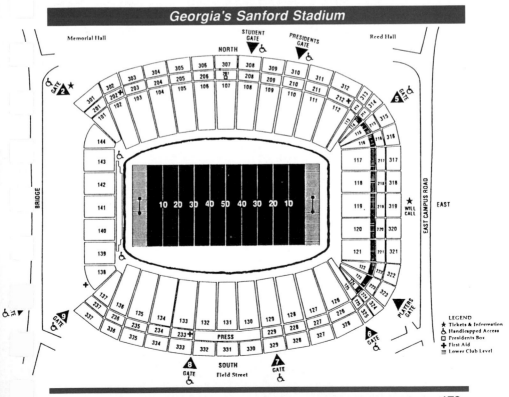

Larry Munson - Play-By-Play
Phil Schaefer - Pre-Game/Halftime Interviews
Loran Smith - Sideline Color

GEORGIA RADIO NETWORK

AM Stations   FM Stations

CITY	STATE	STATION	FREQUENCY	CITY	STATE	STATION	FREQUENCY
Albany	GA	WGPC	1450	Americus	GA	WDEC	94.3
Athens	GA	WGAU	1340	Athens	GA	WNGC	95.5
Atlanta	GA	WSB	750	Blackshear	GA	WKUB	104.9
Augusta	GA	WGAC	580	Carrollton	GA	WBTR	92.1
Bainbridge	GA	WMGR	930	Cornelia	GA	WCON	99.3
Brunswick	GA	WGIG	1440	Douglas	GA	WDMG	99.5
Calhoun	GA	WJTH	900	Elberton	GA	WWRK	92.1
Claxton	GA	WCLA	1470	Greensboro	GA	WDDK	103.9
Clayton	GA	WGHC	1370	Griffin	GA	WQUL	97.7
Cleveland	GA	WRHW	1350	Hawkinsville	GA	WCEH	103.9
Columbus	GA	WRCG	1420	Jesup	GA	WIFO	105.5
Cornelia	GA	WCON	1450	Kingsland	GA	WKBX	106.3
Dalton	GA	WBLJ	1230	Millen	GA	WMKO	94.9
Dublin	GA	WMLT	1330	Moultrie	GA	WMTM	93.9
Eastman	GA	WUFF	710	Newnan	GA	WMKJ	96.7
Elberton	GA	WWRK	1400	Thomaston	GA	WTGA	95.3
Fitzgerald	GA	WBHB	1240	Thomson	GA	WTHO	101.7
Gainesville	GA	WDUN	550	Tifton	GA	WSGY	100.3
Gordon	GA	WBNM	1120	Warner Robins	GA	WRCC	101.7
Griffin	GA	WKEU	1450	Washington	GA	WLOV	100.1
Hartwell	GA	WKLY	980	Waycross	GA	WKUB	104.9
Hawkinsville	GA	WCEH	610				
LaGrange	GA	WTRP	620				
Louisville	GA	WPEH	1420				
Macon	GA	WMAZ	940				
Milledgeville	GA	WMVG	1450				
Montezuma	GA	WMNZ	1050				
Moultrie	GA	WMTM	1300				
Newnan	GA	WCOH	1400				
Rome	GA	WRGA	1470				
Sandersville	GA	WSNT	1490				
Savannah	GA	WBMQ	630				
Statesboro	GA	WWNS	1240				
Swainsboro	GA	WJAT	800				
Sylvania	GA	WSYL	1490				
Thomaston	GA	WTGA	1590				
Thomasville	GA	WPAX	1240				
Tifton	GA	WWGS	1420				
Valdosta	GA	WVLD	1450				
Washington	GA	WLOV	1370				

*TICKET INFORMATION

Ticket Office: (404) 542-1231

Scalping tickets is illegal in Georgia. Tickets may not be sold for more than the price marked. Violators could be apprehended and prosecuted especially if they scalp on campus. Arrests are made from time to time.

Seating for the Redcoat Band is in section 109. The visiting band sits in section 101 and visiting fans are seated in sections 101-105 and 301-305.

*LOCATING THE STADIUM

Via I-20 from Birmingham take I-20 East and exit at the Conyers Exit (Exit 42, Highway 138). Turn left onto Highway 138 at the light. Continue for approximately 20 miles where Highway 138 merges into Highway 78 East. Highway 78 merges into Highway 29 East (to Athens). Continue past the Georgia Square Mall. Turn right onto the Athens Bypass (signs to Watkinsville). Take College Station Road Exit and turn left at the bottom of the ramp.

Via I-20 from Augusta take I-20 West and exit at Highway 78 North (west) to Athens. Continue on Highway 78 to Athens. Turn left onto the Athens Bypass (signs to Watkinsville) and take College Station Road Exit. Turn right at the bottom of the ramp.

Via I-85 from Atlanta take I-85 North to Highway 316 (signs to Athens). Continue on 316 until it dead ends, take a left and proceed until you reach Highway 29. Turn right, continue for approximately 25 miles passing the Georgia Square Mall and several car dealerships. This becomes Broad Street upon entering Athens.

Via I-85 from Greenville take I-85 South to the Carnesville Exit (Highway 106). Continue on 106 to Athens where it will merge into North Avenue. Continue into downtown Athens on North Avenue which will become Thomas Street and then East Campus Drive.

*PARKING

For visiting fans there are two pieces of advice offered by the University when it comes to parking. First, plan to arrive early, and second, take the shuttle. If you come early enough, you may be fortunate to find a parking space downtown in one of the many individual free public slots. Although the merchants might not like it, all the spots (and we do mean all) are taken long before kickoff. Some businesses and some fraternities open their lots for a fee to early arrivals.

The next best plan is to park in the **Coliseum parking lot** (no charge) near the intersection of Sanford Drive (Field Street) and Carlton Street and take the **free shuttle** to the stadium. Access to Carlton Street may be gained via Lumpkin Street or East Campus Drive. Shuttles run up to 30 minutes before gametime. Unfortunately, because of traffic they do not run after the game and you will be faced with a 15 to 20 minute walk back to your vehicle.

RV operators are encouraged to park in the coliseum lot. They may arrive Friday afternoon after 5:00 PM and stay until Sunday. Parking is free but limited. First come, first served.

Handicapped parking permits are available in advance from the Athletic Department. Permits should be presented at the security office. A map on the permit will direct fans to seven lots closest to the stadium.

*ALL INFORMATION IS SUBJECT TO CHANGE

*Mascot mini-mausoleums honor the memory of previous Uga's
in a corner of Sanford Stadium.*

~**Butts-Mehre Heritage Hall.** This gleaming glass and red marble structure completed in 1987 serves a number of purposes: it is an athletic complex, ticket office and museum. Intersection of Pinecrest Drive & Rutherford Street. Open 8 AM- 5 PM, Monday-Friday, 2 PM - 5 PM Saturday, closed on major holidays. Free. (404) 542-9094.

~**Georgia Museum of Art.** Located in the former University Library, this collection of over 5,000 objects of art includes 19th and 20th century works from the U.S. on permanent display and other changing exhibits. On the Old Quadrangle off Broad Street. Handicapped accessible. Monday-Saturday 9 AM - 5 PM, Sunday 1 PM - 5 PM. Free. Park downtown.

~**The Arch.** Symbol of the University of Georgia, this gateway to the old North Campus from downtown Athens, was erected in either 1857 or 1864, depending on the source of information. For years, freshman were forbidden to walk under the Arch.

~**Chapel and Bell Tower.** The Greek Revival Chapel, built in 1832, gracefully crowns the hill just south of the Arch on Old College. It confidently commands the beautifully landscaped Old Quadrangle. At its rear is the Bell Tower whose bell was first used to signal a Georgia gridiron victory in the 1890's, when the football field was located just to the southwest of the Chapel at Old Herty Field. Back then, freshmen were ordered to do the ringing, sometimes until midnight. Today, anyone can ring the bell to help celebrate a win.

~**Herty Field Historic Marker.** Located on North Campus just southwest of the chapel, this informative sign chronicles the early days of UGA football on the site where the game was first played on the campus.

~**Old College.** The first permanent building on the University of Georgia's campus, Old College was completed in 1806. It still stands although its appearance has changed markedly over the years along with the roles it has been called upon to play.

~**Sanford Stadium.** A sweeping vista of the 6th largest on-campus stadium in the country is afforded when one walks along the elevated section of Sanford Drive and looks through the west end zone. The graceful symmetry of Sanford Stadium makes it one of the more appealing football facilities to view.

~**Dean William Tate Student Center and University Bookstore.** If you turn away from the stadium and walk across the overpass, you will be looking down on the Student Center. If you look over to the right you will see the University Bookstore. Offering bathrooms, meals, and UGA souvenirs, these buildings are popular on game day.

~Tennis fans will want to check out the **NCAA Tennis Hall of Fame** and the indoor and outdoor courts of UGA's championship tennis teams. Located near the Coliseum off Rutherford Street.

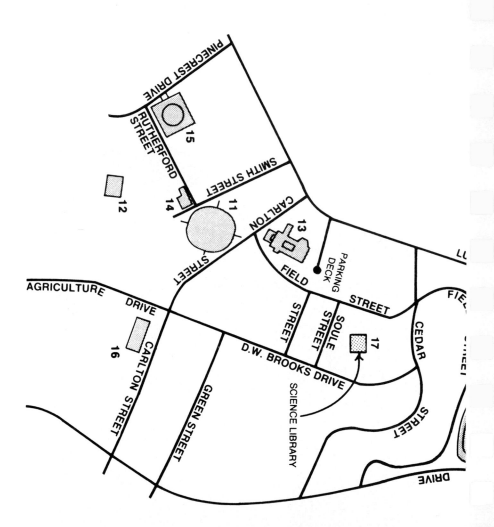

UNIVERSITY OF GEORGIA

1. Arch
2. Chapel
3. Ga. Museum of Art
4. Main Library
5. Academic Building
6. Bookstore
7. Gilbert Health Center
8. Fine Arts Auditorium
9. Tate Student Center
10. Sanford Stadium
11. Coliseum
12. Henry Feild Tennis Stadium
13. Ga. Center for Continuing Education
14. Alumni House
15. Butts-Mehre Heritage Hall
16. School of Veterinary Medicine
17. Science Library

P = Public Parking

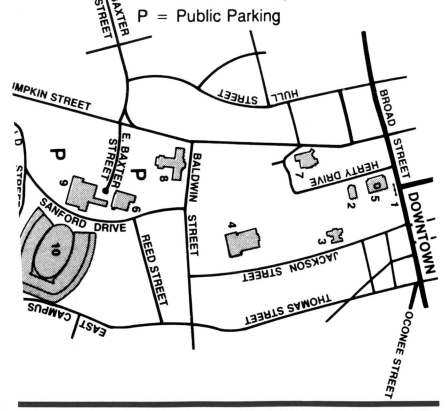

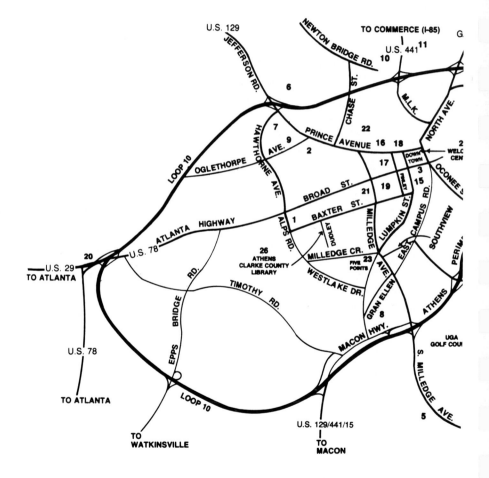

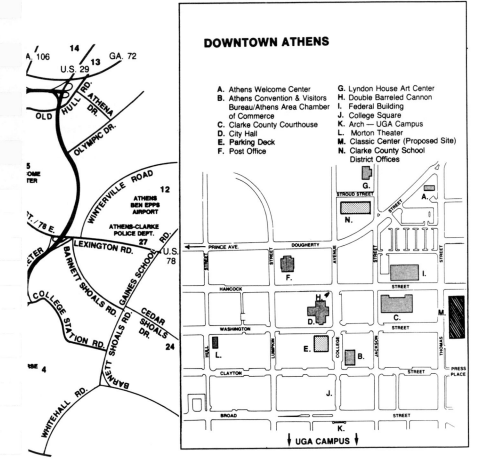

DOWNTOWN ATHENS

A. Athens Welcome Center
B. Athens Convention & Visitors Bureau/Athens Area Chamber of Commerce
C. Clarke County Courthouse
D. City Hall
E. Parking Deck
F. Post Office
G. Lyndon House Art Center
H. Double Barreled Cannon
I. Federal Building
J. College Square
K. Arch — UGA Campus
L. Morton Theater
M. Classic Center (Proposed Site)
N. Clarke County School District Offices

For complete information about Athens' attractions contact the Visitors Bureau and ask for the **"Athens Alive"** brochure:

Athens Convention and Visitors Bureau   (706) 546-1805 / Fax: (706) 549-5636
220 College Avenue / P. O. Box 948
Athens, Georgia 30603

A logical place to start exploring the Athens area is the **Athens Welcome Center** located in the **Church-Waddel-Brumby House**, an 1820 federal period structure. Restored in 1971, this symbol of Athens' Antebellum history is believed to be the oldest surviving residence in the city. Open Mon.-Sat. 9 AM - 5 PM; Sunday 2 PM - 5 PM. 280 East Dougherty Street. (404) 353-1820.

After taking your free tour, you can get ideas about other attractions in the area including the following:

~**College Square** is a revitalized section of Downtown Athens where College Avenue meets Broad Street at the Arch. Restored buildings, extensive landscaping, historic reproduction benches and street lights, specialty shops and dining areas which spill out onto the sidewalks, make this a perfect melting pot of school and town. A *must see* to "savor the flavor" of Athens and the University.

~On the courthouse lawn the world's only **double-barreled cannon** built in 1863 during the Civil War, sits waiting . . . pointed north, just in case the Yankees get any ideas! Corner of Hancock and College Streets.

~Located about two miles south of the Georgia Campus, the **State Botanical Garden of Georgia** is, nevertheless, located on University property. With over 300 acres of land, the garden encompasses three ecological areas: the river flood plain, the slopes, and the upland plateaus, each with hundreds of native plant species, many taxonomically labeled. Other features: five miles of nature trails and a visitor center with cafe. Visitor Center open Monday-Saturday, 9 AM - 4:30 PM and Sunday 11:30 AM - 4:30 PM. The Garden is open daily from 8:00 AM to dusk. Free. (404) 542-1244.

~Athens is fortunate to have northeast Georgia's largest mall, **Georgia Square** on its western edge. With over 100 stores including several large department stores, the facility can provide entertainment for and meet the needs of travelers of all ages and tastes. Open Monday-Saturday, 10 AM - 9 PM; Sunday 1-6 PM. 3700 Atlanta Highway. (404) 543-7910.

~**Five Points** is a community within a community southwest of downtown and the University. Complete with locally-owned antique shops, specialty shops, boutiques, bookstores, old-fashioned soda fountains and curbside cafés, the area is known for quaint shops, gingerbread houses and friendly shop owners. At the intersection of Milledge Avenue, Milledge Circle and Lumpkin Street.

~The **Taylor-Grady House** was built in the mid-1840's by General Robert Taylor and later was the home of Henry W. Grady who, as managing editor of the "Atlanta Constitution," became the spokesman of the New South. Noted for its 13 Doric columns, the home has been designated as a National Historic Landmark. Open 10:00 AM - 3:30 PM, Monday-Friday. 634 Prince Avenue. Admission $2.50.

Save your Confederate money boys . . . the South has a secret weapon and it's in Athens! The world's only double-barreled cannon. Fired only once, it cut down several saplings, tore up some land and killed a cow -- "the first herd shot 'round the world."

Where to Eat and Sleep in the Athens Area

For its size, Athens has a good variety of restaurants and motel accommodations. As with many college towns however, home football weekends stretch the capacity of these facilities to the bursting point, causing fan patronage to spill over into surrounding communities as far away as Atlanta. Since Athens is not on an interstate highway, this can become a problem if fans do not allow adequate travel time in getting to the game. Even though Athens is served by several U. S. highways and state roads, the system is strained by the huge crowds that attend Georgia games. Time spent planning for accommodations and routing to the game will pay dividends.

If you are unable to find accommodations in Athens for game weekend, don't give up. You will probably find vacancies in nearby towns such as Commerce, Conyers, Gainesville, and of course, Metro Atlanta, which is near enough to Athens (about 60 miles) to offer its many attractions, accommodations and restaurants conveniently. For more information about the excitement in Atlanta contact the **Atlanta Convention and Visitors Bureau, (404) 521-6600.**

K
E
N
T
U
C
K
Y

Memorial Hall, at the University of Kentucky, has
become a widely used symbol of the school.

Hold your horses! This can't be right...but it is! In horse-happy Kentucky, there's nothing out of place in this picture. They even sing "My Old Kentucky Home" just like at the Kentucky Derby. I'm not from Kentucky, but it still brought a tear to my eye.

The Lexington campus is the flagship of the 70,000 student University of Kentucky system. Boasting 24,200 students, UK at Lexington ranks as the sixth largest school in the SEC and follows very closely on the heels of the schools ranked 2nd through 5th.

The University of Kentucky was not the first college in Lexington. Transylvania University, founded in 1780, predates UK by 85 years! It was not until 1865 that State College, which officially became the University of Kentucky in 1916, was founded. UK was established as a Land Grant college and continues to offer programs unique in Kentucky on its 673 acre campus.

Today the UK system enrolls 38 percent of all students of higher education in the Commonwealth. The institution has grown to encompass 17 academic colleges and a graduate school. Included among these in Lexington are the Schools of Medicine, Dentistry, Nursing, Pharmacy and Allied Health Professions. Altogether, 108 undergraduate majors are offered. Emphasis of late has been place on research with UK being listed among the top 100 research schools in the nation and one of only 45 public universities to be classified as a Research University of the First Class.

Lexington is located in north-central Kentucky in the heart of the "Bluegrass" region which is noted for its lush, rolling green hills, tobacco fields, black curing barns and beautiful horse farms with their endless white, wooden fences. The city is just a stone's throw from Boonesborough State Park, site of Daniel Boone's pioneer settlement. Traveling around the Lexington area it is easy to see why Boone was so taken with the beauty and promise of the "Bluegrass."

UK is the northernmost school in the SEC, with Cincinnati, Ohio, only an hour and a half drive away up Interstate 75. To the west, along Interstate 64 and also about an hour and a half away, is Louisville. The great location is only one factor which makes Lexington a super place to be if you are a college student. With a quarter million residents, the city is large enough to offer a variety of cultural, social and shopping activities, while small enough to be "manageable" and easily learned.

One thing that helps in this department is the very practical road and street system which appears to be based on a spoked wheel design. A circular roadway loops the city's central core linking together all the traffic arteries radiating from downtown. This arrangement makes getting around Lexington fairly simple and convenient, especially since many shopping centers and major businesses are located at the intersection of New Circle Road and major streets around the perimeter of Lexington.

The Wildcat cheerleaders have won national recognition for their routines and spirit!

Blue and White have been the official colors of the University of Kentucky since 1892. The previous year, when football reappeared on the Lexington campus after a nine year absence, students had chosen "blue and yellow" to represent their team for the big game against in-state rival, Centre College. The question arose, "What color blue" would be most fitting?

At that point in the discussion, Richard C. Stoll, who would letter in football in 1893-94 and for whom the playing field was later named, removed his necktie and held it aloft. The color of Stoll's tie, a "blue" between royal and navy, was then and there chosen as Kentucky's "blue."

The following year students picked "white" to replace the yellow and for 101 years now, "Kentucky Blue and White" have symbolized UK. The PMS Color for Kentucky Blue is #293.

"Wildcats" is the first and only nickname of the University of Kentucky athletic teams. It seems that the label was initially used in 1909 when UK was still known as State College.

At a chapel service, Commandant Carbusier, who was then head of the Military Department at the school, reflected on a recent 6-2 football victory over Illinois, declaring the Kentucky team, "fought like wildcats."

The nickname immediately caught on with the student body and with the media. It has since come to refer to all University of Kentucky athletic teams.

Although he doesn't show it in this shot, the Kentucky Wildcat can be a real "pussycat," delighting the crowd with his playful antics.

University of Kentucky Mascot - "The Wildcat"

Several real-life wildcats (also known as bobcats or lynx) have served as Kentucky's symbol of fighting spirit over the years. The first one, known as "Tom," was given to the university in 1921, but unfortunately, survived only a short time in captivity.

He was followed by "TNT" and several others including "Whiskers," "Hot Tamale" and "Colonel." The latter was the last real life wildcat to serve as mascot as best we can tell. He was given to SUKY, a student pep organization by an alumnus in 1947, and served as mascot for about 8 years until his death in early 1955.

Some of the earlier mascots had been returned to the wilds of the Kentucky mountains after they failed to thrive away from their natural habitat. Perhaps the difficulty of keeping the real animals healthy in captivity has led to the present UK mascot. The Wildcat mascot now seen cavorting at all Kentucky football games first appeared during the 1976-77 year. He was first "brought to life" by Gary Tanner who set the tone for subsequent mascots with antics and highjinks which have come to characterize the Kentucky Wildcat.

In the 1980's, Terry Barney started a tradition which continues today. After every UK score the Wildcat is held aloft on a platform by the cheerleaders in front of the student section. As the crowd counts, the Wildcat performs a one-arm push-up for each point scored by Kentucky up to that moment. Then the mascot leads the crowd in spelling out "C-A-T-S." The record for one-arm push-ups in one game? 184, against Utah State in 1987 in a game won by Kentucky 41-0!

Wildcat workout. Held aloft by the cheerleaders,
the Wildcat performs a one-armed push-up for each point scored.
The students in the crowd keep him honest by counting along!

The

University of Kentucky

"Wildcat"

marching band

excites

the "home folks"

at

Commonwealth

Stadium.

The University of Kentucky "Wildcat" Marching Band was recently ranked by Southern Living Magazine as one of the "Top 10 Bands in the South!" It's no wonder since the more than 250 member group is considered one of the most progressive and innovative in the country. Their challenging and contemporary marching styles are enjoyable, as are their show designs and musical arrangements.

The "Wildcat" Band plays at all home football games and several away games each year featuring the 24-member flag corps, 10 majorettes, 2 feature twirlers and the 32-member UK Percussion Line which has been recognized in competitions throughout the United States for its ability.

Under the direction of Band Director Richard S. Clary and Assistant Director Bradley P. Ethington, the band thrills the fans and visitors alike with a wide variety of music from jazz to pop to the classics . . . and of course, "My Old Kentucky Home." So don't stay too long in the popcorn line and miss the great musical performances of the UK "Wildcat" Marching Band.

University of Kentucky "Alma Mater"

Hail Kentucky, Alma Mater!
　Loyal sons and daughters sing;
Sounder her praise with voice united;
　To the breeze her colors fling.
To the blue and white be true;
　Badge triumphant age on age;
Blue the sky that o'er us bends;
　White, Kentucky's stainless page.

University of Kentucky Fight Song "On, On, U of K"

On, on, U of K,
We are right for the fight today,
Hold that ball and hit that line;
Ev'ry Wildcat star will shine;
We'll fight, fight, fight,
for the blue and white
As we roll to that goal, Varsity,
And we'll kick, pass and run,
'till the battle is won,
And we'll bring home the victory.

"My Old Kentucky Home"

The sun shines bright on the old Kentucky home,
'Tis summer, the people are gay;
The corntop's ripe and the meadows in the bloom,
While the birds make music all day.

CHORUS:　　Weep no more, my lady,
　　　　　　Oh! Weep no more, today!
　　　　　　We will sing one song for my
　　　　　　　old Kentucky home,
　　　　　　For my old Kentucky home far away.

The young folks roll on the little cabin floor,
All merry, all happy, and bright;
By-n-by hard times come a-knocking at the door,
Then, my old Kentucky home, good-night!

TM ©University of Kentucky 1986

Staking their tailgating turf,
rival camps fly competing banners
in the great parking lot of Commonwealth Stadium

The University of Kentucky may be the northernmost SEC school, but it is not lacking in Southern hospitality nor a love of football! It is true, UK football has to compete with a strong basketball program and a devotion to horse racing, but the Wildcats are proud to have a "good team, not in a football state," as Tom Wilson, Jr., of Lexington said.

SEC fans who travel to Lexington for a game will not be disappointed because the Wildcats come ready to play and are "still looking for a winning season," as UK fan Martin Clough of Cynthiana says. So don't underestimate your enemy! Kentucky fans expect to win and it may not be long before they have their winning season!

And don't think it's easy to get tickets for the game, because UK fans really support their team. If you do get tickets you will certainly enjoy the whole football experience in Lexington, especially the ease with which you can travel to and from the stadium, park your vehicle, and tailgate.

As for the Southern hospitality, UK fans have some of the best tailgating foods in the conference and you'll wish they would invite you to join them for country ham and biscuits, a bourbon ball, or one of those little cheese biscuits and some corn pudding! Other favorite gameday foods are chili (unique and delicious!), kabobs, bar-b-que and of course, hot dogs! We even saw fans cooking eggs and grits in a cast iron skillet on a grill, while others tempted us with German sausages and homemade sauerkraut! It's no wonder that "tailgating" is a favorite tradition and what UK fans most enjoy besides the game itself! If you want to eat out, however, Kentucky fans recommended Logan's, The Ketch, Pure Gold, Fifth Quarter and Outback Steakhouse. Oh, by the way, you will find that it's a "tradition" for the children of Lexington to sell boxed candy before the games to help support their own little league teams!

Kentucky also has some unique and enjoyable traditions during the game. For example the game does not begin until the bugler from Keeneland Race Park gives the "call" most often associated with horseracing. Fans also look forward to singing "My Old Kentucky Home," and so will you! Other favorites are the "team walk" to the stadium which Coach Curry began, the cannon blast and the Wildcat "one-arm push-ups" for each home team score. Caywood Ledford, long-time announcer for UK, is dearly loved and respected by fans who consider him a "tradition."

As for rivalries, you may not be surprised to know that Kentucky and Tennessee share a heated one! Each year before their game, both schools have blood drives (UK won in 1992!), and Kentucky calls their's the "Blue Crush." Both teams battle on the football field for the right to keep the "Beer Barrel" trophy which is awarded at the end of the game. Southeastern Conference teams have great rivalries and celebrations to accompany them!

There is much to do in Kentucky and to enjoy at a UK football game. Make sure that you travel to Lexington and experience some great football tradition and maybe even attend a horserace later! You will find, as we did, many loyal fans such as Helen Parrent of Frankfort. She talked eagerly about her love and devotion to Kentucky **football**, and gave me a unique "Wildcat" pin which serves as a reminder that all SEC fans have two things in common: pride in their tradition and a desire to win!

With their background in hunting and horse racing, Kentucky folks do know how to party with class in the great outdoors! Here color-coordinated tents and pavilions are set up outside Commonwealth Stadium prior to game time.

*Coach Curry
gives
personal attention
to his quarterback
at halftime
on a rainy game in
Knoxville.*

Head Coach:

Birthday: October 21, 1942
Hometown: College Park GA

Bill Curry (Georgia Tech, 1965)
Georgia Tech Assistant, 1976;
Green Bay Assistant (NFL), 1977-79;
Georgia Tech Head Coach, 1980-86;
Alabama Head Coach, 1987-89;
Kentucky Head Coach, 1990-present

Assistant Coaches

Mike Archer (Miami, Fla., 1975)	Defensive Coordinator/Linebackers
Daryl Dickey (Tennessee, 1985)	Offensive Coordinator/Quarterbacks
Ray Dorr (West Virginia Wesleyan, 1965)	Runningbacks
Bill Glaser (Bellarmine, 1965)	Special Teams Coordinator/Defensive Tackles
Tommy Limbaugh (Alabama, 1967)	Assistant Head Coach/Recruiting/Tight Ends
Joker Phillips (Kentucky, 1986)	Wide Receivers
Don Riley (East Tennessee State, 1956)	Offensive Line
Rick Smith (Florida State, 1971)	Defensive Backs
David Turner (Davidson, 1985)	Defensive Ends

A view of Commonwealth Stadium on a grungy day. The skyline of downtown Lexington peers over the lower deck. Even with clouds, Lexington is one of our favorite places to be.

Commonwealth Stadium has been the home of the Wildcats since it was constructed at a cost of $12 million in 1973. The twenty year old facility is graceful in its symmetry, and in fact, has been called the "prettiest in America" from an aesthetic standpoint by Coach Bill Curry. Being the second newest stadium in the conference, it also ranks high in fan convenience with modern restrooms, adequate and well-placed concession areas and an excellent system of access ramps and walkways.

Located on the South side of the University's campus, the stadium is constructed on 86 acres of land which used to be part of UK's Experimental Station Farm grounds. Vehicular access to the site is among the best of any stadium in the conference. U.S. Highway 27, also known as, Nicholasville Road, and Alumni Drive border the property on two sides. Parking rates near the top also, being both plentiful, reasonable and relatively uncomplicated.

From the first days of Kentucky football until Commonwealth Stadium opened, games were played at a site which became known in time as Stoll Field/McLean Stadium. This facility was located across from Memorial Coliseum on the East side of the campus. Although the first UK football game was played there in 1881, the name "Stoll Field" was not used officially until 1916 when it was dedicated in honor of alumnus and benefactor, Judge Richard C. Stoll. In 1924 concrete stands were constructed and dedicated as

McLean Stadium in memory of Price Innes McLean, a member of the 1923 squad who died as a result of injuries suffered in the Cincinnati game. Ultimately, McLean Stadium's capacity grew to 37,000. It was last used in 1972.

One tradition which began in the old stadium and has continued into the new facility is playing October home games at night. Kentucky was one of the first colleges to play a game under the lights, defeating Maryville 40-0 on October 5, 1929. In 1949 October games were moved to the evening to accommodate horse racing fans who wanted to attend afternoon races at nearby Keeneland, whose racing season extended into the tenth month. Kentucky is unique in being the only school in the Southeastern Conference where football must show deference to two other sports: basketball and horse racing.

Commonwealth Stadium ranks fifth in size among SEC stadiums with its present capacity of 57,800. Plans exist for enclosing the south end zone which would increase seating to 72,000. Luxury suites and boxes may also be added in the future. In 1990 a new scoreboard/message center was installed helping to make Commonwealth Stadium one of the nicest places to enjoy a football game in the country.

Stadium Stats

Capacity:	57,800
First game:	September 15, 1973; Kentucky 31, Virginia Tech 26
Largest crowd:	58,345; October 12, 1985,
	Kentucky 33, Mississippi State 19
Stadium record:	(125 games) 1973-1992: W-71 L-50 T-4 (Pct. .584)
Playing surface:	Natural Grass / Bermuda, which turns brown in November

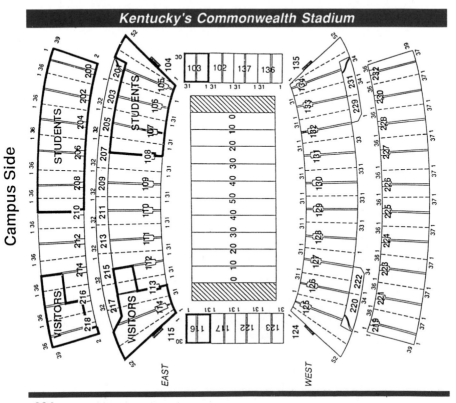

Kentucky's Commonwealth Stadium

Campus Side

Press Box Side

EAST

WEST

Ralph Hacker	-	Play-By-Play/Hosts the Bill Curry pre-game and post-game radio shows
Charlie McAlexander	-	Color Commentary/Hosts "Wildcat Warm-Up" and "Wildcat Wrap-Up" shows
Dave Baker	-	Color Analyst
Rob Bromley	-	Sideline Reporter
Dick Gabriel	-	Sideline Reporter
Tom Leach	-	Hosts halftime and postgame "Scoreboard Shows"

Kentucky Football Radio Network

AM Stations

CITY	STATE	STATION	FREQUENCY
Ashland	KY	WCMI	1340
Bardstown	KY	WBRT	1320
Benton	KY	WCBL	1290
Bowling Green	KY	WKCT	930
Brandenburg	KY	WMMG	1140
Cadiz	KY	WKDZ	1110
Cincinnati	OH	WCKY	1530
Corbin	KY	WCTT	680
Cumberland	KY	WCPM	1280
Danville	KY	WHIR	1230
Eminence	KY	WKXF	1600
Frankfort	KY	WFKY	1490
Franklin	KY	WFKN	1220
Harlan	KY	WHLN	1410
Harrodsburg	KY	WHBN	1420
Hartford	KY	WLLS	1600
Hawesville	KY	WKCM	1160
Henderson	KY	WSON	860
Hindman	KY	WKCB	1340
Hopkinsville	KY	WHOP	1230
Lebanon	KY	WLBN	1590
Lexington	KY	WVLK	590
London	KY	WFTG	1400
Louisa	KY	WVKY	1270
Louisville	KY	WHAS	840
Louisville	KY	WWKY	790
Manchester	KY	WWXL	1450
Mayfield	KY	WNGO	1320
Maysville	KY	WFTM	1240
Middlesboro	KY	WMIK	560
Morganfield	KY	WMSK	1550
Mt. Sterling	KY	WMST	1150
Murray	KY	WSJP	1130
Owensboro	KY	WOMI	1490
Paducah	KY	WPAD	1560
Paintsville	KY	WSIP	1490
Pikeville	KY	WPKE	1240
Prestonsburg	KY	WDOC	1310

FM Stations

CITY	STATE	STATION	FREQUENCY
Ashland	KY	WCMI	92.7
Bardstown	KY	WOKH	96.7
Benton	KY	WCBL	102.3
Bowling Green	KY	WDNS	98.3
Brandenburg	KY	WMMG	93.5
Cadiz	KY	WKDZ	106.3
Campbellsville	KY	WCKQ	104.1
Central City	KY	WKYA	101.9
Corbin	KY	WCTT	107.3
Danville	KY	WMGE	107.1
Dry Ridge	KY	WNKR	106.5
Elizabethtown	KY	WASE	105.5
Glasgow	KY	WGGC	95.1
Grayson	KY	WUGO	102.3
Greenup	KY	WLGC	105.5
Hardinsburg	KY	WXBC	104.3
Harrodsburg	KY	WHBN	99.3
Harrogate	TN	WXJB	96.5
Hartford	KY	WLLS	106.3
Hallsville	KY	WKCM	102.9
Hazard	KY	WSGS	101.1
Hindman	KY	WKCB	107.1
Hopkinsville	KY	WHOP	98.7
Jamestown	KY	WJRS	104.9
Lebanon	KY	WLSK	100.9
Leitchfield	KY	WKHG	104.9
Lexington	KY	WVLK	92.9
London	KY	WWEL	103.9
Louisa	KY	WSAC	92.3
Madisonville	KY	WKTG	93.9
Manchester	KY	WWXL	103.1
Mayfield	KY	WXID	94.7
Maysville	KY	WFTM	95.9
McKee	KY	WWAG	107.9
Middlesboro	KY	WMIK	92.7
Monticello	KY	WKYM	101.7
Morganfield	KY	WMSK	95.3
Mt. Sterling	KY	WMST	105.5

Kentucky Football Radio Network (continued)

AM Stations				FM Stations			
CITY	STATE	STATION	FREQUENCY	CITY	STATE	STATION	FREQUENCY
Princeton	KY	WPKY	1580	Owingsville	KY	WKCA	107.1
Shelbyville	KY	WCND	940	Paintsville	KY	WSIP	98.9
Somerset	KY	WSFC	1240	Pikeville	KY	WDHR	92.1
Whitesburg	KY	WTCW	920	Prestonsburg	KY	WQHY	95.5
Williamsburg	KY	WEZJ	1440	Princeton	KY	WPKY	104.9
				Providence	KY	WHRZ	97.7
				Richmond	KY	WMCQ	101.7
				Shelbyville	KY	WCKP	101.3
				Somerset	KY	WSEK	97.1
				Whitley City	KY	WHAY	105.9
				Whitesburg	KY	WXKQ	103.9
				Williamsburg	KY	WEZJ	104.3

University of Kentucky - Gameday Information

*Ticket Information

Ticket Office: (606) 257-1818

SEATING: At Commonwealth Stadium the Kentucky Band sits in section 108. The visiting band sits in section 114 and visiting fans sit in section 113, 114, 115, 216 and 218.

*Stadium Policies

Umbrellas, horns and artificial noisemakers are prohibited. Signs may be hung at the stadium, but may not restrict the view of others.

*Parking Information

About 6,500 parking spaces around Commonwealth Stadium are reserved, but there is still ample, good parking. The general public lots open three hours before the game and it costs only $3.00 to park in these lots. Access to stadium parking lots is primarily from Tate's Creek Road or Nicholasville Road off New Circle 4. Signs will be in place directing traffic to parking areas. All lots need to be closed after the game. In the event you have automobile problems, raise the hood of your vehicle and free assistance will be provided.

RV's need to approach their lot via Nicholasville Road ONLY. Signs are put up the night before. On Saturday morning someone will come around to collect $10.00 for RV parking.

Parking at Commonwealth Stadium was very convenient. It was easy to get to the stadium and out of the area after the game.

*ALL INFORMATION IS SUBJECT TO CHANGE

The Lexington campus of the University of Kentucky system is as handsome as its host city. Heart of the "Bluegrass" area of Kentucky, Lexington is a great college town in many respects: beauty, size, location and outlook.

~**The University of Kentucky Art Museum** features a permanent collection of over 3,500 works from the old masters to contemporary paintings and photographs. Open year round, Tuesday-Sunday, Noon to 5 PM. Free admission. Rose Street and Euclid Avenue. (601) 257-5716.

~**The University of Kentucky Museum of Anthropology** houses exhibits on the cultural history of Kentucky, kinship, art and religion, archaeology and physical anthropology. Located at 201 Lafferty Hall in the central UK campus. Open year round, Monday-Friday, 8 AM - 4 PM. Free admission. (601) 257-7112.

~**The University of Kentucky Visitors Center** is located on the first floor of the Student Center addition South Limestone Street. Tours 10 AM and 2 PM on weekdays; 11 AM on Saturdays. (606) 257-9000.

~**Commonwealth Stadium**, located on Alumni Drive off Nicholasville Road. Home of the Wildcats!

University of Kentucky
campus map

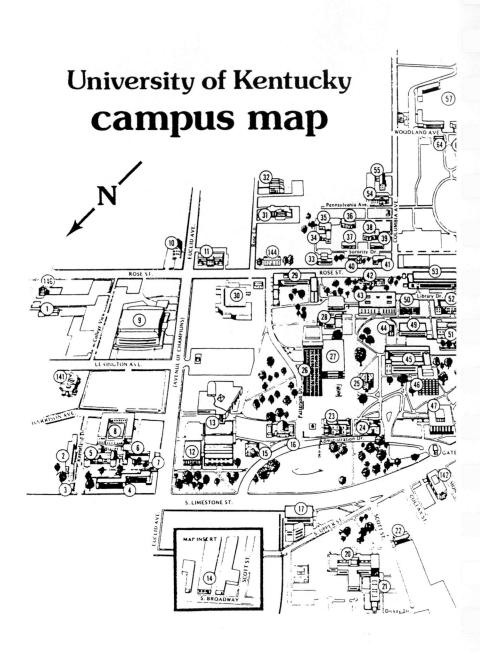

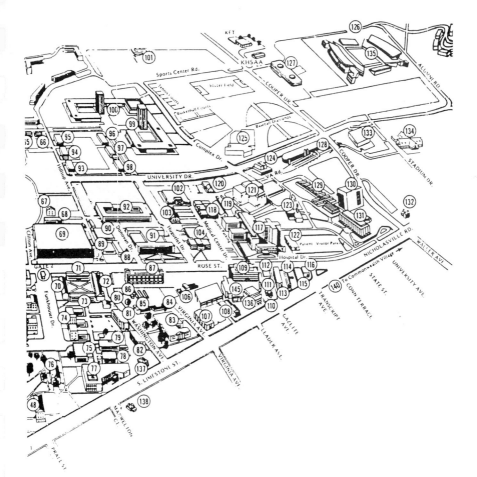

CAMPUS MAP LEGEND

LEXINGTON

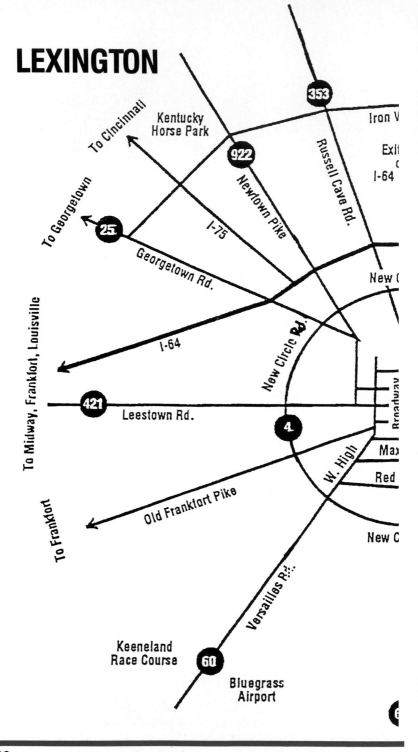

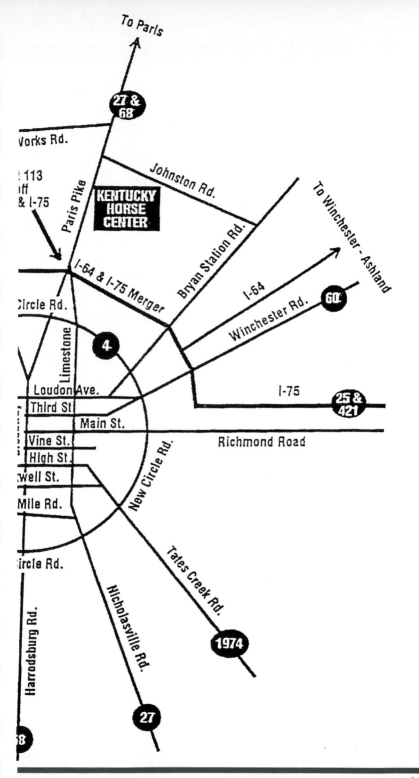

Lexington isn't called "The Horse Capital of the World" for nothing. There are a number of educational and/or exciting places around the city relating to horses.

~**Keeneland Race Course,** the "class" of the thoroughbred tracks. Located on U.S. 60 West, 4201 Versailles Road. Early morning workouts may be watched free. Photographs permitted. (606) 254-3412 or 1-800-456-3412.

~**The Kentucky Horse Center**, located at 3380 Paris Pike, offers tours of a thoroughbred training facility. Catered meals (breakfast, lunch & dinner) are available at a reasonable cost, and feature Kentucky specialties such as country ham and bread pudding with bourbon sauce. (606) 293-1853.

~**The Kentucky Horse Park** celebrates the horse and his special relationship to humans through museum, films, etc. Horseback riding and surrey rides. Gift shop, restaurant and campground on premises. 4089 Iron Works Pike, exit 120 off I-75. (606) 233-4303.

~**The Red Mile Harness Track**, located at South Broadway and Red Mile Road, offers Fall Grand Circuit Racing. The public is welcome year-round to morning workouts. (606) 255-0752 or 1-800-354-9092.

~**Waveland State Historic Site** features an 1847 Greek Revival Antebellum home beautifully restored and furnished. Located at 255 Higbee Mill Road, (606) 272-3611.

~**Rupp Arena**, located downtown at 430 West Vine Street. Serves as the basketball home of the Kentucky Wildcats . Seating 23,000. (606) 233-4567.

~**The Star of Lexington** is a 540 passenger riverboat that takes visitors on a most interesting two hour tour through the awesome palisades of the Kentucky River. The cruises feature food and live music. (606) 263-STAR.

~**Fort Boonesborough State Park** is a reconstructed fort up the hill from the site where Daniel Boone built his pioneer settlement. Demonstrations of weaving, spinning, quilting, woodworking, soap, broom candle and doll making, and pottery. A camping area and sand beach are located nearby at the fort's original site. (606) 527-3131.

~**The Shaker Village of Pleasant Hill** interprets the impact of the Shakers on American culture. Encompassing 33 original buildings dating from the 19th century, the village features live demonstrations of crafts and self-guided tours which teach about Shaker history, architecture, and craftsmanship. In Harrodsburg, Kentucky, 25 miles from Lexington. (606) 734-5411.

~**Toyota Plant Tours** are available at the Toyota facility which produces Camrys in Georgetown, Kentucky. Free tours call for info (502) 868-3027.

For complete information contact:

Greater Lexington Convention & Visitors Bureau
Suite 363, 430 West Vine Street
Lexington, KY   40507
(606) 233-1221 or 1-800-84-LEXKY

NOTES

L

S

U

*Memorial Tower was dedicated in 1926
and rededicated 50 years laterduring America's Bicentennial.
It is a fitting symbol for a great University.*

*Sorority houses dot the shoreline of beautiful University Lake
along University Lakeshore Drive . . . a magnificent setting for a college community.*

The Louisiana State University and Agricultural and Mechanical College is the official name of the oldest and largest institution in the LSU system which is composed of eight schools with ten campuses in five cities. Located on the south side of Baton Rouge, capital of Louisiana and the state's second largest city (metropolitan-area population of more than 500,000), LSU is home to 26,000 students. Although the campus controls more than 2,000 acres of land, most of the important facilities are located on a 650 acre tract bordered on the west by the Mississippi River and on the north, east and south by Baton Rouge's business and residential areas.

LSU began as the Louisiana State Seminary of Learning and Military Academy. Only nineteen students were in attendance when the school opened on January 2, 1860 near Pineville, Louisiana. When the Civil War broke out a year later, the school's first superintendent, William Tecumseh Sherman, resigned to take a command in the Union Army. Most of the students enlisted in the Confederate forces!

In 1869, following a fire which destroyed the Seminary building, the school was moved to Baton Rouge where it occupied several "temporary" campuses. In 1870, the Seminary was renamed Louisiana State University and in 1877 it merged with the Agricultural and Mechanical College then located in New Orleans.

Plans for a new campus were begun in 1914 and construction of the present campus started in 1922 with the first buildings occupied in 1925. Construction of the original phase was completed in 1932.

LSU is probably one of few colleges in the country whose football teams have worn the school colors since the beginning of gridiron competition. It seems that the custom of wearing the colors of Mardi Gras on LSU athletic uniforms was begun by the baseball team in the Spring of 1893. Those who are familiar with the Gulf Coast festival know that, by tradition, purple, gold and green are the hues associated with Mardi Gras.

On November of that same year, for LSU's first football game ever, the team's coach, Dr. Charles Coates, took some players into town to purchase ribbons to be worn on the squad's gray jerseys. Apparently, only purple and gold ribbon was available and those were the colors worn in that New Orleans game against Tulane. Later, at the suggestion of Dr. Coates, Royal Purple (PMS # 268) and Old Gold (PMS #129) were adopted as the official school colors.

Football at LSU . . . they love it with a purple passion!

Mike the Tiger, LSU's lovable mascot, gives a pre-game wave to the student section.

The nickname of LSU athletic teams, "Fighting Tigers", has a long and historic attachment to LSU and the people of Louisiana. In 1896, after three years without a nickname, the LSU football squad decided to adopt the "tiger" as their animal identity.

It would not have been unusual if the "Tigers" nickname had come purely from the jungle cat variety of tiger. Many teams of the day were seeking out names of ferocious beasts with which to identify, hoping to strike fear in their opponents. Actually, however, LSU's nickname came from a group of Civil War soldiers from New Orleans and Donaldsonville who had fought gallantly and earned the name, "The Fighting Band of Louisiana Tigers." So it was only natural that the "Tigers" nickname was chosen.

It was not until 59 years later, in 1955, that the adjective, "Fighting," was added to "Tigers" to complete the present nickname, "Fighting Tigers." In that year, the football team established a reputation of playing especially hard in the fourth quarter. This fighting spirit inspired the expanded nickname.

*MIKE V shows no respect as the LSU cheerleaders
escort him past Alabama fans in the south end zone.*

The mascot of LSU is a Bengal Tiger named "Mike" who first appeared in Baton Rouge in 1935. He replaced a lifelike papier-mâché tiger that had served as an ersatz mascot for more than ten years. Prior to that time, only the nickname, "Tigers," was available to conjure images of cat-quick and ferocious footballers in the minds of friend and foe alike. Mike, or Mike I, as this original live tiger came to be known later, was bought by the LSU student body from the Little Rock Zoo for $750.00. He was soon placed in a specially built home near Tiger Stadium. Mike I's former name had been "Sheik," but by request of the students, his name was changed to "Mike" after Mike Chambers, the popular Athletic Trainer at LSU. Mike I reigned as mascot for 20 seasons until his death in 1957.

Mike II was a native Louisianian, having been born in the Audubon Park Zoo in New Orleans. Unfortunately, his tenure was very brief. The Spring after the 1957 season, he died of pneumonia.

Mike III arrived just before the 1958 season from the Seattle Zoo. He was purchased with $1,500 in student donations. Mike III served for eighteen years. He died after the 1975 season during which the "Tigers" went 5-6, the only loosing season Mike III ever experienced!

In late August of 1976, Mike IV reported for duty, just in time for the new football season. He was donated to the University by August Busch, III and the Dark Continent Amusement Park in Tampa, Florida. After fourteen years as mascot, Mike IV was retired to the Baton Rouge Zoo.

The present mascot, Mike V, was donated by Dr. Thomas and Caroline Atchison of the Animal House Zoological Park in Moulton, Alabama. He assumed his duties on April 30, 1990, moving into his newly refurbished home outside the northwest corner of Tiger Stadium while just six months old. Today, at age four, he tips the scales at almost 500 pounds!

Many exciting traditions were associated with LSU football and the Tiger mascot. Prior to each game, for example, Mike's cage-on-wheels is placed strategically by the visiting team's locker room. No doubt the psychological effect on opponents having to walk so near such an intimidating beast has been an important factor in LSU's home field advantage over the years!

Later, as gametime approaches, Mike's cage is pulled around the perimeter of the football field with the cheerleader squad on top. This stirring sight never fails to excite the crowd. A long-held belief around Tiger Stadium is that for every pregame growl offered up by Mike, a touchdown will be scored later in the game. Years ago Mike was coerced into growling by having the cheerleaders rock his cage. When this treatment was deemed cruel, recorded growls, played to the crowd over the P.A. system were substituted for a short period.

Today, neither method of producing growls is used. Mike V does roar, but only when HE chooses. One occurrence that never fails to elicit a ferocious roar from the "real" Mike, is when he spots his imitator, a human dressed up in a tiger suit. Whether he senses a challenge to his "turf" by this interloper, or if he is merely offended at being represented by the comedic, two-legged tiger, we can only speculate. However, as one who has stood five feet from Mike's cage when he growled, I can tell you, whatever the meaning of his message, it must be taken seriously!

When LSU's Golden Girls perform, concession stand workers can take a break.
Nobody leaves their seats. The band's not bad either!

LSU's "Golden Band from Tigerland" turns 100 this year having been founded in 1893 by two of the school's cadets, Wylie M. Barrow and Ruffin G. Pleasant. That original band had only nine members with Pleasant serving as director. This same enterprising Ruffin G. Pleasant went on to become a member of the LSU Athletic Hall of Fame and eventually, Governor of Louisiana!

In the 1930's another Governor of the state, Huey Long, showed a strong interest in the LSU Band, so much so that he helped then band director, Castro Carazo, write two songs for the band and school: "Touchdown for LSU" and "Darling of LSU."

Today the LSU band ranks near the top of all college bands nationwide from the standpoint of both musical excellence and ability to excite the crowd. In addition to the marching musicians, the 300 member unit includes the LSU Golden Girls and the Tiger Band Color Guard. About 70 percent of the band's members are non-music majors who represent almost every field of study offered by the University.

Over its long history the band has had 17 different directors. Since 1980 the Director of Bands at LSU has been Frank Wickes. He is assisted by Assistant Director of Bands, Linda Moorhouse.

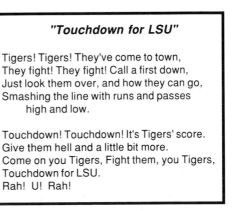

"Touchdown for LSU"

Tigers! Tigers! They've come to town,
They fight! They fight! Call a first down,
Just look them over, and how they can go,
Smashing the line with runs and passes
    high and low.

Touchdown! Touchdown! It's Tigers' score.
Give them hell and a little bit more.
Come on you Tigers, Fight them, you Tigers,
Touchdown for LSU.
Rah! U! Rah!

LOUISIANA STATE UNIVERSITY
"Alma Mater"

Where stately oaks and broad magnolias
    shade inspiring halls,
There stands our dear Alma Mater
    who to us recalls
Fond memories that waken in our hearts
    a tender glow,
And make us happy for the love
    that we have learned to know.
All hail to thee our Alma Mater,
    molder of mankind,
May greater glory, love unending
    be forever thine.
Our worth in life will be thy worth
    we pray to keep it true,
And thy spirit dwell in us forever...L-S-U.

LSU'S FIGHT SONG
"Fight for LSU"

Like Knights of old, Let's fight to hold
The glory of the Purple Gold.

Let's carry through, Let's die or do
To win the game for dear old LSU.

Keep trying for that high score;
Come on and fight,
We want some more, some more.

Come you Tigers, Fight Fight! Fight!
For dear old L - S - U.
RAH!

"Hey, Fightin' Tigers"
*(Adapted from the original composition
Hey, look Me Over" from the
Broadway production "Wildcat".)*

Hey, Fightin' Tigers, Fight all the way
Play Fightin' Tigers, win the game today.

You've got the know how, you're doing fine,
Hang on to the ball as you hit the wall
And smash right through the line

You've got to go for a touchdown
Run up the score.
Make Mike the Tiger stand right up and roar.
ROAR!

Give it all of your might as you fight tonight
and keep the goal in view.
Victory for L - S - U!

TIGER RAG
"Hold That Tiger"

Long ago, way down in the jungle
Someone got an inspiration for a tune,
And that jingle brought from the jungle
Became famous mighty soon.

Thrills and chills it sends thru you!
Hot! so hot, it burns you too!

Tho' it's just the growl of the tiger
It was written in a syncopated way,
More and more they howl for the "Tiger"
Ev'ry where you go today
They're shoutin'

Where's that Tiger! Where's that Tiger!
Where's that Tiger! Where's that Tiger!
Hold that Tiger! Hold that Tiger!
Hold that Tiger!

Coach Hallman prepares to enter Tiger Stadium after leading his team on a "Tiger Walk," one of LSU fan's favorite traditions.

Clearly the most unique gameday experience (in our estimation) is found in Baton Rouge. The atmosphere of Mardi Gras pervades the whole event from LSU's school colors to the music outside the stadium to the Cajun cuisine. There is so much to occupy you that you may find yourself forgetting the pressures---not only of the combat to take place on the field, but of life itself. Everywhere on campus you can experience the attitude of Louisianians which permeates their life-style: "Joie de vivre"* (Zhwah duh viv-re), or "The joy of living."

Right outside "Death Valley" there is jambalaya, crawfish pie and other delicacies to eat. A live band entertains the crowd, always spicing up their set with some Cajun music, and eventually getting some of the crowd to dance. Even the visiting fans get caught up in the fun. Waiting for the appearance of the LSU Band and The Golden Girls who herald the walk of the coaches and team down the hill to the stadium is reminiscent of New Orleans revelers anticipating the arrival of Rex! The "Tiger Walk," as this event is called, is an important tradition and rivals the team walk "through the Grove" at Ole Miss for fan support. It really is quite regal with the Golden Girls in their capes and the Golden Band from Tiger Land playing as though for a coronation. (We witnessed the band's entrance when they visited Florida and found they enter stadiums on the road in the same regal manner!) Nearly 25% of the LSU fans we interviewed said this was one of their favorite traditions associated with Tiger football, and expressed their pride in the Golden Girls and Golden Band as well. As Russell G. Mixon of Baton Rouge says, "It's a Cajun good time!"

Other favorite traditions at LSU are Mike the Tiger and his "stroll" around the stadium before the game (in his cage of course!), the purple and gold colors, and most notably, night games in Death Valley! Dan and Luanne Farmer of Gulf Shores, Alabama, said there is nothing like the "excitement and noise of LSU fan(atic)s" in Tiger Stadium. Betsy Terrill of Clewiston, Florida, agrees saying "there's just nothing like it!" To prove that she drives over 2,000 miles, round trip, several times a season to support her Tigers.

Dr. John Parsons of Siesta Key, Florida, reminds us of another important and unique gameday tradition at LSU: Po-Boy Sandwiches! LSU fans love to tailgate and enjoy some of the usual fare, hot dogs, fried chicken and bar-be-que; but by far, Cajun cuisine is the favorite! Tiger fans also love to eat out and suggest Ralph & Kacoo's, Mulatte's, Mike Anderson's, Louie's and Linny's for visiting fans to try. On campus you can enjoy the Plantation Room, The Chimes or buy from a vendor.

Maybe it's their watery environment which helps the people of Louisiana enjoy life so fully, but whatever the influence, they are able to *laissez les bon tons rouler** ("lay-zay lay bawn tawn roulay" ---let the good times roll) through their love of good food, good music and the outdoors. It reminds me of the words in an old Hank Williams' song: "Son of a gun we'll have big fun on the bayou!"

When you do visit the Bayou Bengals you'll understand why Jodie R. Smith, III (whose grandmother, Maggie Smith, was voted the "most loyal LSU fan during WWII") believes "there's no place you would rather be on a Saturday night than Tiger Stadium." In spite of the heat, the "atmosphere of Saturday night in Death Valley can't be beat" says Ed Valek, II, of Sarasota, Florida, and Byron Bajoie of Shreveport thinks everything can be enjoyed at LSU football games and if the Tigers win that's a *Lagniappe* **("la n yap" --- something extra)! The authors would have to agree with Mary Medlen and Deedy Curline of Plaquemine, Louisiana, who said: "It's a Winner!"

*Louisiana Office of Tourism
**From THE ENCYCLOPEDIA OF CAJUN & CREOLE CUISINE" by John D. Folse

The three men in this picture were probably:
A. Released for a day's outing, due back at 5.
B. Not drinking what they were selling at the concession stand.
C. Paid a lot of money for posing like that.
D. Normal LSU fans.

If you folks watching at home think THIS is impressive,
wait 'til the sun sets and the night rules Death Valley!

Head Coach

Curley Hallman, Texas A&M (1970)
  Texas A&M Graduate Assistant, 1969;
  Texas A&M Volunteer, 1970;
  Alabama Assistant, 1973-76;
  Memphis State Assistant, 1977-78;
  Clemson Assistant, 1979-81;
  Texas A&M Assistant, 1982-87;
  Southern Mississippi Head Coach, 1989-90;
  LSU Head Coach, 1991-present.

Birthday:	**September 3, 1947**
Hometown:	**Northport AL**

Assistant Coaches

Phil Bennett (Texas A&M, 1978) — Assistant Head Coach/Outside Linebackers

Jerry Baldwin (Miss. Valley State, 1975) — Assistant Head Coach/Inside Linebackers

Lynn Amedee (LSU, 1962) — Offensive Coordinator/Quarterbacks
Mike Bugar (Florida State, 1969) — Defensive Coordinator/Defensive Line
Steve Buckley (Southern Mississippi, 1985) — Running Backs/Special Teams
Larry Edmonson (Texas A&M, 1983) — Wide Receivers
Larry Zierlein (Ft. Hays State University, 1971) — Offensive Line
Darrell Dickey (Kansas State, 1984) — Tight Ends
Steve Davis (Livingston, 1975 — Defensive Backs/Special Teams

Fans begin to gather long before gametime in the area between Tiger Stadium and the Pete Maravich Assembly Center. (Note the dorm rooms built under the old stands.)

To longtime SEC fans the name, Tiger Stadium, is almost magical in its ability to evoke memories of pressure-packed night games boomed across the Southland on WWL radio from the darkened frenzy of "Death Valley." So vital to the success of the "Bayou Bengals" has been the stadium with its rabid fans, and so feared by opponents the volatile atmosphere, that in a 1987 coaches' poll it was named the most dreaded road-playing site in America! Truly, Tiger Stadium defines "Home Field Advantage."

The site of Tiger football since 1924, the stadium in its original design seated about 12,000 in the east and west stands. While other SEC schools can rightfully claim that they have played football longer at their present stadiums than LSU, none can claim that its stadium is actually older than the campus on which it is located. None except LSU, that is! For Tiger Stadium was packing them in two years before the relocated LSU campus was dedicated and six years before the facilities were fully occupied.

In 1928, four years before Tiger Stadium opened, the sideline stands were lengthened to the goal lines and additional rows were built to provide 10,000 more seats almost doubling the capacity to 22,000. This expansion was made possible when T. P. "Skipper" Heard, then Graduate Manager of Athletics and later Athletic Director, convinced the University's President that money could be saved if needed campus dormitories were built into the enlarged stadium.

Ultimately, some 1,500 dorm rooms were completed within Tiger Stadium, making it unique in that regard.

On October 3, 1931, when outdoor sports lighting was in its infancy, (major league baseball was not played at night until 1935) the same T. P. Heard began what has become one of LSU's most enduring traditions: night football. On that evening, LSU defeated Spring Hill 35-0 and to this day statistics prove that LSU becomes a different team "under the lights" (see below). Heard promoted night games for three reasons: 1. to avoid the heat and humidity, 2. to avoid scheduling conflicts with Tulane and Loyola, and 3. to allow fans who tended the plantations to see LSU play.

In 1936, just eight years after the first expansion, the north end zone was enclosed joining the east and west stands and creating a horseshoe-shaped facility. At this time, capacity stood at 46,000. Seventeen years passed before further construction enclosed the South end of the horseshoe, completing the bowl configuration and raising the number of seats to 67,720 in 1953. At this point, even if Tiger Stadium had never been expanded further, it would still be larger than five other stadiums in the SEC. To have had a complete bowl this size forty years ago is a testament to the high regard in which Tiger fans hold the game. "Death Valley" had arrived!

1978 saw the addition of the upper deck atop the west stands. The 8,000 regular seats, along with approximately 2,000 seats at the club level on either side of the press box, increased the capacity to about 78,000.

Although Tiger Stadium is a large structure, space is somewhat constricted on the playing surface. In fact, the arena area is the most confined of all the stadiums in the SEC. In 1986 the playing field was moved 11 feet to the south, centering it in the arena and providing a better distribution of space on side lines and end line areas.

Constant upgrading of the facility, such as waterproofing (1985 & 1987), addition of 25,000 chairback seats (1985), redecoration of the press box (1987) and improvements to restrooms over several seasons, have enabled Tiger Stadium to comfortably meet the needs of greater and greater throngs of fans.

With the addition of a few more rows of seats in the lower west stand and a complete renumbering of all seats to provide uniform size in 1987, and with extra bleacher seating added in 1988, the stadium attained it present size of 80,140. Plans exist to increase the east side stands by 1,500 seats in the near future.

Stadium Stats

Capacity:	80,140
Largest crowd:	82,390; September 24, 1983; LSU 40, Washington 14
Stadium Record:	1924-1992; W-286 L-113 T-18 (Pct. .707)
Playing Surface:	Natural Grass

Home attendance has averaged almost 68,000 per game since 1957. LSU usually ranks among the top 15 colleges nationally in average home game attendance and was ranked #2 for the 1963 season.

LSU'S Tiger Stadium

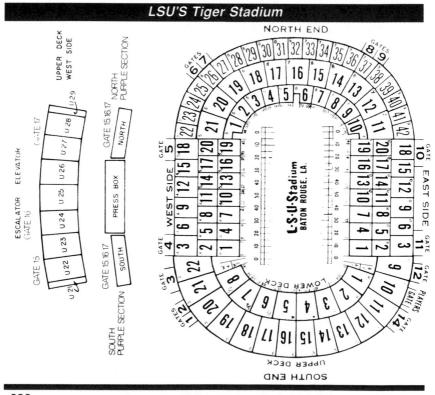

Louisiana State University - Sports Network

Jim Hawthorne	-	Play-By-Play/"Voice of the Tigers"
Doug Moreau	-	Analyst
Kevin Ford	-	Pre-game, halftime and post-game shows

LSU Sports Network (Radio Affiliates)
AM Stations   FM Stations

CITY	STATE	STATION	FREQUENCY	CITY	STATE	STATION	FREQUENCY
Alexandria	LA	KSYL	970	Bogalusa	LA	WBOX	92.9
Amite	LA	WABL	1570	Bunkie	LA	KEZP	104.3
Baton Rouge	LA	WJBO	1150	Columbia	LA	KCTO	103.1
Bogalusa	LA	WBOX	920	Deridder	LA	KEAZ	101.7
Covington	LA	WARB	730	Donaldsonville	LA	KKAY	104.9
Deridder	LA	KDLA	1010	Farmerville	LA	KWJM	92.7
Eunice	LA	KEUN	1490	Hammond	LA	WHMD	107.1
Flowood	MS	WPBQ	1240	Jena	LA	KJNA	99.3
Hammond	LA	WFPR	1400	Jonesboro	LA	KTOC	104.9
Jena	LA	KJNA	1480	Lake Providence	LA	KLPL	92.7
Jonesboro	LA	KTOC	920	Leesville	LA	KVVP	105.5
Lake Charles	LA	KLCL	1470	Many	LA	KWLV	107.1
Lake Providence	LA	KLPL	1050	Marksville	LA	KAPB	97.7
McComb	MS	WHYN	1250	Minden	LA	KASO	97.7
Many	LA	KWLA	1400	Moreauville	LA	KLIL	92.1
Marksville	LA	KAPB	1370	Morgan City	LA	KFXY	96.7
Minden	LA	KASO	1040	Natchez	MS	WQNZ	95.1
Mobile	AL	WKRG	710	Oak Grove	LA	KWCL	96.7
Monroe	LA	KMLB	1440	Springhill	LA	KTKC	92.7
Morgan City	LA	KMRC	1430	Tallulah	LA	KBYO	104.5
Natchez	MS	WNAT	1450	Thibodaux	LA	KXOR	106.3
Natchitoches	LA	KNOC	1450	Ville Platte	LA	KVPI	93.5
New Iberia	LA	KNIR	1360	Winnfield	LA	KVCL	92.1
New Orleans	LA	WWL	870	Winnsboro	LA	KMAR	95.9
Opelousas	LA	KSLO	1230				
Shreveport	LA	KWKH	1130				
Springhill	LA	KBSF	1460				
Tallulah	LA	KBYO	1360				
Winnfield	LA	KVCL	1270				
Winnsboro	LA	KMAR	1570				

Are these some serious football fans or what?!

*Ticket Information

    LSU football tickets are available at TicketMaster outlets throughout Louisiana and along the Gulf Coast, or through the **LSU Ticket Office,** open 8:00 AM - 4:30 PM Monday through Friday, at **(504) 388-2184.** For 24-hour schedule and ticket information call the **LSU Tiger Hotline (504) 388-6951.**

    By Louisiana statute it **is unlawful to sell tickets for more than the printed face value.** At LSU, this law is enforced by Sheriff's undercover detectives who look mainly for those attempting to profit from the practice. Like many other SEC venues, a few arrests are made from time to time to keep scalping activity down. Of course, **buying a ticket for a premium price** is not illegal.

*Seating Information

At Tiger Stadium the visiting band sits in south stadium, section 2. Visiting fans sit in south stadium, sections 1-3, 19-21 and 22-27.

*Parking Information

From the north use either River Road or Nicholson Drive, Highland Road or Dalrynmple Drive. On Nicholson Drive parking is available near the new Fieldhouse, at Kirby South Dormitory lots off Aster and Roosevelt Streets, and at the Pleasant Hall lots on Dalrymple Drive.

From the east or south use either College Drive, Acadian/Stanford Exit, Highland Road or Burbank Drive and Nicholson Drive. Parking for these routes is available on Nicholson Drive Extension south of the stadium, off Nicholson Drive by the baseball stadium, on South Stadium Road near the Mississippi River and the lots in the vicinity of the John M. Parker Coliseum.

Fans coming from the South on Nicholson Drive or Burbank will be routed to Gourrier Lane, the River Road and onto South Stadium Road. At 5:30 PM Saturday police will direct one-way traffic ONLY toward Tiger Stadium on Highland Road from Lee Drive, on West Lakeshore Drive from Stanford, on Nicholson Drive Extension from Parker Boulevard, on Dalrymple Drive from the I-10 overpass.

Fans arriving early at LSU games will find one of the best parking situations in the SEC. Few lots are reserved and it is possible to park very close to Tiger Stadium.

RV operators without permits may park, for a $20.00 fee, in in the ROTC reserved lot located on Nicholson Extension . **Free RV parking** will be provided in the "Traveling Tiger" lot behind Alex Box Stadium with overflow directed to the large grass lots across from the School of Veterinary Medicine. Parking of vehicles on the neutral ground (islands) on Nicholson Drive is prohibited. RV operators desiring to park in areas other than those designated for RV parking may continue to use areas around Pleasant Hall, the Agricultural Center and east of Tower Drive.

*ALL INFORMATION IS SUBJECT TO CHANGE.

The REAL Mike the Tiger . . . up close and personal! Nice Kitty ! ? ? !

Walking tour of the campus . The unique beauty of the LSU campus deserves a close look and the best way to achieve that is by taking a leisurely stroll around the central campus core. Among the sights of interest:

~**Memorial Tower.** Hours 9 AM - 4PM weekdays; 10 AM - Noon, 1PM - 4 PM Saturday; 1 PM - 4 PM Sunday. Built between 1923 and 1926 as a monument to Louisianans who died in the first World War. In 1976 the Tower was rededicated in its fiftieth year and the Nation's Bicentennial.

~**Greek Theater.** Natural amphitheater with seating for 3,500. Once used for commencement exercises.

~**Huey P. Long Fieldhouse.** Includes once largest outdoor pool in the nation when built in the early 1930's (180' by 48'). Long was a Louisiana Governor, Senator and *GREAT* LSU supporter.

~**Bernie Moor Track Stadium.** Named after one-time head football coach. Seats 5,680.

~**Pete Maravich Assembly Center.** Site of LSU basketball, graduations and concerts. Seats 14,164.

~**Tiger Cage - Where Mike lives.** Located between the Assembly Center and the Northwest end of Tiger Stadium.

~**Tiger Stadium.** Home of the "Fighting Tigers."

~**T-33 Jet.** Monument to LSU graduates who have died in defense of their country during the jet age.

~**Cannons.** Used to fire on Fort Sumter at the beginning of the Civil War. Presented by General William T. Sherman, first superintendent of LSU.

~**Sugar Kettle.** Thought to be the original kettle first used to successfully granulate sugar in Louisiana in 1795.

~**LSU Union.** Hours 7AM - 11 PM Monday through Friday; 11 AM - 11 PM Saturday and Sunday. A massive facility containing eating and recreational areas, theaters, post office, bookstore, etc.

~**LSU Gift Center.** 2 locations: Within Tiger Stadium and near the Tiger Cage. Open on football, basketball and baseball game days. All sorts of LSU clothing and memorabilia.

Can this be venerable Tiger Stadium? Yes it is!
Renovations have made the old girl more modern and fan-friendly.
She still has more mystique than any stadium in the league in my book.

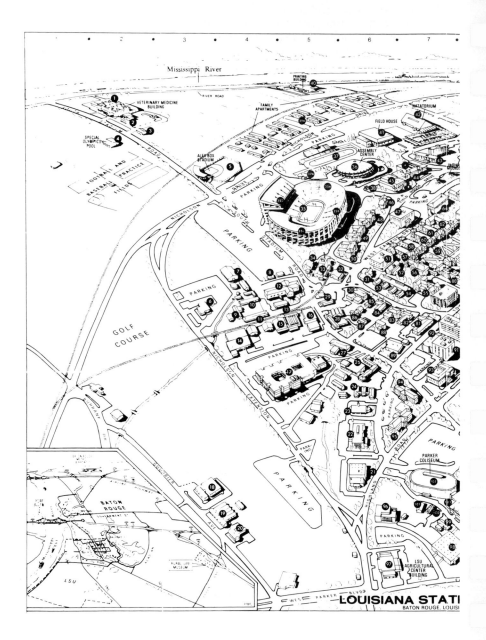

LOUISIANA STATE
BATON ROUGE, LOUISI

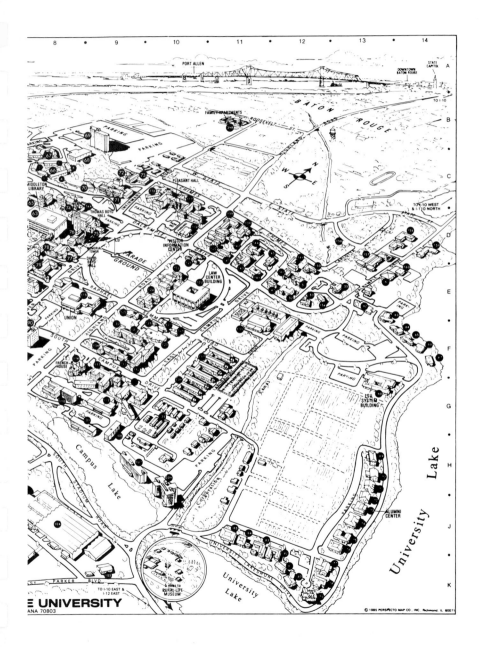

GREATER BATON ROUGE

Points of Interest

1. Old State Capitol
2. Magnolia Mound Plantation
3. Louisiana State University
4. LSU Rural Life Museum
5. Cortana Mall
6. Bon Marche Mall
7. Baton Rouge Metro Airport
8. Cohn Memorial Arboretum
9. Greater Baton Rouge Zoo

10. Southern University
11. Visitor Information Center/
State Capitol
12. Port of Baton Rouge
13. Heritage Museum
14. McHugh House
15. LSU Hilltop Arboretum
16. Baton Rouge Gallery
17. Celebration Station

18. Blue Bayou Water Park
19. Landmark Antique Plaza
20. Westmoreland Antique Gallery
21. Jimmy Swaggart Ministries

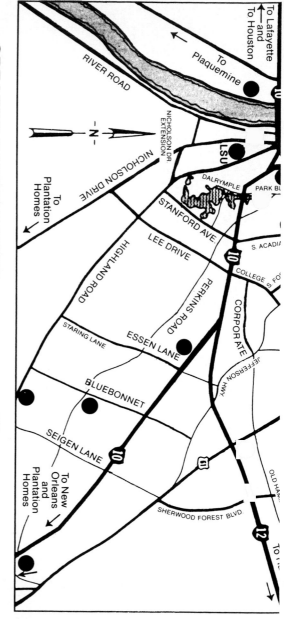

Baton Rouge

THE FLAVOUR OF LOUISIANA

BATON ROUGE AREA CONVENTION & VISITORS BUREAU, INC.

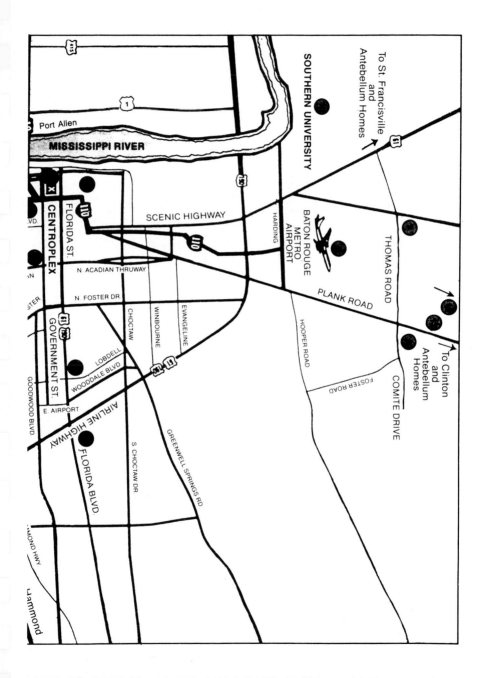

Tour any of numerous old river plantations. Baton Rouge is close to several, among them:

Destrehan Plantation	(504) 764-9315
San Francisco Plantation	(504) 535-2341
Oak Alley Plantation	(504) 265-2151
Tezcuco Plantation	(504) 562-3929
Houmas House Plantation	(504) 437-7841
Nottoway Plantation	(504) 545-2730

LSU Rural Life Museum. An outdoor complex of 19th century furnished building of the rural South. Essen Lane at I-10 in Baton Rouge. (504) 765-2437.

Louisiana's old State Capitol. Due to reopen this year after a 16 million dollar renovation. Hands-on exhibits. 100 North Boulevard at River Road in Baton Rouge. (504) 922-0403.

Louisiana State Capitol. Interesting architecture, observation deck. The nation's tallest state capitol. Visitor Information Center located inside. State Capitol Drive in Baton Rouge. (504) 342-7317.

Swamp Tours. Tour the Atchafalaya Basin. Whiskey River Landing. I-10 at Henderson, Louisiana. (318) 667-6135.

Greater Baton Rouge Zoo. Zoo-choo train goes through zoo with guided tours. Thomas Road, one mile east of LA 19, Baker, Louisiana. (540) 775-3877.

Where to Eat and Sleep in the Baton Rouge Area

"Many and varied" describes the dining and hotel accommodations in and around Baton Rouge. Try to make reservations for hotels in advance in order to insure type and location of your choice during football weekends.

For complete information contact:

Baton Rouge Area Convention and Visitors Bureau
P. O. Box 4149
Baton Rouge, LA 76821
1-800-LA-ROUGE / 1-800-527-6843

Ask for free *"Visitors Guide"*.

NOTES

The Lyceum was the first building on any state campus in Mississippi.
Built in 1848, it is a widely recognized symbol of Ole Miss.

Ventress Hall houses a beautiful stained beautiful stained glass window honoring the memory of the "University Grays."

The histories of the University of Mississippi and its host city, Oxford, have been intertwined almost from the beginning in a true symbiotic relationship. Less than a quarter century apart in age, the two have grown up together and today the university and the town are about the same size with 11,000 students and citizens respectively.

When the city of Oxford was founded it was named after the famous center of education in England in the hope that the name would attract an educational institution. Sure enough, in 1841, Oxford was selected over several rival towns to be the site of the future University of Mississippi. The school was officially chartered three years later in 1844. The first students were admitted in 1848 and the first class was graduated in 1851. In 1854, the School of Law, the fourth oldest state-supported law school in the nation, was established. From 1848 to 1871 the University of Mississippi was the only institution of higher learning in the state.

Hard times hit the school and Oxford in 1861 when the Civil War broke out and the University was closed for the duration, reopening in 1865. At the outbreak, cadets from the college had formed a military unit known as the "University Grays." This same group of young men was involved in the Battle of Gettysburg in 1863 and suffered almost 100% casualties. The town of Oxford fared little better, falling to the torch of invading Union armies.

In the 1880's the University made history in the South by becoming one of the first institutions of higher learning in the region to admit women (1882) and the first to have a woman faculty member when Sarah McGehee Isom joined the staff in 1885.

The first quarter of the twentieth century saw a great deal of progress in the University's growth. The School of Engineering was established in 1900 followed by the Schools of Education and Medicine in 1903. The School of Pharmacy followed in 1908 and nine years later the School of Business Administration was formed.

Although, like many Southern universities, Ole Miss underwent a great deal of social change in the 1960's, the school has come through the period with grace and optimism. In the mid-nineteen fifties the School of Medicine had relocated to Jackson. In the early 70's, the Schools of Health Related Professions and Dentistry were added to the Jackson campus. Since then, the quality of medical education offered by the University has been a source of pride for all Ole Miss students and alumni.

They are also proud of the overall academic excellence of the University. If questioned about Ole Miss' reputation as a "party school," they admit that having a good time is important to them and they know how to do it, but academics are a higher priority! This is borne out by the facts. Although Ole Miss is not a huge school, it ranks 17th in the production of Rhodes Scholars among all U.S. colleges and universities with 23.

Today Oxford is recognized as the "most cultured" of all smaller cities in Mississippi. This is primarily due, of course, to the presence of the University in the community. Meanwhile, Ole Miss students love Oxford. When questioned about the possible limiting aspects of a small town on a young person's social and cultural life, the overwhelming response was, "we wouldn't have it any other way: Oxford is great!"

If Oxford's founding fathers could see their city today, they would no doubt be overjoyed that their hopes and dreams for Oxford have been realized.

A Rebel cheerleader strikes a defiant pose as her
team-mates rally the crowd against Alabama.

When Ole Miss' first football team was organized a hundred years ago, much thought was given to the choice of colors which would represent the squad. The first manager-coach of the tame, and in fact, its organizer, Dr. A. L. Bondurant, suggested that a joining together of "the Crimson of Harvard and the Navy Blue of Yale would be very harmonious, and that it was well to have the spirit of both of these good colleges."

Originally the colors of only the football team, crimson (now cardinal*) and navy have since become the official colors for the total university athletic program. The official Ole Miss red is "cardinal" (PMS number 185). The blue is "navy" (PMS number 282.5).

Colonel Rebel and the Ole Miss cheerleaders lead their team onto the field as competing banners seem to vie for attention in the foreground.

For a short time in the 1930's the Mississippi football team was known as "The Flood." Since 1936 Ole Miss football teams have officially been nicknamed "Rebels." In that year Judge Ben Guider of Vicksburg provided the winning suggestion from over 200 proposed nicknames in a contest sponsored by the student newspaper, "The Mississippian." The idea was to submit the list of names to a group of Southern sportswriters to see which one they preferred. Twenty-one newsmen responded and of these, eighteen chose "Rebels."

University Nickname - "Ole Miss"

The endearing nickname, "Ole Miss," has been officially associated with the University of Mississippi since 1896 when a contest was held to suggest a name for the yearbook. The winning name was entered by Miss Elma Meek of Oxford. "Ole Miss" was an expression servants in plantation homes used in referring to the lady of the house. Her daughter was called "Young Miss."

Although originally associated only with the student publication, the name "Ole Miss" has come to symbolize all aspects of the University. Perhaps a proper understanding of the relationship between "Ole Miss" and "the University" is best had by reading what the late Frank E. Everett, Jr. (Class of '32) wrote:

There is a valid distinction between The University and Ole Miss even though the separate threads are closely interwoven. The University is buildings, trees and people. Ole Miss is mood, emotion and personality. One is physical, and the other is spiritual. One is tangible, and the other intangible. The University is respected, but Ole Miss is loved. The University gives a diploma and regretfully terminates tenure, But one never graduates from Ole Miss.

Colonel Rebel, the Ole Miss mascot, is the hilarious caricature of a Southern gentleman and is widely known and admired throughout the SEC.

The personification of the Ole Miss Rebel spirit is provided by "Colonel Rebel," a larger-than-life caricature of the true Southern Gentleman, who presides at all University of Mississippi football games. Jeff Hubbard, a former Ole Miss cheerleader, is credited with creating the mascot in 1979 and portrayed the Rebel until 1982.

Originally known as "Johnny Rebel," the present name, "Colonel Rebel," is actually older, having first been used in the 1938 Ole Miss yearbook with the illustrations upon which today's mascot is based.

The Ole Miss "Rebel Band" energizes the crowd with sound and motion.

The Ole Miss Rebel Band is a thrilling sight with its 200 members performing precise routines. With an exciting sound to match the band provides wonderful entertainment both pregame and at halftime. The colorful bright red and blue uniforms enhance the band's on-field presence.

Fronting the band is the Rebelette dance team, one of the many facets of the University Band organization. Other components include the "Rebel Rebound Sound" (basketball pep band) and three concert ensembles---Wind Ensemble, Symphonic Band and Concert Band.

Members of the band entertain fans in the grove before and after the games at Ole Miss. Altogether, gameday in Oxford is very much enhanced by their on-the-field and off-the-field presence.

Director of bands at Ole Miss is David Wilson.

UNIVERSITY OF MISSISSIPPI
"Alma Mater"

Way down south in Mississippi,
There's a spot that ever calls,
Where among the hills enfolded,
Stand old Alma Mater's halls,
Where the trees lift high their branches
To the whispering Southern breeze,
There Ole Miss is calling, calling
To our hearts fond memories.

OLE MISS' FIGHT SONG
"Forward Rebels"

Forward Rebels, march to fame,
Hit that line and win this game,
We know that you'll fight it through
For your colors red and blue---Rah, rah, rah,
Rebels, you're the Southland's pride,
Take that ball and hit your stride,
Don't stop 'til the victory's won
for your Ole Miss.

Rebel Rousers . . . Ole Miss fans cheer for the "red and blue."

In our opinion, "The Grove" at Ole Miss sets the standard for tailgating in the SEC. Silver service and candelabras are not uncommon in this tradition-rich setting.

Johnny Vaught said in his book, "Rebel Coach: My Football Family,"
I know without any doubt whatsoever that Ole Miss football is more of a family affair than at any other institution in the country.
This has been called the "Mississippi mystique" and is the attitude which "bind{s} Ole Miss to family and state." It is very real . . .and when you travel to Oxford for a football game you will enjoy that experience too. As Johnny Ferguson (an Ole Miss fan who lives in Searcy, Arkansas) says, it is "South and proud of it!"

As true Southerners, born and bred, the authors have experienced the prejudice of those who think that being "South" is not something to be proud of. True, we have a history that is tarnished, but if I read my history books correctly, so does the North! Nevertheless, Ole Miss is a real "Southern experience" that can make you proud of and help you enjoy all the good and wonderful attitudes which make the South so great! There is a sense of history and tradition here that is different from all other SEC schools. You will also find more "traditions" here, and we enjoyed every one of them!

For example, as you arrive on campus you immediately see "The Grove," a beautiful, wooded area which invites you to relax and enjoy the whole gameday experience. This is the heart of tailgating in Oxford. For years families drove their vehicles into the area and many have been meeting under the same tree for over 25 years! However, last year, in order to conserve the beauty of the grass, sprinklers were installed, so no vehicles are allowed in the grove. In our estimation this only enhances the experience, because without the vehicles which are so prominent at other SEC tailgating areas, we thought The Grove had a wonderful, old-fashioned picnic atmosphere.

Other notable differences in Ole Miss tailgating are the beautifully decorated tables (some included silver chafing dishes and many had fresh flower arrangements) and the gentile dress of the fans. At most SEC games colorful T-shirts, sweats and blue jeans are the staple, but at Ole Miss you will find fans who "dress" for the occasion. Tailored skirts and blouses, and soft cotton dresses for the ladies and khaki pants with oxford (of course) cloth shirts for the men, with many wearing a coat and tie for the game. Students at many schools dress for football games, but here--it IS the dress for a game! Finally, it was clear where I had gotten my desire to dress up for football games! You see, this author was born in northern Mississippi and she really felt at home in Oxford; and her husband finally understood the pressure he was under to wear a double-breasted blazer when escorting her!

The "Hotty Toddy" cheer is a traditional favorite of Ole Miss students and fans.

Ole Miss fans are excited about football and really want to win, but they make the whole day special. Great Southern food is to be found on these picnic tables such as fried chicken, pimento cheese sandwiches, deviled eggs, and special home-made cakes and cookies. We enjoyed a cup of "tea punch" with Elise and Cavett Otis and Fred and Carol Pitts from Tupelo, a delicious "buffalo chip cookie" with Molly and R. J. Hornsby of Jackson, Tennessee, and a "traditional" pimento cheese sandwich with Gerald and Frances Drury of Collierville, Tennessee. You will find bar-b-que, hamburgers and hot dogs, and maybe even some fried catfish. It was not a surprise to find people enjoying mint juleps in this beautiful setting!

For those who want to try some local restaurants, Ole Miss fans suggest The Downtown Grill, Café Ole, McAlister's, The Beacon, and Cobb's Seafood. Take the short drive to Taylor for a catfish dinner at Taylor Grocery---that's right---a grocery, where the fish is fresh, the tea is cold, and the chocolate chess pie is delectable! You can even get a fried bologna sandwich, if you're southern enough!. It's a true "experience" but be sure to call ahead for reservations, especially on game weekends.

Colonel Lee M. Jones of Oxford confirmed what most Ole Miss fans said: "the favorite traditions associated with Rebel football are "Dixie, the Confederate battle flag and tailgating in The Grove." When one born in the South hears the band play "From Dixie With Love," well, it's an experience that brings chills even now. Gameday at Ole Miss is a reminder of all that makes the South so special: family, good food, a laid-back afternoon with friends, and a pace of life which allows one to ponder "why we are here." It certainly can help Southerners regain an appreciation of their heritage.

A football game in Oxford is not to be missed. The Rebels have a past tradition of winning and expect to rise to those "glory days" again, so you can count on a good game and great day. Jerome Trahan of Meridian echoed the sentiments of many Ole Miss fans who said the part they "least enjoyed about attending Ole Miss football games" was leaving Oxford! The University of Mississippi is like a family and family is always welcome. So don't be surprised to find yourself, even a rival fan, taken in by the warmth and tradition to be experienced at Ole Miss!

The traditional "Rebel Walk" through "The Grove"
is probably the best attended of the team walks in the SEC.

The Ole Miss coaching staff has the Rebel program heading in the right direction.
Bowl games have once again become an annual part of football at Oxford.

Head Coach

Billy Brewer (Ole Miss, 1961)
Southeastern Louisiana Assistant, 1972-73;
Southeastern Louisiana Head Coach, 1974-79;
Louisiana Tech Head Coach, 1980-82;
Ole Miss Head Coach, 1983-present

> **Birthday: October 8, 1935**
> **Hometown: Columbus MS**

Assistant Coaches

Larry Beckish (Wichita State, 1964)	Offensive Coordinator/Quarterbacks
Jim Carmody (Tulane, 1956)	Assistant Head Coach/ Defensive Line
Keith Daniels (Mississippi College, 1969)	Running Backs
Joe Lee Dunn (Chattanooga, 1968)	Defensive Coordinator/ Inside Linebackers
Freeman Horton (Southern Mississippi, 1979)	Outside Linebackers
Ken Matous (Wichita State, 1979)	Wide Receivers
John Neal (Brigham Young, 1980)	Defensive Backs
Melvin Smith (Millsaps, 1982)	Tight Ends
Joe Wickline (Florida, 1983)	Offensive Line

Vaught-Hemingway Stadium occupies the site where Ole Miss football has been played since 1915.

Home Stadium - "Vaught-Hemmingway Stadium"

Football has been played on the same site at Ole Miss since 1915. In that year, students helped construct the first stands for football on the spot now occupied by Vaught-Hemmingway Stadium. During the Great Depression, construction of a permanent facility became a three year, federally funded project. Completed in 1941, the stadium's original capacity was 24,000.

It was named for the late Judge William Hemmingway who had died in 1937, after serving for many years as professor of law and chairman of the university's Committee on Athletics. In 1982, former Ole Miss coaching great, John Howard Vaught, was honored for his 190-61-11 record and 1960 National Championship team by having his name added to the stadium.

In 1950, one of the longest press boxes found anywhere was built, stretching some 80 yards. In 1988, the structure was completely redone incorporating a club level section which seats 100. Like many colleges across the country, Ole Miss at one time opted for artificial turf, but later abandoned the choice. From 1970 through the 1983 season, Astro-Turf gave Ole Miss the only artificial playing surface in the state. In the Summer of 1984, natural turf returned. One additional change at Vaught-Hemmingway took place in 1990, when lights were installed and night football came to Ole Miss.

Over the years, several renovations and expansion projects have increased the stadium's capacity to 43,577. The largest crowd ever to witness a game at Vaught-Hemmingway was the 1989 LSU matchup viewed by 42,354.

Stadium Stats

Capacity:	42,577
Five Largest Crowds:	1992 - 42,847 vs Memphis State
	1989 - 42,354 vs LSU
	1984 - 41,564 vs Memphis State
	1992 - 41,500 vs Mississippi State
	1980 - 41,412 vs Memphis State
Playing surface:	Natural grass

Mississippi Veterans Memorial Stadium - Jackson

Historically, Ole Miss' "Home away from home" has been Mississippi Veterans Memorial Stadium in Jackson. With the movement of the Ole Miss-Mississippi State rivalry to a home and home format in 1991, however, the importance of the site has diminished. The "Battle of the Golden Egg" or "Egg Bowl," as the season-ending grudge match is known, was played at Mississippi Memorial Stadium from 1973 through 1990.

The Jackson stadium is Mississippi's largest, with a capacity of 60,549. Constructed in 1953 with seating for 22,000, the stadium has undergone several expansions, reaching a peak size of 62,500 in 1980. The largest crowd ever to watch a sporting event in Mississippi (63,522) attended the Arkansas-Ole Miss game. Horseshoe-shaped, the stadium resembles (at least in part) the great bowls in Pasadena and Ann Arbor. The present configuration was achieved when the west end zone was enclosed in the 1980 expansion. Capacity was reduced somewhat in 1990 when the east end zone stands were removed.

The playing field at Memorial Stadium is named for long-time SEC football official and former member of the Mississippi House of Representatives, Butch Lambert.

Stadium Stats

Capacity:	60,549
The 5 largest crowds:	1981 - 63,522 vs Arkansas
	1980 - 62,520 vs Mississippi State
	1982 - 62,385 vs Alabama
	1982 - 61,286 vs Mississippi State
	1981 - 61,153 vs Mississippi State
Playing surface:	Natural Grass

Vaught-Hemmingway Stadium

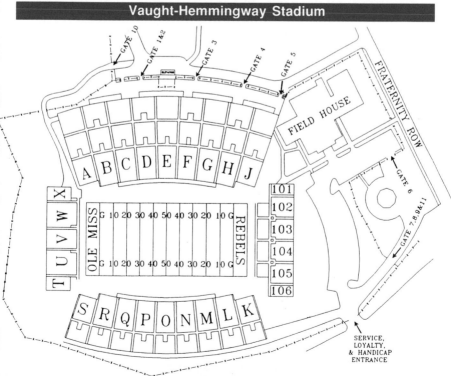

Mississippi Veterans Memorial Stadium in Jackson

David Kellum - Play-By-Play/"Voice of the Rebels"
Lyman Hellums - Color Commentator
Stan Sandroni - On-The-Field Analyst

Ole Miss Radio Network

AM Stations				FM Stations			
CITY	STATE	STATION	FREQUENCY	CITY	STATE	STATION	FREQUENCY
Aberdeen	MS	WWZQ		Amory	MS	WAFM	
Biloxi	MS	WVMI		Bay Springs	MS	WIZK	
Birmingham	AL	WCEO		Booneville	MS	WBIP	
Clarksdale	MS	WROX		Columbia/Prentiss	MS	WJDR	
Columbia	MS	WCJU		Columbus	MS	WJWF	
Forest	MS	WQST		Corinth	MS	WXRZ	
Houston	MS	WCPC		Greenville	MS	WIQQ	
Jackson	MS	WJDS		Greenwood	MS	WYMX	
Lexington	MS	WXTN		Hattiesburg	MS	WHSY	
Louisville	MS	WLSM		Holly Springs	MS	WKRA	
McComb	MS	WAPF		Indianola	MS	WNLA	
Memphis	TN	WMC		Jackson	MS	WJDX	
Pascagoula	MS	WGUD		Meridian	MS	WZMP	
Philadelphia	MS	WHOC		Natchez	MS	WTRC	
Picayune	MS	WRJW		Oxford	MS	WQLJ	
Starkville	MS	WSSO		Tupelo/New Albany	MS	WWKZ	
Tylertown	MS	WTYL		Vicksburg	MS	WBBV	
Walnut	MS	WLRC					
Waynesboro	MS	WABO					
West Point	MS	WROB					
Winona	MS	WONA					

*Ticket Information

Ticket office phone numbers: 1-800-843-7709 / (601) 232-7167

The state of Mississippi has an **anti-scalping** law which controls the price which may legally be charged for tickets. Basically, it is illegal in Mississippi to sell a ticket at any amount over face value. It is not illegal to buy a ticket over face value nor is it a crime to buy a ticket for less than face value and then sell it for a profit if the second sales price is no greater than face value. Ole Miss campus police will actively enforce the anti-scalping law at big games which are sell outs. At other games, tickets are generally available at the ticket office near the stadium, the area around the stadium, the Grove and the Student Union.

Visiting fans are seated in sections P, Q, S and the end zone. The visiting band has a choice of where they would like to be seated in these sections.

*Parking Information

The best approach to football parking areas at Ole Miss is from State Road 6 (the By-pass) on the south side of town. Unless fans arrive very early they should avoid approaching the stadium from the town side. The campus may be accessed off the By-pass via Old Taylor Road which dead ends at University Avenue. A left turn will place you on the campus. Once on campus, The Grove Loop is to the right off University Avenue and leads around by the Ole Miss {Student} Union. The Grove is no longer open to vehicles but is still the center of tailgating activities. Vehicles may park in campus parking spaces and off-street areas throughout this part of the campus.

Fraternity Row, which is on the left off University Avenue and passes Vaught-Hemmingway Stadium, is closed to traffic before the game (except for those with permits to park around the stadium). You will find parking lots on the left and right sides of Old Taylor Road as you approach University Avenue. You may park in any of these lots and then walk a reasonable distance onto the campus proper and to the stadium.

A new road and parking area has been completed near the Coliseum. Take the Hathorn Road exit off State Road 6 (the By-pass) and turn right by the Acoustics Building to reach the new area. **RV's** are allowed to park free in this lot and may arrive early. At times, depending on the game, **private shuttles** are operated from the Mall or from downtown, but this cannot be counted on.

RV's are allowed to park in the core campus area on gameday only, but they may not park along the streets. They may arrive as early as they wish in the outlying lots. **RV's** may park for free in the lot on the left across from the Oxford- University Baseball Stadium and may arrive as early as they like before the game, even a day or two.

At present, campus parking spaces marked for the **handicapped** are not restricted to vehicles with handicapped stickers on gameday. However, this policy is being reviewed and is subject to change. **Handicapped parking permits** may be obtained from the Athletic Department in advance or from campus security on gameday. The Ole Miss Police Department is located in Odom Hall between Library Loop and Sorority Row North. Handicapped fans may be dropped off near the stadium if their vehicle has a license plate handicapped sticker.

*ALL INFORMATION IS SUBJECT TO CHANGE.

Sorority and Fraternity houses, such as these, do little to diminish Ole Miss' reputation as a "party school;" but students are quick to point out they know how to study as well as party!

~**The Center for the Study of Southern Culture** is housed in Barnard Observatory which dates from 1848. The Center serves as a teaching and research institute of the study of the South and offers weekly brown bag lunch speakers, special films, videos, lectures and exhibits. Tours are available by appointment. Hours: Monday-Friday, 8:15AM-4:45PM. (601) 232-5993.

~**The Grove** is a park-like area near the University Avenue entrance to Ole Miss and is the spiritual heart of the campus.

~**The Lyceum** was the first building on the Ole Miss campus. Constructed in 1848, it now serves as the administration building.

~**The J. D. Williams Library, Archives and Special Collections** feature the permanent exhibition of William Faulkner's Nobel Prize, signed first editions and manuscripts. Many other works of Mississippi authors are also included. Hours: Monday-Friday, 8:30-5:00. Phone (601) 232-5861.

~Other **University Museums** offer permanent and special exhibits including a Southern Folk Art Room, an extensive collection of Greek and Roman antiquities and scientific instruments from the 17th and 18th centuries. (601) 232-7073.

~**The Old Chapel** is the second oldest building on campus dating from 1853. Originally planned as a dormitory, it was redesigned to serve as a student assembly building.

~**Barnard Observatory** was built 1857-59 to help make the University a leading center of American science. Plans called for the installation of the world's largest telescope. The beginning of the Civil War caused it to be diverted to Northwestern University in Illinois. During the Civil War the observatory served as a hospital and morgue. It now houses the Center for the Study of Southern Culture.

~**Ventress Hall,** originally constructed in 1889 as a library, now houses the University Art Department. Its Gothic architecture makes it one of the most distinctive buildings on campus.

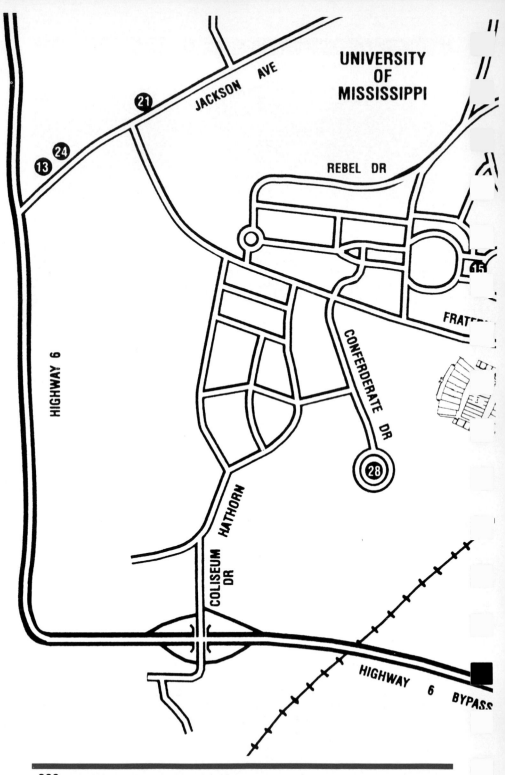

UNIVERSITY
OF
MISSISSIPPI

JACKSON AVE

REBEL DR

HIGHWAY 6

CONFERDERATE DR

FRATER

COLISEUM
DR

HATHORN

HIGHWAY 6 BYPASS

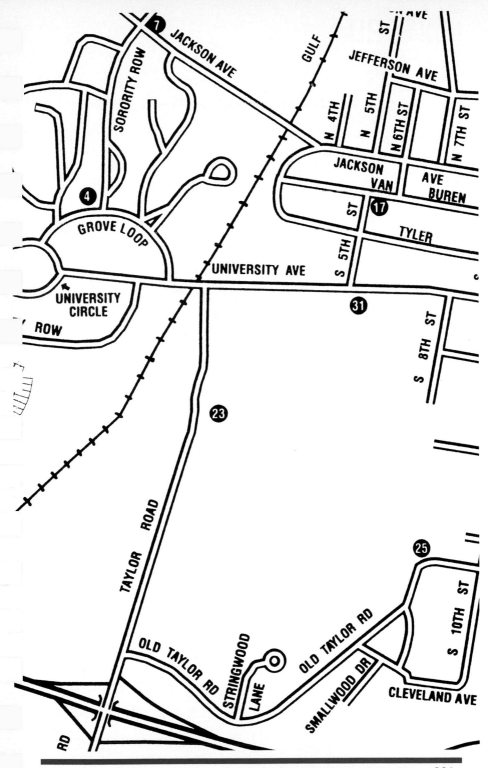

OXFORD

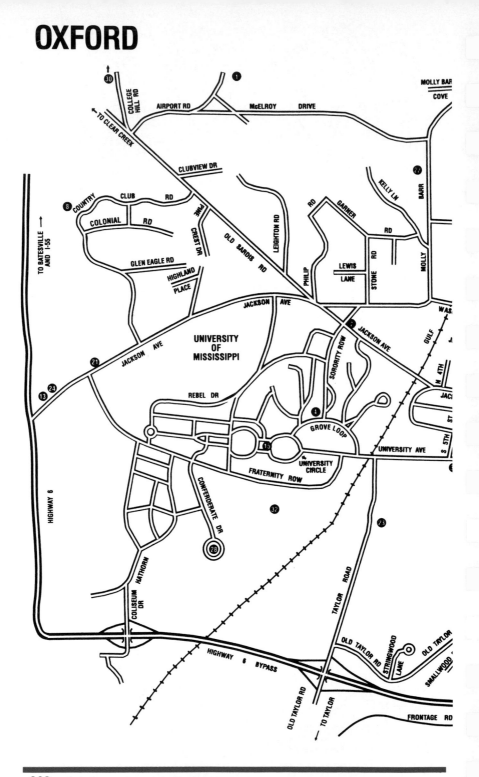

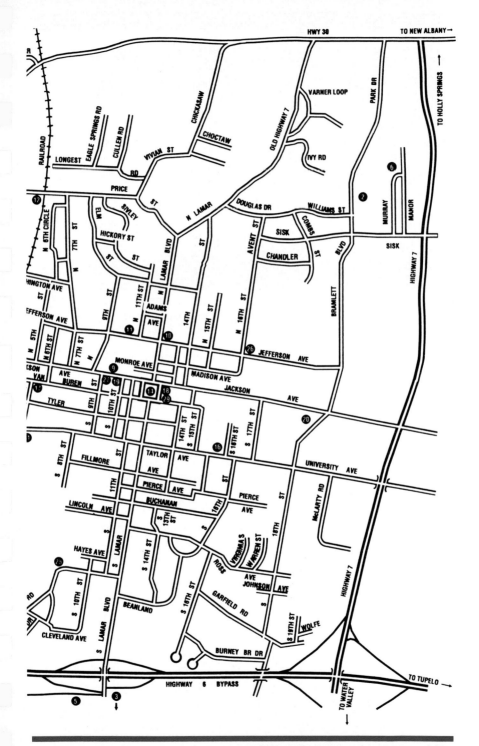

Rowan Oak

Take a **Walking Tour of Downtown Oxford.** The Oxford Tourism Council provides self-guided maps for several "tours" of the historic community. For more information, contact:

Oxford Tourism Council - Phone **(601) 234-4651 or Fax (601) 234-4655**
P. O. Box 965 (299 Jackson Avenue)
Oxford, MS 38655

~Begin at the **Historic Public Square.** All roads lead to and from this part of town which has been designated a National Historic District.

~The **Lafayette County Courthouse** was the inspiration for its fictional counterpart in William Faulkner's Yoknapatawpha County. This building, built in 1873, replaced one burned by Union troops in 1864.

~**Rowan Oak**, the home of William Faulkner, Nobel Prize winning author, is kept just at it was when he wrote many of his masterpieces. Closed holidays. Open 10 AM - 12 Noon and 2:00 - 4:00 PM, Tuesday thru Saturday. (601) 234-3284.

~**First Saturday** is a lively celebration of arts and crafts and music. On selected football weekends.

~**John W. Kyle State Park**. 9 miles east of Sardis on State Road 315, and **Wall Doxey State Park**, 7 miles south of Holly Springs off State Road 7. Each offers camping, picnicking, fishing, swimming and cabins. 1-800-647-2290.

Where to Eat and Sleep in the Oxford Area

Don't despair if you find you can't get rooms in Oxford. Most rooms are reserved from year to year by Ole Miss fans who faithfully attend their home games. However, you can find rooms in nearby Granada, Tupelo or even Memphis, Tennessee. That's right . . . many fans stay in Memphis for the night and drive down to Oxford for gameday activities.

There are many restaurant choices in Oxford, so if you decide not to picnick or tailgate, you will have no problem finding something to please your palate.

Jackson is a growing center of Mississippi Government and regional commerce. For a complete run-down of attractions contact:

Metro Jackson Convention & Visitors Bureau
(601) 960-1891 in MS / 1-800-354-7695 outside MS
P. O. Box 1450
Jackson, MS 39215

~**The Mississippi Governor's Mansion**, 300 E. Capitol Street, has been the official residence of all Mississippi governors since 1842. One of only two executive residences designated a National Historic Landmark. Open Tuesday through Friday, tours each half hour from 9:30-11:00 AM. Prior notice needed for groups of 5 or more. Free. (601) 359-3175.

~**The State Capitol**, 400 High Street, was completed in 1903 and is based on the plan of the national Capitol. It was extensively renovated in the early 1980's. Free.

~**The Oaks House Museum**, 823 N. Jefferson Street, is located in the oldest house in Jackson. General Sherman occupied the building in 1863 during the Siege of Jackson. Open Tuesday through Saturday, 10 AM - 4 PM, Sunday 1:30 - 4:00 PM. Admission: adults $2.00, children $1.00. (601) 353-9339.

~**The Jackson Visitor Information Center,** located at 1150-1/2 Lakeland Drive, is a replica of the trading post on Le Fleur's Bluff that was chosen as the site of the state capital in 1821. The staff is eager to help you explore Jackson. Open Monday-Friday, 8:30 AM - 4:30 PM until Labor Day. Also open Saturday 8:30 AM - 4:30 PM and Sunday 1:30-4:30 PM. (601) 960-1800.

~For an out-of-this-world experience, a visit to the **Russell C. Davis Planetarium** at 201 E. Pascagoula Street, is a must. Boasting the largest planetarium in the Southeast and one of the least equipped theatres in the world, the facility offers programs that the whole family will enjoy. Open M-F with showtimes at 12:00, 2:00 and 8:00 PM; Sat. 2:00, 4:00 and 8:00 PM; Sunday 2:00, 4:00 PM. Admission: adults (13 up) $4.00, children and senior citizens $2.50. (601) 960-1550.

~**The Jackson Zoological Park**, 2918 W. Capitol Street, claims one of the finest collections of wild animals from around the world. A special discovery zoo is just for children. Open Memorial Day to Labor Day, daily from 9:00AM-6:00PM. Remainder of the year 9:00AM - 5:00PM. Adults $3.50, children 3-12 & senior citizens $1.75, children under 2 free. (601) 351-2580.

~**The Mississippi Museum of Art**, 201 E. Pascagoula Street, houses an extensive collection of American and European masterworks. Unique exhibit and demonstration areas involve visitors with the arts first hand. Open Monday-Friday 10 AM - 5 PM, Sat & Sun 12 - 5 PM. Adults $3.00, children $2.00. (601) 960-1515.

~**The Mississippi Crafts Center** on the Natchez Trace Parkway at Ridgeland (take Natchez Trace exit 105-A from I-55 North) is a showplace for traditional and contemporary folk arts and crafts of Mississippi. Informative exhibits and live demonstrations, sales gallery. Open daily 9:00AM-5:00PM. Free. (601) 856-7546.

~**The Mississippi Museum of Natural Science**, 111 N. Jefferson Street, contains a quarter million specimens of Mississippi flora and fauna. Open M-F 9:00AM-5:00PM, Sat 9:30 AM - 4:30 PM. Closed Sun. Free. (601) 354-7308.

~**The Old Capitol Museum**, 100 S. State Street, features exhibits which tell the story of Mississippi from the Spanish explorers to the modern era. Bookstore and gift shop. Open Mon-Fri 8AM - 5PM, Sat 9:30AM - 4:30PM, Sun 12:30-4:30 PM. Free admission. (601) 359-6920.

METRO JACKSON

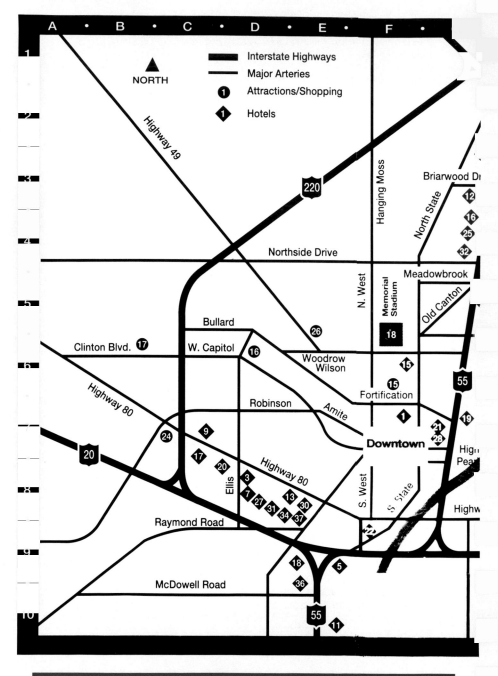

NORTH

- ▬▬ Interstate Highways
- ─── Major Arteries
- ❶ Attractions/Shopping
- ◆ Hotels

Highway 49

220

Hanging Moss

North State

Briarwood Dr

12
16
25
32

Northside Drive

N. West

Meadowbrook

Memorial Stadium

Old Canton

Bullard

Clinton Blvd. 17

W. Capitol 16

26

Woodrow Wilson

18

15

55

Highway 80

Robinson

Amite

15

Fortification

20

24

9

17

20

3

Ellis

Highway 80

1

21
28

19

Downtown

High Pea

7 27 31 34 37
13 30

S. West

S. State

Raymond Road

32

Highw

McDowell Road

18

5

36

55

11

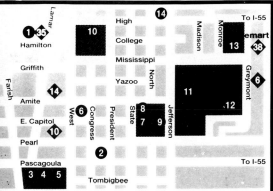

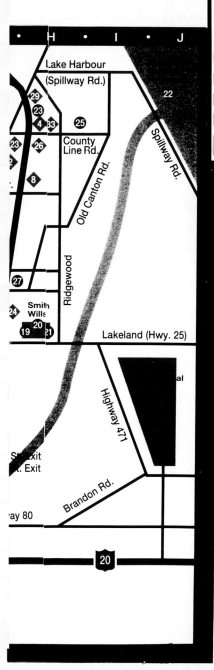

ATTRACTIONS
1. Smith-Robertson Museum
2. City Hall
3. Davis Planetarium
4. MS Museum of Art
   (Arts Center)
5. Municipal Auditorium
6. Governor's Mansion
7. Old Capitol Museum
8. War Memorial Building
9. MS Natural Science Museum
10. MS State Capitol
11. MS State Fairgrounds
12. MS State Coliseum
13. MS Trade Mart
14. The Oaks
15. Manship House
16. Jackson Zoological Park
17. Mynelle Botanical Garden
18. MS Memorial Stadium
19. MS Agriculture and
    Forestry Museum
20. Smith-Wills Stadium
21. Dizzy Dean Museum
22. Ross Barnett Reservoir
23. WaterLand USA

SHOPPING
24. MetroCenter Mall
25. NorthPark Mall
26. Jackson Mall
27. Highland Village

*The Chapel of Memories, built with bricks from a
historic dorm which was destroyed by fire,
has become a landmark of the MSU campus.*

Lee Hall, located at the heart of the MSU campus, reflects the level of pride taken in the buildings and grounds at the school.

With an enrollment of 13,700 at the Starkville campus, Mississippi State is the largest university in the state. The population of MSU's host city is only slightly larger than the student body at 16,700. Nevertheless, Starkville, located near the intersection of U. S. Highway 82 and alternate 45 in the eastern part of North-Central Mississippi, offers cultural amenities which satisfy a growing and ever more divergent campus community.

MSU, founded in 1878 as the Agricultural and Mechanical College of the State of Mississippi, was one of the National Land Grant Colleges established after Congress passed the Morrill Act in 1862. The school's original mission was to offer training in "agriculture, horticulture and the mechanical arts..., without excluding other scientific and classical studies, including military tactics." The first students arrived in 1880, and for many years the students were referred to as cadets. The role of the military, through ROTC, is still prominent on the campus today.

Federal legislation continued to stimulate growth of the school in its early days. In 1888, the Agricultural Experiment Station was established. In 1914, the Extension Service was begun which links the University to each county of the state. Three years later teacher training in vocational education was funded.

In 1932 the school's name was changed by the state legislature to Mississippi State College. Twenty-six years later, in 1958, the name was again changed to the current Mississippi State University. The new name reflected the school's growth with the addition of advanced degrees and several other schools and colleges.

To say MSU is proud of its academic and social strides. For several years now, the schools' incoming freshman class has scored an average 23.1 on the ACT: highest of the eight state-supported institutions in Mississippi. In addition, Mississippi State has the largest honors program with more than 600 students participating. The University's minority enrollment also continues to grow. Black student numbers are up by 37% over the last five years and now make up almost 15% of the total enrollment. In 1992, MSU ranked 81st in the nation in the number of Black students who were graduated.

With students from every county in Mississippi, all fifty states and many foreign countries, each working in wide-ranging degree programs and research endeavors, it is obvious that Mississippi State is reaching out to embrace the three purposes stated on the school seal: Learning, Research and Service.

MSU's arched cafeteria displays the state and national flags of all its students.
The food is as impressive as the architecture.

Preparing for their inaugural football contest in 1895, the student body and team of Mississippi A & M College, as Mississippi State University was called back then, realized they needed team and school colors. The selection of colors was left by the student body to the football team which, in turn, bestowed the honor on the team's captain, W. M. Matthews. According to reports, Matthews, without hesitating, chose maroon and white, and since that time every MSU team, except one has worn those colors.

In 1938, without consulting anyone, football coach, Spike Nelson, ordered cardinal and gold uniforms. Met with a hostile reaction, neither the uniforms nor coach Nelson returned for the 1939 season.

The official MSU "maroon" is PMS Color #202.

Bully holds forth on an end zone platform
while an MSU cheerleader demonstrates pride for his school!

Mississippi State's newest nickname, "Bulldogs," is also one of its oldest. The origin of the Bulldog moniker can be traced to a defeat of Ole Miss in Jackson in 1905 by the team from Mississippi Agricultural and Mechanical College, now MSU. Feeling their oats and no doubt deciding to "rub in" the 11-0 victory, cadets from A & M secured a coffin, decorated it with University of Mississippi colors, placed a bulldog pup on top and proceeded to have a military funeral complete with brass band and funeral march to show "sympathy for the dead athletic spirit" of Ole Miss, according to the student newspaper, "The Reflector." Because of the "bulldog" style of football exhibited by the A & M team that day, the bulldog was adopted as the school's first mascot.

For a number of years thereafter, teams from Mississippi A & M were known as both or either "Bulldogs" or "Aggies." When the school name changed in 1932 from Mississippi A & M College to Mississippi State College, the "Aggies" nickname was dropped.

Although athletic teams from Starkville continued to be called "Bulldogs," from 1935-1960 the nickname "Maroons" was predominant. Of course "Maroons" was in reference to the school's colors, maroon and white. Around 1960, a movement surfaced to drop the nickname "Maroons" and to adopt "Bulldogs" as the official and only nickname. While the source of this movement is hazy, with the support of university officials and the Alumni Association it was agreed to use the name on a trial basis during the 1960 season. The following fall (1961) the change was made permanent.

Pound puppies at play.

Profiles in courage . . . as well as determination, loyalty and real friendliness.
These two "Bullys" were favorites of ours.

At least 19 live bulldogs have served as mascot for MSU if you count the bulldog pup who topped the coffin in the 1905 victory parade (see "Nickname" section), the one who appeared in a pre-game parade/rally before the 1926 Alabama game and the one who inspired the 1935 team to a 20-7 victory over Alabama (a team the "Bulldogs" or "Maroons," as they were more properly called, had not beaten in twenty years).

This last dog, although serving only a one-game reign as mascot, was probably the greatest factor in establishing an unbroken line of mascots with the same name. It seems that the 1935 squad, needing inspiration or a good luck charm, dispatched coach Ralph Sasse to Memphis with instructions not to return without a mascot unless he wanted the team to refuse to play. Coach Sasse returned to the campus with "Ptolemy," a gift of the Edgar Webster family. The charm worked. The long losing string against Alabama was ended!

Soon after another great Mississippi State victory, this one by a 13-7 score over powerful Army, the first of the bulldog mascots to carry the name "Bully" was acquired. Bully I was the "brother" of Ptolemy and achieved "star" status on campus. He was free to roam around, receiving attention and handouts from students. Unfortunately, this freedom led to Bull I's demise. He was killed by a campus bus, causing the students to mourn for days. They placed Bully in a glass-topped coffin, carried his remains on a half-mile funeral procession, complete with the college band and R.O.T.C. escort, and buried him beneath the Mississippi State players' bench on the fifty yard line at Scott Field. "Life" magazine covered the funeral. At least one other "Bully" was buried at the stadium. Others have been laid to rest near various dorms, frat houses and halls near the school.

The practice of letting mascots roam free finally ended when various fraternities began to provide for their care and housing. In the mid-1970's, the Pre-Vet Club began taking care of Bully and now the mascot lives the real "dog's life," receiving excellent care from MSU's School of Veterinary Medicine.

Being MSU's mascot can be risky. Several "Bully's" have been victims of actual or attempted "dognappings," usually perpetrated by students from Ole Miss or Southern Miss. In 1951, Bully VI was taken to Oxford for a short time. The last caper took place before the 1974 Ole Miss game.

The current mascot, Bully XVI, is a brindle bulldog, as opposed to UGA V of the University of Georgia, who is white. Bully is very gentle, although strong-willed. His human counterpart, played by David Longstreet in 1992, was one of our favorites, staying constantly in character and always displaying that bulldog "attitude."

The MSU cheerleaders encourage Bully and members of the Cadet Corps as they perform push-ups tallying the total after each Bulldog score.

The "Famous Maroon Band" of Mississippi State University has been entertaining crowds for about ninety years, but it hasn't always been famous or maroon! Originally it was a military style band with the bandsmen in cadet uniforms. In 1926 in a competition with the University of Alabama, the band wowed the crowd by appearing unexpectedly in maroon jackets and white pants, the same color combination the band wears today. Mississippi A & M (as MSU was known then) won the trophy and a nickname when a sports writer coined the moniker, "The Famous Maroon Band."

Present membership in the MSU Band is approximately 325. Like many SEC bands, Mississippi State's is made up of students with diverse academic interests, but a common interest in music and performance.

Director of Bands at MSU is Dr. Kent Sills.

MISSISSIPPI STATE UNIVERSITY'S ALMA MATER
"Maroon and White"

"In the heart of Mississippi,
Made by none but God's own hand,
Stately in her natural splendor
Our Alma Mater proudly stands.
State College of Mississippi
Fondest memories cling to Thee.
Life shall hoard thy spirit ever,
Loyal sons we'll always be.

"Tho' our lifesome power may vanish
Loyalty can't be o'errun.
Honors true on Thee we lavish,
Until the setting of the sun.
Live Maroon and White forever,
Ne'er can evil mar Thy fame.
Nothing us from Thee can sever,
Alma Mater we acclaim,

CHORUS:
    Maroon and White
    Maroon and White
    Of Thee with joy we sing,
    Thy colors bright,
    Our souls delight
    With praise our voices ring."

2nd CHORUS:
    Maroon and White,
    Maroon and White,
    To Thee our hearts will cling,
    Thy sons will fight
      with all their might,
    For Thee in everything."

MSU'S FIGHT SONG
"Hail State"

Hail dear 'ole State
Fight for that victory today;
Hit that line and 'tote that ball;
Cross the goal before you fall,
And then we'll yell, yell, yell!
For dear 'ole State
We'll yell like hell!
Fight for Mississippi State,
Win that game today!

MSU's "Famous Maroon Band" shows why it's famous
with a stirring halftime performance.

What makes Mississippi State unique in the SEC? Well, David W. Allen of Ocean Springs says it's "the <u>cowbell</u>, and <u>undying</u>, non-fair-weathered fan support!" That's certainly part of it, but we discovered a lot that is unique in Starkville. For example, they have a most beautiful campus, award winning in fact, and some unbelievable reproductions of Mediterranean ruins...not exactly what you'd expect to find in the heart of Mississippi! A trip to State for a football game is great fun and you can certainly expect a hard-fought game of football, too!

Besides the usual tailgating fare, you will certainly enjoy visiting The Cafeteria located near the stadium. There is food for every taste under the magnificent arched ceiling, and whatever you eat, try the chess pie! Bulldog fans travel across country for a slice! We also ate some WONDERFUL homemade pecan pies made and sold by the ROTC on gameday, and hope they are back next year!!! State fans enjoy bar-b-que, chicken, ham, turkey, and homemade potato salad, but Pete and Betty Norman of Summit, Mississippi, fed us the best seafood gumbo we've ever eaten (not counting family recipes!). For local dining treats, fans recommend Harvey's, Oby's and Little Dooey's Bar-B-Q!

You will find that more Mississippi State fans, per capita in the SEC, travel and party with friends in their own motor homes, and those fans are what made Starkville special for us. They were warm and friendly, but knew how to use those cowbells to their advantage to intimidate rival fans! There was much controversy within the conference about the use of cowbells, and they have been outlawed in the stadium, much to the disappointment of State fans and the delight of the other schools. We noted very few in the stands, and those were confiscated quickly! However, we liked the cowbells when used outside and found them quite effective against visiting fans. Devoted Mississippi State fans have certainly taken a part of their heritage which is used to put them down and made it a battle tactic. As Stephen C. Pounders of Bear Creek, Alabama, says, "We are proud of our Land Grand Institution," and we found that pride to be empowering!

Being from Mississippi, it was like coming home and being with family. State fans are hard-working, fun loving and want the other SEC schools to know there is more to them than just cowbells. When asked if they wear school colors to the games, several replied, "Yes, yes, yes!" In the same vein another fan, Neil Hilliard of Aberdeen, said his favorite traditions associated with MSU football were "Bully," "Bully," and "Bully," and his favorite gameday food was "Bulldog meat!" They love their Bulldog image and Bully plays it to the max! When you see him in action you'll understand why the fans are so proud of him!

State fans are Bulldog tough and tenacious. They may have a smile on their face and a warm handshake, but don't be deceived. They are serious about their football. Hardy Tingle of Starkville summed it up this way when asked why he would be upset if his child decided to attend in-state rival, Ole Miss: "All the shame and embarrassment to the family not to mention the realization that she had lost her mind."

Just a friendly reminder that there are two, count them, two Southeastern Conference schools and football programs in the State of Mississippi, and State fans think their "southern tradition" is just as deep and as important for you to experience. The authors would have to agree!

An MSU tradition, the Bulldog Battery provides excitement
by punctuating the game's highlights with canon fire.

Bully surveys the action in last year's watershed game against Alabama.

Head Coach

Jackie Sherrill (Alabama, 1966)
Alabama Graduate Assistant, 1966;
Arkansas Assistant, 1967-68;
Iowa State Assistant, 1968-73;
Pittsburgh Assistant, 1973-75;
Washington State Head Coach, 1976;
Pittsburgh Head Coach, 1977-81;
Texas A&M Head Coach 1982-88;
Mississippi State Head Coach, 1991-present.

Birthday:	
Hometown:	**Biloxi MS**

Assistant Coaches

Bruce Arians (Virginia Tech, 1974)	Offensive Coordinator/ Quarterbacks
Ricky Black (Mississippi State, 1971)	Tight Ends
Rick Christophel (Austin Peay State, 1975)	Wide Receivers
Bill Clay (Arkansas, 1963)	Defensive Coordinator/ Defensive Backs
Jim Helms (Texas, 1967)	Assistant Head Coach/ Running Backs
Pete Jenkins (Western Carolina, 1963)	Defensive Line
Denver Johnson (Tulsa, 1981)	Offensive Line
Ken Pope (Oklahoma, 1973)	Outside Linebackers
Jim Tompkins (Troy State, 1962)	Inside Linebackers

Scott Field is a jewel of a place to watch a college football game.

Since 1914, Scott Field has been the home of Mississippi State football. The facility is named in honor of Don Magruder Scott, an Olympic sprinter and one of the University's first football heroes. From a gridiron and section of bleachers, the beautiful stadium has grown through the years to a present capacity of 41,200. Major expansions occurred in 1936 and 1948, and from that latter year until 1986, the stadium was capable of holding 32,000 fans.

With the growth of the University's football program, the 1986 expansion was greatly needed. Included in the 9,000 additional seats was a west side upper deck providing 5,500 seats, 1,700 chairback seats on the first level below and 1,000 chairback seats on the press box level. The chairback seats are protected from the elements by the upper deck.

Also included in the '86 facelift were two 1,700 seat extensions on the east side stands which made the stadium more symmetrical. These improvements, along with the new scoreboard and landscaping in the north end zone, the impressive Leo Seal M-Club Center in the Turman Fieldhouse in the south end zone and the excellent Bob Hartley Press Box, named for MSU's long-time Sports Information Director, combine to make Scott Field a jewel of a place to play and watch football.

Stadium Stats

Capacity:	41,200
Largest crowd:	42.700 October 25, 1986 vs Auburn
	42,700 November 1, 1986 vs Alabama
Playing surface:	Natural grass

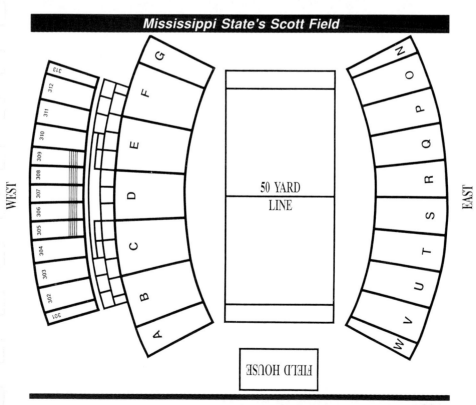

Mississippi State's Scott Field

Jack Cristil - Play-By-Play/"Voice of the Bulldogs"
Jim Ellis - Color Analyst
John Correro - Sideline Reporter
Steve Ellis - Producer/Engineer

Mississippi State Radio Network

AM Stations				FM Stations			
CITY	STATE	STATION	FREQUENCY	CITY	STATE	STATION	FREQUENCY
Bay Springs	MS	WIZK	1570	Aberdeen	MS	WWZQ	105.3
Booneville	MS	WBIP	1400	Batesville	MS	WBLE	100.5
Columbia	MS	WFFF	1360	Carthage	MS	WSSI	98.3
Corinth	MS	WKCU	1350	Clarksdale	MS	WAID	106.3
Forest	MS	WQST	850	Cleveland	MS	WMJW	107.5
Gulfport	MS	WROA	1390	Columbus	MS	WMBC	103.1
Holly Springs	MS	WKRA	1110	Drew	MS	WKZB	95.3
Houston	MS	WCPC	940	French Camp	MS	WFCA	107.9
Indianola	MS	WNLA	1380	Greenville	MS	WDMS	100.7
Memphis	TN	WHBQ	560	Greenwood	MS	WGRM	93.9
Picayune	MS	WRJW	1320	Hernando	MS	WVIM	95.3
Ft. Gibson	MS	WKPG	1320	Jackson	MS	WIIN	98.7
Vicksburg	MS	WQBC	1420	Laurel	MS	WNSL	100.3
Wiggins	MS	WIGG	1420	Lexington	MS	WAGR	102.5
				Louisville	MS	WLSM	107.1
				McComb	MS	WAKH	105.7
				Meridian	MS	WJDQ	101.3
				Pascagoula	MS	WGUD	106.3
				Philadelphia	MS	WWSL	102.3
				Starkville	MS	WMXU	106.1
				Tupelo	MS	WZLQ	98.5
				Tylertown	MS	WTYL	97.7
				Waynesboro	MS	WABO	105.5
				West Point	MS	WKBB	100.9
				Winona	MS	WONA	96.7
				Yazoo City	MS	WJNS	92.1

*Ticket Information

Ticket office phone number is (601) 325-2600.

The State of Mississippi has an anti-scalping law which controls the price which may legally be charged for tickets. Basically, it is **illegal** in Mississippi to sell a ticket at any amount over face value. It is not illegal to buy a ticket over face value, nor is it a crime to buy a ticket for less than face value and then sell it for a profit if the second sales price is no greater than face value.

BUT!!! HOWEVER!!! Mississippi State University (with one of the strictest ticket policies in the SEC) actively discourages not only the illegal scalping of tickets on university property, but also enforces a ban on even the legal sale of tickets for fear that such sales will eventually result in scalping.

So, if you are looking for a ticket prior to gametime, you had better look off campus!

*Parking Information

Visitors who arrive at the Scott Field area prior to gametime should not be deterred when they notice fans parking on the town side of State Road 12. Usually all this means is that the "free" parking on campus has been claimed. In all likelihood, if they drive onto campus and follow the signs designating "Open Lot Parking," they will find a place to park fairly close to the stadium. The only catch is that there is a $4.00 charge.

Many fans choose to park farther away on the Collegeview Street or University Drive approaches, for example, to avoid the charge, or perhaps to avoid the traffic after the game by getting a head start should they leave the game early. There are two large "open parking" lots on the north and south ends of the stadium area. One is located near the soccer field past the McArthur Athletic Dorm (north end) and the other is located on the south end off the farm road.

RV's without permits should proceed to the Humphrey Coliseum parking lot. This area is best approached via Collegeview Street off State Road 12. There is no official opening time for this lot. Fans can come plenty early to enjoy all the "atmosphere" of a Bulldog football weekend. Mississippi State and some other SEC schools located in small towns have raised footballing in motorhomes to an artform. In many cases this has been made necessary by the lack of motel rooms, but even as more motel rooms are built in places like Starkville, the SEC's fascination with RV's continues to grow.

Parking in the coliseum lot is free for motorhomes and no permit is required.

Vehicles with license plate **handicapped** stickers should approach the north or south end of B. S. Hood Road which lies along the immediate west side of Scott Field. This road is blocked on both ends and manned by campus police. With proper license plate, vehicles with handicapped drivers/passengers will be allowed to pass and park close-in. B. S. Hood Road may be approached via University Drive and Lee Boulevard on the southwest corner of Scott Field, and via Collegeview Street on the northwest corner.

*ALL INFORMATION IS SUBJECT TO CHANGE.

*Civil War ruins? Hardly! These are Mediterranean ruins reproduced in Mississippi.
The MSU campus has much to interest archaeology buffs.*

A visitor's first impression of the MSU campus might well be the beauty of the landscaping and the care which is shown to the maintenance of the flowers, shrubs, trees and buildings. If so, that impression is well-founded, because the school has won a national award for the best maintained university grounds in the United States. This is no mean feat since the University's total land holdings in and around Starkville exceed 4,000 acres!

Mississippi State houses a number of interesting and educational attractions right on campus for the benefit of visitors. These include the following:

The **Cobb Institute of Archaeology Museum** features reproductions and artifacts from the Holy Land and Near East as well as North American artifacts. Open on academic schedule. Free. (601) 325-3826.

The **Dunn-Seller Museum** exhibits items relating to paleontology, mineralogy and geology. Open on academic schedule. Free. (601) 325-3915.

Bug lovers will itch to visit the **Mississippi Entomological Museum** which includes literature, displays, live exhibits and over 700,000 specimens. Open year round. Monday-Friday 8 AM - 5 PM by appointment. You won't get stung by the admission--it's free! (601) 325-2085.

The MSU Art Gallery offers monthly exhibitions and is open on the academic schedule. Free. (601) 325-6900.

Those who rave over Ragtime will run to the **Templeton Music Museum** and Archives which is home to a collection of ragtime phonographic instruments, roller organettes, music boxes, recordings, sheet music, player piano and player organs. Tours by appointment. Free. (601) 325-8301.

If you're exhausted after all that toe tapping and need to restore your energy level, stop off at the **Fredrick Herman Herger Dairy Science Building.** Tour a dairy manufacturing plant and purchase milk, cheese and ICE CREAM actually processed on campus. (Take that, Ole Miss!) Store open Monday-Friday 8 AM - 5 PM. Tours by appointment. Free. (601) 325-2440.

The **Rose Garden and Plant Science Research Center** allows visitors to drive through. Most flowers bloom in the late spring, but there are flowers until frost. Free. (601) 325-3138.

For wine connoisseurs, the **A. B. McKay Food and Enology Laboratory** is home to research facilities used to improve food, develop new products, improve grape quality and develop Mississippi wines. Tours by appointment. Free. (601) 325-2440.

"Bully" recommends that you visit the **School of Veterinary Medicine**. Tours by appointment. Free. (601) 325-1418.

The Chapel of Memories has become a widely recognized symbol of Mississippi State. With its majestic tower, the structure dominates the central core of the campus. The building was constructed with the bricks from a huge dorm which housed thousands of MSU students over many years. The dorm was lost to fire over three decades ago. Open 24 hours.

The Cafeteria, a nondescript brick building on the outside, will wow you with its sweeping wood beam Gothic arches on the inside. With sunlight filtering through the beautiful stained glass windows and illuminating the colorful flags of many nations representing the native lands of the University's foreign students, the dining hall seems a strangely exotic place to eat down-home cookin'. Don't miss the MSU produced ice cream and baked goods (fans return to Starkville just for a piece of their chess pie!).

The Colvard Union Building features the Union Grill with a menu of specialty sandwiches, vegetables, and salad plates. The Snack Shop offers popcorn, candies and assorted snacks. The main location of the student bookstore with its large variety of MSU souvenirs is also located here. Open game day.

Mississippi State University

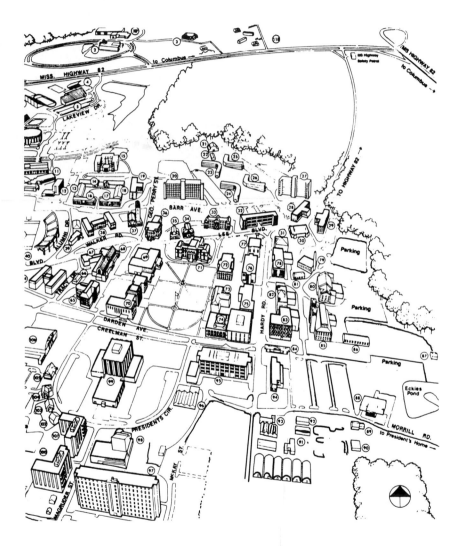

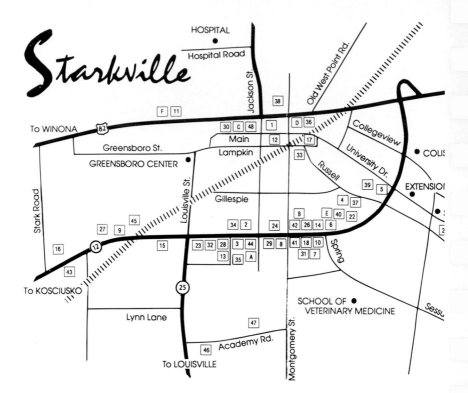

RESTAURANTS

Family Dining

1	Allgood's Burgers	323-1323
2	Back Yard Burgers	324-0111
3	Baskin Robbins	323-0331
4	Blue Goose	324-2603
5	Bulldog Deli	324-3354
6	Burger King	323-2225
7	C J's Pizza	323-8897
8	Captain D's	323-0689
9	Christy's Hamburgers	323-6497
10	Danver's	323-4051
11	The Derby	324-1309
12	Domino's Pizza	324-2100
13	A Gold Star Restaurant	324-3135
14	Hardee's	323-8047
15	Kentucky Fried Chicken	323-1944
16	Little Caesar's Pizza	324-3244
17	Little Dooey B-B-Q	323-6094
18	McDonald's	323-1706
19	Mr. Cook	323-7354
20	MSU Cafeteria	325-2965
21	MSU State Fountain	325-2967
22	Pizza Hut East	323-6340
23	Pizza Hut West	323-8373
24	Popeye's Fried Chicken	324-3537
25	Petty's Bar-B-Q	323-8901
26	Quincy's Family Steakhouse	324-0053
27	Serendipity Bakery	323-5320
28	Shoney's	323-2211
29	Sonic Drive-In	323-3448
30	Starkville Cafe	323-1665
31	Subway Sandwich	323-6210
32	Taco Bell	323-5174
33	TCBY	323-3996
34	Wendy's	324-0029
35	Western Sizzlin'	323-8432

Food and Drink

36	Bully III	323-8251
37	Cheers	324-2129
38	Choices	323-0782
39	Cotton District Grill	323-6062
40	District Cafe	323-9696

RECREATIONAL FACILITIES

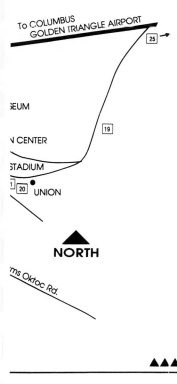

To COLUMBUS
GOLDEN TRIANGLE AIRPORT
25

;EUM

19

J CENTER

STADIUM

1 20 UNION

NORTH

ms Oktoc Rd.

▲▲▲

41	Harvey's	323-1639
42	Holiday Inn	
	Restaurant	323-6161
43	House of Kong	323-4477
44	J. C. Garcia's	323-3066
45	Mulligan's	324-3095
46	Oby's Deli	323-0444
47	Richey's	324-2737
48	Waverley Restaurant	
	(Ivy Guest House)	323-2000

ACCOMMODATIONS ▲

A	Best Western	324-5555
B	Holiday Inn	323-6161
C	Ivy Guest House	323-2000
D	The Regal Inn	323-8251
E	University Inn	323-9550
F	University Motel	323-1421
	Bed & Breakfast	323-3322

Starkville Visitors and Convention Council
601-323-3322

Mississippi State University
Golf Course 325-3028
18-hole championship golf course. Open to the public.

Carl Maddox Track 325-2892
Mississippi State University

Anatomies 323-4455

Skate Odyssey 329-1881

Cinema 12 Four Theatre 323-7222

Rock Hill Stables 327-7820
Horseback riding by appointment.

Noxubee Wildlife Refuge 323-5548
Hunting, fishing, picnicking, hiking and bird watching. Located 8 miles south of Starkville.

Oktibbeha County Lake 323-3350
Fishing, swimming, waterskiing, camping and picnicking. Located 8 miles northwest of Starkville.

John W. Starr Memorial Forest 325-2191
Hunting, picnicking, hiking, fishing and overnight camping. Located 3 miles southwest of Starkville.

Dorman Lake Lodge 325-2191
Available for rental.

SHOPPING ▲▲▲

College Park - 100 Russell Street
Downtown Starkville - Main Street
La Galerie Shopping Mall - Russell Street
Starkville Crossing - Hwy 12 West
Southdale Shopping Center - Hwy 12
State Shopping Center - Hwy 12 West
University Square Shopping Center - Hwy 12
Village Shopping Center - Hwy 12 West
82 Plaza Shopping Center - Hwy 82

What to See and Do in the Starkville Area

If you want to unwind in a laid-back, downhome atmosphere, Starkville, Mississippi is the place for you. Aside from Southeastern Conference sports action, most of the attractions and events in the area are geared toward education or relaxation. Many of the places visitors frequent in and around Starkville offer insight into the East Mississippi prairie culture of which the residents are justly proud.

In your travels through the area note how forestry and agriculture, including dairying, compliment the rolling landscape. An auto trip through Starkville and environs might include the following stops:

~From Starkville, take U.S. Highway 82 west to the **Natchez Trace Parkway**. Follow this beautiful and historic trail south to Kosciusko where the Trace Museum and Visitor Center is located. The drive from Starkville takes from 45 minutes to an hour. (601) 289-2981.

~Then turn east toward Louisville on State Highway 14 and north on Highway 25 to traverse the **Noxubee National Wildlife Refuge**. Noxubee is home to many waterfowl and affords an excellent opportunity for a picnic or nature walk. Fishing and hunting are permitted in season. Free. (601) 323-5548.

~Continue north toward Starkville to **Gentry's General Store** for a look at how country shopping used to be in a really rustic setting. (601) 323-1278.

~If you liked Gentry's, you'll also enjoy the **Artesia Hardware Store** on alternate U.S. Highway 45 in Artesia, southeast of Starkville. This 1890's vintage business offers many unusual products for sale. Closed Thursday afternoons and Sundays. (601) 272-5281.

~A few miles farther south on 45 in Macon, the **Touch of Country** offers handmade crafts by local artists and has everything from candy to quilts to dolls. 8:30 AM - 5 PM, Monday-Friday. (601) 726-4392.

~Go a few miles farther southeast on Highway 45 and you arrive in **Columbus, Mississippi**, where you can drive down street after street lined with more than 100 Antebellum homes and many Victorian structures. (The town was spared by the Yankees). Some of the houses are open for daily tours. Tour maps and information are available. 1-800-327-2686.

~In Starkville, check out the **Oktibbeha County Heritage Museum** which is located at the intersection of Fellowship and Russell Streets. The collection features local artifacts exhibited in a restored train depot. (601) 323-0211.

~If you're still in a museum mood, but need a soft drink first, why not satisfy both thirsts at the **C. C. Clark Memorial Coca-Cola Museum**. Located at the Northeast Mississippi Coca-Cola Bottling Company on State Highway 12 west, it displays more than 2,300 items of Coca-Cola memorabilia. Open year-round by appointment only. Free. (601) 323-4150.

Special Fall Events

September -- *Boardtown Jubilee*. Festival gets its name from Starkville's original name, Boardtown, because it was home to two saw mills.
October-November -- *Oktoc Country Store*. Atmosphere reminiscent of country stores of yesteryear. Don't miss the Brunswick stew!
November-December -- *Union Crafts Fair* at Mississippi State University.

For more information contact:

Starkville Visitors and Convention Council
Post Office Box 2720
Starkville, Mississippi 39759
(601) 323-3322

Where to Eat and Sleep in the Starkville Area

Starkville offers a good variety of places to eat on game day. Some are located right on campus. They include:
    The Cafeteria which has a full-line menu from salads to
    sandwiches, to char-grilled entrees and homestyle meals!
    Mazzio's Pizza located in the south end of the cafeteria
    serves pizza, sandwiches, salads and assorted Italian entrees.
    The Union Grill is located in the Colvard Student Union and
    features many specialty sandwiches made with MSU baked rolls,
    as well as, hot entrees, vegetables and salad plates.
Many of Starkville's eateries are concentrated along State Highway 12 between University Drive and State Highway 25, just to the west of the MSU campus and are easy to locate.

Hotel and motel rooms may be scarce in Starkville on game weekends, but don't let that stop you! Rooms can be found in nearby Columbus, Winona, West Point, Kosciusko or Louisville. These cities are close enough so that you will be able arrive in time to enjoy the afternoon tailgating, meeting friends or making new acquaintances.

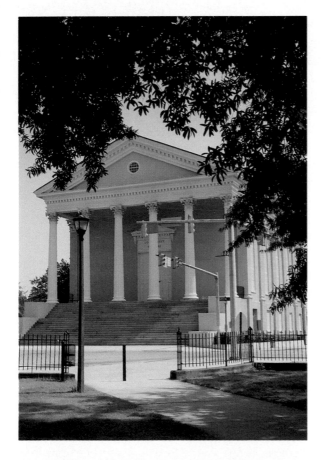

The graceful Longstreet Theatre, dating from 1855, houses the Department of Theatre, Speech and Dance, and is the oldest building on campus not located on the Horseshoe.

*One of the entrances to "The Horseshoe," historical and spiritual heart
of the University of South Carolina campus.*

The University of South Carolina is located in the heart of Columbia, the state's bustling capital city, which in turn, is located in the heart of the Palmetto State. Columbia was one of the first planned cities in the United States, having been designed in 1786 by the South Carolina General Assembly to be centrally located for the convenience of the people. Today the once sleepy town has become a center not only of government and education, but banking, commerce and industry as well. Columbia boasts a growing metro population of 440,000. All of these factors make the downtown 242 acre campus an exciting place to visit.

The USC campus in Columbia is one of nine located throughout the state which together form the University of South Carolina system. Over 26,000 of the system's 41,000 students attend classes in Columbia.

The University was founded in 1801 as South Carolina College and is the oldest school in the United States to be continuously supported by public funding. The original campus surrounded a parklike area known as "The Horseshoe" and even today that part of the school remains its sentimental, if not literal, heart. The restored buildings alongside "The Horseshoe" date from the early days of the school and today house the South Carolina Honors College, one of the finest of its type in the nation.

The University of South Carolina's Columbia campus is made up of 17 academic units including the schools of Law and Medicine. Altogether, seventy-eight programs lead to undergraduate degrees. The Masters degree may be earned in 163 fields and the doctorate is awarded in 63. Many of the schools and programs at USC have received honors and recognition as well as high ranking in various polls. For example, the Master of International Business Studies program has been ranked best in the nation several years running. In addition, the Marine Science program is ranked fourth best in the U.S., while the Marketing Department of the School of Business Administration and the advertising track in the School of Journalism and Mass Communications have both been ranked eighth.

With such an admirable record of academic achievement and a long tradition of solid athletic performance, it is no wonder that the University of South Carolina was courted by the Southeastern Conference when the league considered expansion. After the first year of Gamecock football in the SEC, with the excitement of five wins in the last six contests, the wisdom of that union became apparent!

In a serious moment, the South Carolina cheerleaders salute their Alma Mater.

Garnet and Black have been the official colors of the University of South Carolina's athletic teams since early in the century. They were chosen because they are the dominant colors found on the feathers of gamecocks, the school's mascot and nickname.

Recently, "black" has been emphasized more than "garnet" for two reasons. One, with South Carolina's and Arkansas' entry into the SEC, there are now six teams out of the twelve with red, crimson, maroon or garnet as the colors of their home uniforms. It was thought that since these colors are similar, it would be easier to create and maintain a distinct image for South Carolina within the league by wearing black, a color worn by only one other SEC team, Vanderbilt.

And two, this allowed for a revival of "Black Magic," a mystique first created by the black uniforms of the 1984 team which went 10-2 and ended up ranked 13th in the nation--the most successful season ever by a Gamecock team!

South Carolina's "garnet" is PMS Color #201.

Aside from Jacksonville State University in Alabama, the University of South Carolina is the only college in the nation with "Gamecocks" as its nickname. South Carolina's use of the unique moniker began more than 90 years ago. Actually, the official name of USC's athletic teams is "Fighting Gamecocks."

For those who are not familiar with that term, it should be explained that a gamecock is a fighting rooster know for its spirit and courage. In parts of the South, and especially in the Carolinas, cock fighting had long been important historically and culturally. Although it is now illegal due to concerns over humaneness and peripheral issues such as gambling, it is still practiced surreptitiously. One of its early proponents, General Thomas Sumter, was a Carolina patriot whose guerrilla fighting tactics during the Revolutionary War earned him the nickname, "The Fighting Gamecock."

For more than ten years after the introduction of football at USC the team had no official nickname. Various labels were used, perhaps the most common being "Jaguars." When South Carolina teams first began to be called by their present nickname, the term was written as two separate words, "Game Cocks." In 1903, this was shortened to one word by a Columbia newspaper, "The State," and the nickname has been "Gamecocks" ever since.

Members of the SEC will soon become familiar with the thundering roar of South Carolina fans yelling "Go Cocks!" And, if she is a true fan, even the finest, southern, South Carolina lady can be heard leading the familiar cry!

Tennessee may have Rocky Top . . . but South Carolina has "COCKY-TOP!"

"Cocky" (the name says it all) is South Carolina's feisty, award-winning mascot! The colorful and sassy bird can be seen from all parts of Williams-Brice Stadium strutting his stuff and alternately preening or ruffling garnet feathers, depending upon how USC's fortunes are going at the moment.

If the ability to convey emotions to the crowd is a prime requirement for mascots, then surely, Cocky is one of the best. He's certainly one of our favorites!

Cocky takes the lead in cheering for the Gamecocks!

The renowned Carolina Band performs before a packed house at Williams-Brice Stadium.

The Carolina Band is considered one of the nation's finest college marching bands and first performed as a uniformed group during the 1923-24 season. It is no wonder that USC fans spoke with pride about their band!

During the pregame show, the band forms an unusual "tunnel" through which the football team enters the playing field to the piped-in strains of "2001." When the stadium settles down to a roar, the Carolina Band takes the field and keeps the excitement going! Another great pre-game tradition is when the Band and a member of USC's voice faculty join together to perform the Alma Mater and National Anthem

The 300 member band, which includes a 24 member Flag Corps and a dance line called the "Coquettes," is under the direction of Jim Copenhaver, their leader for the past 18 seasons, On gameday they break into 3 "pep bands" and tour the parking area entertaining and leading with pep rallies before the game begins. Besides performing at all home football games the Carolina Band travels to four away games. Smaller groups, 75-100, entertain at pep rallies and at all men's and women's basketball games.

In honor of USC's entry into the SEC, the band has adopted a new name, "The Mighty Sound of the Southeast," which these authors think is very appropriate! Be sure to get your popcorn and cold drink early so you won't miss a minute of this important part of "Gamecock spirit."

UNIVERSITY OF
SOUTH CAROLINA
"Alma Mater"

We hail thee, Carolina,
and sing thy high praise,
With loyal devotion
rememb'ring the days
When proudly we sought
thee, thy children to be.

Here's a health, Carolina,
Forever to thee!

Since pilgrims of learning,
we entered thy walls,
And found dearest
comrades, in thy classic halls,
We've honored and loved
thee, as sons faithfully.

Here's a health, Carolina,
Forever to thee!

UNIVERSITY OF
SOUTH CAROLINA
"Fight Song"

Hey, Let's give a cheer,
Carolina is here,
The Fighting Gamecocks
Lead the way.
Who gives a care,
If the going gets tough,
And when it is rough,
That's when the 'Cocks get going.
Hail to our colors
Of Garnet and Black,
In Carolina pride have we.
So, Go Gamecocks
Go---FIGHT!
Drive for the goal---FIGHT!
USC will win today---GO COCKS!
So, let's give a cheer,
Carolina is here.
The Fighting Gamecocks
All The Way!

Tailgating along the Cockaboose Railroad outside Williams-Brice Stadium.

South Carolina is one of two new entries into SEC football competition and we think they will be a great addition! They bring some exciting and unusual traditions which we think SEC fans will enjoy when they visit Columbia or have the Gamecocks in town. Now there's the first "uncommon" thing about USC football, their nickname! You may have expected another dog, perhaps a lion, even a bear . . . but get ready the Gamecocks are coming and they know how to fight! Just look at their first SEC season, it looked like a slow start but they came back with an astonishing finish.

USC also has a tailgating tradition unrivaled in the conference. An enterprising couple saw some use for the old railroad tracks beside the stadium. Twenty-two cabooses line the tracks, now called the Cockaboose Railroad, and have been converted by individuals and groups who use them for gameday get-to-gathers! These "Cockabooses" are quite attractive and lend an atmosphere of importance and permanence to Gamecock football.

However, South Carolina fans enjoy their tailgating whether in a Cockaboose, from the back of their station wagon, or picnicking under a tree! More than one fan said, as did Michael Stumbris from Olympia, SC, that their favorite traditions associated with Gamecock football were "Tailgating," "Tail-gating," and "Tailgating." South Carolina fans enjoy fried chicken and potato salad, bar-b-que, sandwiches and chips, hot dogs and hamburgers and even steaks! Favorite local restaurants are California Dreaming, the Peddler, Al's Upstairs, Columbia's, J. Paul's Steakhouse and the Elite Epicurean. Whatever your choice, tailgating or eating out, be sure to come early to find parking, because Gamecock fans SUPPORT THEIR TEAM and there is very little parking available! When we arrived we were thrilled with the wide open space for parking, but we learned quickly that most of it is reserved parking for devoted fans.

How devoted are they? Well, Shep and June Headley said "our blood runneth Garnet & Black" and to prove it they postponed their marriage for a week waiting until South Carolina had an open football weekend! Now that's some serious devotion! Jenny Thompson told us she had been a fan since she was born because her parents were "discussing their USC-Clemson tickets" while waiting for her arrival! Well, first things first!

Another interesting tradition is "Black Magic." When South Carolina decided to join the SEC they realized that many of the schools use some shade of red. So, in order to set themselves apart, they chose to go with their other color . . . black . . . which had not been used as their home color since 1989. It has returned now and with it seems to be some good fortune

So if you are looking for a good time at an SEC football game we'd advise you to travel to Columbia. The opening "2001" entrance of the football team is a real excitement builder complete with stirring music and a smoke screen which fills the stadium. It really gets your blood to pumping! You will certainly enjoy the friendly rivalry with USC fans.

Columbia is a beautiful southern city with a lot of history for you to explore. And surprisingly enough, USC actually has more antebellum buildings on campus that any other SEC school. Many of them were spared while those in Alabama and Mississippi were burned and had to be rebuilt.

Though Bert Dooley of Lexington, South Carolina, said what he least enjoyed about attending South Carolina football games was "usually the score," we say don't count on it! As another fan put it "We are eager to be the best. The SEC is the best conference and competing will make us work harder to be the best."

The band takes a breather, but the excitement builds as smoke and the piped-in theme from
2001 dramatically signal the entrance of the Gamecocks.
"Black Magic." It's an electric moment!

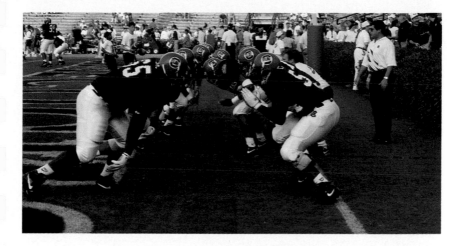

Under the watchful eyes of coaches, Gamecock linemen prepare for trench warfare. After a disappointing start, the South Carolina squad won five of their last six games!

Head Coach

Sparky Woods (Carson-Newman, 1976)
Tennessee Assistant, 1976;
Kansas Assistant, 1977;
North Alabama Assistant, 1978;
Iowa State Assistant, 1979-82;
Appalachian State Assistant, 1983;
Appalachian State Head Coach, 1984-88;
South Carolina Head Coach, 1989-present.

> **Birthday: December 20, 1953**
> **Hometown: Oneida TN**

Assistant Coaches

David Bibee (Tennessee, 1977)	Assistant Head Coach/Secondary
Miles Aldridge (Gardner-Webb, 1971)	Defensive Coordinator/ Inside Linebackers
Rich Bisaccia (Yankton College, 1983)	Running Backs/Special Teams
John Gutekunst (Duke, 1966)	Defense/Outside Linebackers
Tim Harkness (Johnson C. Smith, 1977)	Wide Receivers
Brad Lawing (Lenoir-Rhyne, 1979)	Defensive Line
Carroll McCray (Gardner-Webb, 1983)	Tight Ends/Tackles
Mark McHale (Shepherd College, 1977)	Guards/Centers
Art Wilkins (Bucknell, 1972)	Offensive Coordinator/Quarterbacks

Williams-Brice Stadium is the only home stadium in the SEC not located directly on campus. It lies south of downtown Columbia, adjacent to the State Fairgrounds.

For the first 32 of its 59 years, Williams-Brice Stadium was known as Carolina Stadium. It was constructed in 1934 as a WPA Project, making it one of the older stadiums in the SEC. And yet, when viewed from any angle today, the stadium appears to be completely modern, even futuristic, if you focus on the angular sweep of the light standards which crown the arc of its upper decks.

From an original capacity of 17,600, the stadium has been expanded and renovated several times so that today 72,400 gridiron fans can each witness the game from a comfortable vantage point. One of the largest expansion projects came in 1971-72, and not only resulted in raising the number of seats from about 43,000 to more than 54,000, but gave the facility a new name. A gift from the estate of Mrs. Martha Williams Brice was responsible. It seems that Mrs. Brice's husband, Thomas H. Brice, had been a three-year letterman at South Carolina in the 1920's. Mrs. Williams' family operated the Williams Furniture Company and she was able pass on a large inheritance to her nephews, Thomas W. and Phillip L. Edwards. They, in turn, passed much of it on to the University of South Carolina and to the stadium project. On September 9, 1972, during the season opener with Virginia, the name was officially changed from Carolina Stadium to Williams-Brice Stadium.

Although it is "Home Sweet Home" to Gamecock football, housing locker rooms, weight training facility, meeting rooms and Captains' and Team Halls, Williams-Brice Stadium is not really at "home." That is, it is not located on the University campus as are all eleven other SEC stadiums. Instead, it is situated a couple of miles to the South at the State Fair Grounds.

Stadium Stats

Capacity:	72,400
Largest Crowd:	75,043; November 21, 1987; South Carolina 20, Clemson 7
Playing surface:	Natural grass; artificial playing surface was removed in 1984

South Carolina's Williams-Brice Stadium

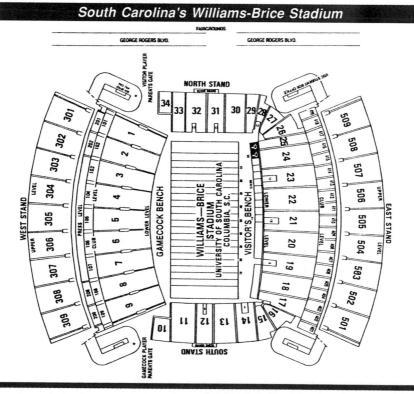

Bob Fulton	-	Play-By-Play/"Voice of the Gamecocks"
Tommy Suggs	-	Color Analyst
Todd Ellis	-	Sideline Reporter
Jim Powell	-	Network Host

Gamecock Radio Sports Network
AM Stations   FM Stations

CITY	STATE	STATION	FEQUENCY	CITY	STATE	STATION	FEQUENCY
Allendale	SC	WDOG	1460	Aiken	SC	WKSX	92.7
Batesburg	SC	WBLR	1430	Allendale	SC	WDOG	93.5
Charlotte	NC	WCNV	1480	Anderson	SC	WRIX	103.1
Chester	SC	WGCD	1490	Bamberg	SC	WWBD	92.1
Columbia	SC	WVOC	560	Barnwell	SC	WBAW	99.1
Florence	SC	WJMX	970	Beaufort	SC	WSHG	104.9
Fountain Inn	SC	WFIS	1600	Camden	SC	WPUB	94.3
Jacksonville	FL	WPDQ	690	Charleston	SC	WYBB	98.1
Kingstree	SC	WDKD	1310	Gaffney	SC	WAGI	105.3
Newberry	SC	WKDK	1240	Georgetown	SC	WSYN	106.5
Rock Hill	SC	WRHM	1340	Greenville	SC	WESC	92.5
Spartanburg	SC	WSPA	950	Greenwood	SC	WMTY	103.5
Union	SC	WBCU	1460	Orangeburg	SC	FroggyFM	105.1
				Scranton	SC	WSQN	102.9
				Seneca	SC	WBFM	98.1
				Sumter	SC	WIBZ	99.3
				Walterboro	SC	WONO	105.3

*Ticket Information

Ticket Office:
(803) 777-4274

State law prohibits the sale of tickets for more than $1.00 over face value. **Scalping** has not been a problem at Gamecock games in the recent past, but watch out as the program builds! USC fans are very loyal and there may not be many tickets for sale on gameday.

*Seating

At Williams-Brice Stadium the "Mighty Band of the Southeast" sits in section 16. The visiting band and fans sit in sections 24, 25, 26 27-29 and 30.

A peek inside one of the Cockabooses, used for tailgating USC style.

*Parking Information

From I-20 (heading east). Take the U.S. 1 exit into Colmbia. Turn right on Assembly Street. The stadium is three miles on the right.

From I-26 (heading west). Take Highway 478 exit. Go approximately four miles and take Bluff Road exit. Turn left onto Bluff Road. The stadium is two miles on the right.

Parking at Williams-Brice Stadium is deceptive. While there are vast acres of open space at the Fairgrounds, little, if any is available to unpermitted vehicles. Most all of the space around the stadium and across the way at the Fairgrounds is reserved for Gamecock boosters.

There are a few lots behind the east side of the stadium which are attended and charge around $5.00. Be careful not to park too far away from the stadium or in an unattended area. This is especially important for night games. The key is to arrive early and then to enjoy the atmosphere and not worry about parking or the safety of your vehicle.

*ALL INFORMATION IS SUBJECT TO CHANGE.

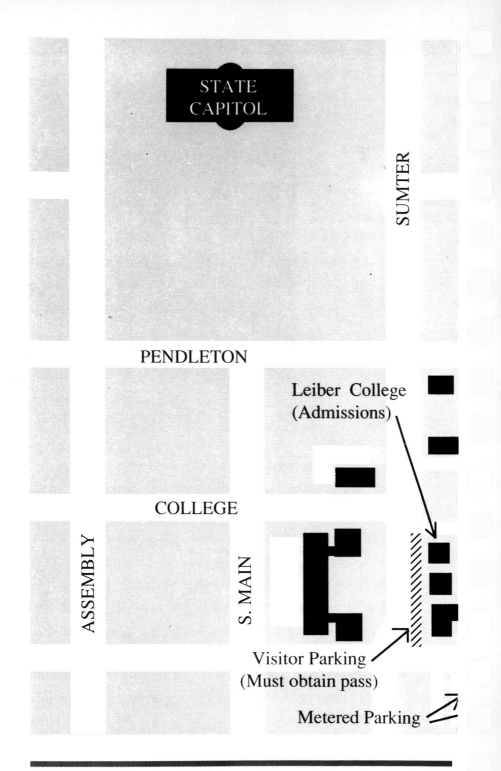

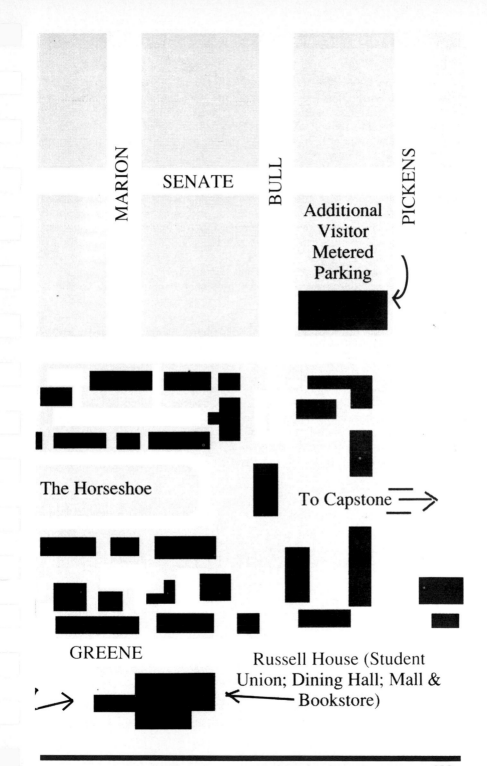

MARION

SENATE

BULL

PICKENS

Additional
Visitor
Metered
Parking

The Horseshoe

To Capstone

GREENE

Russell House (Student
Union; Dining Hall; Mall &
Bookstore)

~From 1805 to 1850 **The "Horseshoe"** served as the original part of the University of South Carolina campus. This park-like area surrounded by historic early buildings of the university is the sentimental heart of USC. Located at the intersection of College and Sumter Streets, the Horseshoe offers visitors and students a place to relax and reflect on the early history and traditions of a great university.

~**McKissick Museum** is located at the head of the Horseshoe and stands on the site of the original president's house. Completed in 1940 as the university's library, the structure was converted to museum use in 1976. Permanent exhibits feature Southern culture and folk art with emphasis given to South Carolina. The University's history is also highlighted. An extensive collection of Movietone newsreels is housed here as well. Other temporary exhibits are displayed on a changing schedule. Open Monday-Friday, 9 AM - 4 PM, Saturday 10 AM - 5 PM, Sunday 1 - 5 PM. Free admission. (803) 777-7251.

~**The Carolina Coliseum** is the site of Gamecock basketball games and is located on Assembly Street between Greene and Blossom Streets.

~**Longstreet Theatre** constructed in 1855, is the only one of the original campus buildings not located on the Horseshoe. Situated at the corner of Greene and Sumter Streets, the facility at one time served as a gymnasium for USC basketball and now houses the Department of Theatre, Speech and Dance.

~**Capstone House** is a high-rise residence hall and conference center which has often been used as a landmark symbol of the university. Located on Barnwell Street between Pendleton and Greene.

~**Campus tours** are offered by the Admissions Office twice daily at 10 AM and 2 PM, Monday through Friday. Call 1-803-777-7700. In South Carolina call 1-800-922-9755.

Parking for campus visits Monday through Friday is most easily done at the Park and Devine Streets lot. A free shuttle bus runs from 7:30 AM - 5 PM every 15-18 minutes.

Where to Eat and Sleep in the Columbia Area

Columbia is the capital city of South Carolina and is accustomed to hosting large groups for conventions, state fairs and sporting events. Therefore, you will probably be able to find lodging even at the last minute. A wide range of accommodations is available from economy to luxury suites. For the same reasons, you will be able to find many restaurants to tempt you if your decide not to tailgate.

Access to the stadium is easy because of its location on the south side of Columbia, so even if you travel from some distance it will be easy to find.

The Greater Columbia Convention and Visitors Bureau offers an excellent guide entitled "The Book on Hospitality." (1-800-264-4884)

~Take a walking tour of the **Main Street District.** Secure a map from the Historic Columbia Foundation at 1601 Richland Street (803-252-7742) and view interesting and historic building.

~**The State House** or Capitol Building, bears six bronze stars where the still unfinished walls were pounded by Union cannon fire in 1865. Begun in 1854, the Italian Renaissance structure was not completed until 1907. On Gervais Street between Assembly and Sumter Streets. Free. (803) 734-2430.

~**The South Carolina State Museum** located at 301 Gervais Street, has been adapted for its present used as an exhibition hall for South Carolina's cultural and natural history, science and technology and art. Originally it housed the world's first all-electric textile mill built 1893-96. Nominal entry fee. (803) 737-4921.

~**The Robert Mills House** was designed by Robert Mills, the first Federal architect of the United States. He designed the Washington Monument and U.S. Treasury Building. One of the few residences designed by Mill, this house features curved walls, venetian windows and Regency furniture. Situated at 1616 Blanding Street. (803) 252-1770.

~**The Mann-Simons Cottage** at 1403 Richland Street is a Columbia Cottage home built about 1850 and is unique in that it is the only ante-bellum house in Columbia owned by an Afro-American. Bought by Celia Mann, a former slave who also purchased her freedom, the house remained in her family and/or that of her son-in-law for 120 years. Nominal admission charged. (803) 252-1450.

~**The Hampton-Preston Mansion and Garden** at 1615 Blanding Street has served as the home of two of South Carolina's most prominent families. Although built 1812-1835, the mansion has been restored to its ante-bellum period, 1835-1855. Many fine architectural and decorating features, as well as personal effects of the famous residents, are present. (803) 252-1770.

~**Woodrow Wilson's Boyhood Home**. A Tuscan villa-style house was the residence of the future president during his teen years, 1872-1874. This is the only home ever owned by the Wilson family which moved frequently since Mr. Wilson was a Presbyterian minister. Located at 1705 Hampton Street. Admission: $3.00.

~**The Columbia Museum of Art** permanently houses the Kress Collection of Renaissance, Baroque and Medieval works as well as temporary exhibits featuring other periods and regions. Artists represented include Monet, Chagall, Renior and Matisse. Located at Bull and Senate Streets. (803) 799-2816.

~**Riverbanks Zoological Park** features over fifteen hundred wild and domestic animals, many in simulated natural environments. Special exhibits include a "farm" with all the barnyard "critters" and an aquarium reptile complex. Open daily. Located at Greystone Boulevard and I-126. (803) 779-8730.

~**Sidney Park** is a 17.5 acre urban green space complete with a 1.5 acre lake. This is a great area for relaxing and picnicking. Beautiful landscaping, waterfalls, flowers and swings from which to watch it all highlight the park. Located at 930 Laurel Street. (803) 733-8331.

~**Columbia Riverfront Park and Historic Columbia Canal** at 312 Laurel Street, combines natural and social history with science and technology in a unique urban park. A great place for picnicking, jogging, cycling or relaxing. (803) 733-8613.

For more information contact:
> **Greater Columbia Convention and Visitors Bureau**
> **P. O. Box 15**
> **Columbia, SC   29202**   **(803) 254-0479 or 1-800-264-4884**

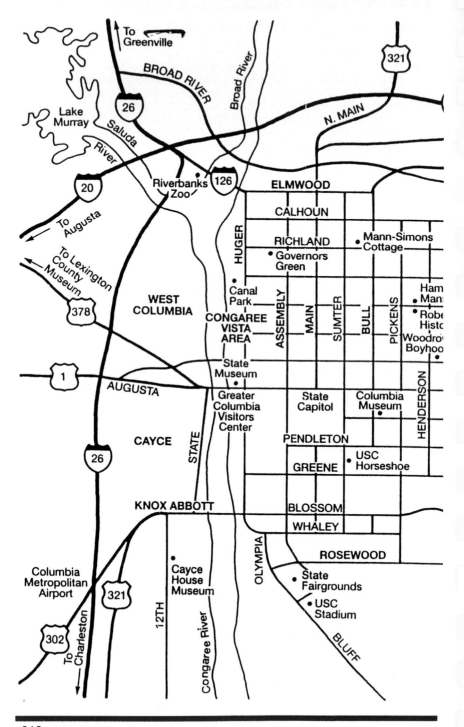

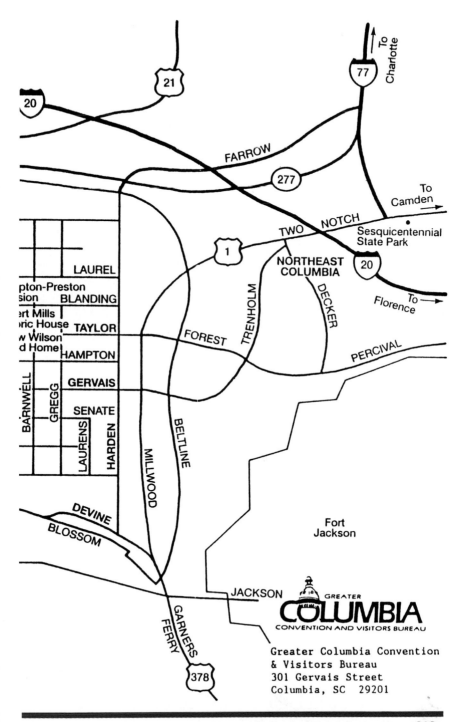

*Ayres Hall, on the crest of "The Hill,"
is UT's most recognized landmark.*

*A view down through time . . . from "The Hill," where it all began,
to the state-of-the-art library beyond.*

The University of Tennessee in Knoxville is the largest of the four campuses in the 40,000 student UT system. Other campuses are located at Chattanooga, Martin and Memphis. With over 26,000 students and 1,400 faculty members, the Knoxville facility offers more than 100 undergraduate majors and 140 graduate programs as well as specialized programs unique to that campus.

In addition to being the largest campus, Knoxville boasts the original campus of the state's university system. Two hundred years ago next year, the university was founded on "The Hill," high above the north bank of the Tennessee River near downtown Knoxville. It was originally known as Blount College and later it became East Tennessee College. Finally, in 1879, the school's official name became the University of Tennessee.

UT is located on a 417 acre campus that accommodates a variety of architectural styles from stately Ayres Hall on "The Hill" to the John C. Hodges Library, an ultra-modern, state-of-the-art facility. The campus extends from the banks of the Tennessee, up The Hill and to the west where most of the campus expansion has occurred since the early days when The Hill encompassed the entire institution.

The University and the city of Knoxville have grown up together. The city was founded in 1786, eight years before the school, when General James

White built a fort for protection of the pioneers in the settlement. Named for General Henry Knox, Washington's Secretary of War, Knoxville served as the capital of Tennessee until 1812. Since that time the city has enjoyed steady growth, attracting a variety of industries and businesses. Located in East Central Tennessee, Knoxville is on the fringe of the Smokey Mountains and is just minutes from the Great Smokey Mountain National Park. Numerous lakes and streams in the area provide a variety of outdoor activities that are enhanced by the mountain vistas.

The progressive outlook of Knoxville's people and government was demonstrated by the city's decision to host the 1982 World's Fair. The fairgrounds, with some structures adapted for a variety of uses, stands mere yards from the UT campus.

University of Tennessee Colors - "Orange and White"

Many athletic teams have selected orange as their color, but only Tennessee has the "particular" orange hue found on their team jerseys. It seems that Charles Moore, a member of UT's first football squad in 1891, selected "orange and white," the colors of the common American daisy which grew profusely on "The Hill." Later, a vote of the student body made the choice official.

It was not until 1922, however, that Vol players first appeared in the now-famous Tennessee orange jerseys.

Tennessee's "orange" is PMS Color #151.

A pregame time to honor the Alma Mater---the great University of Tennessee!

Trio of Tennessee symbols, two "Smokeys" and the "Vol,"
watch the action at Neyland Stadium.

The University of Tennessee's athletic teams take their nickname from the nickname of the state. In the first half of the nineteenth century, whenever our nation found itself in war, Tennessee responded overwhelmingly to the call for volunteers. So many men volunteered for duty in both the War of 1812 and the Mexican War that Tennessee became known as the "Volunteer State." "Vols" is a shortened form of "Volunteers."

Forty years ago, a school opinion poll indicated that the University needed a live mascot. So, in 1953, the UT Pep Club sponsored a contest to choose a fitting coon hound to serve in that capacity. The advertisements for the contest stated, "This can't be an ordinary hound. He must be a 'houn Dawg' in the best sense of the word." The late Rev. W.C. Brooks entered his prize winning blue tick coon hound, Smokey, as a contestant. The contest took place during halftime of a football game. The dogs were positioned along the old cheerleader ramp. Each dog was introduced in turn with the student body cheering for their favorite. Smokey went last. When his name was announced, he barked. The students cheered. Smokey howled and the students roared louder. This continued until it was obvious that UT had found its mascot. Rev. Brooks supplied mascots to the university until his death in 1986, after which his wife, Mrs. Mildred Brooks, and family continued the tradition.

Smokey, the blue tick coon hound, is Tennessee's beloved mascot.

Over the years the various Smokeys have had adventure-filled lives. Aside from appearing before more fans than any SEC mascot each year, the following incidents have occurred:

In 1955, Smokey II was dognapped by the University of Kentucky students. The following year, he survived a confrontation with the Baylor bear at the Sugar Bowl. Smokey VI suffered from heat exhaustion during the 1991 UCLA game when temperatures on the field hit 110 degrees. He was listed on the weekly Vols injury report until he returned to action later in the season.

We personally witnessed Smokey VII hunkering down in the steady rain during the Kentucky game and in the spitting snow of the Vanderbilt game. A mascot's life is not all glamour!

Smokey Stats

Most wins .... 105-39-5 .... Smokey III
Highest winning percentage .... 722 .... Smokey VI
Most SEC championships .... 3 .... Smokey VI

Perhaps Smokey's proudest moment is when he leads the "Vols" through the "T" before each home game. Watching Smokey "dig out" across the checkerboard end zone (his handler likewise flat out and frantic at the other end of the tether) is one of our most enjoyable memories!

Smokey's Reigns

Smokey 1953-54
Smokey II 1955-56
Smokey III 1965-1977
Smokey IV 1978-79
Smokey V 1980-83
Smokey VI 1984-1991
Smokey VII .... 1992 -

The "Pride of the Southland Band" presents an exciting pre-game show culminating in the "running through the 'T'" formation, a Tennessee tradition.

The University of Tennessee's marching band, known as the "Pride of the Southland Band," was organized at the end of the Civil War when the University reopened, making it one of the oldest collegiate bands in the nation. Today, with over 300 members, the UT band is one of the finest and most admired marching bands in America (see "Fan Scan" results).

For over 31 years the band was directed by Dr. W. J. Julian, who retired last year after building the band from 84 members to its present size and after making "Rocky Top" the "unofficial fight song" of Tennessee!

The marching band is only one of several units in the UT band program. Students from all of the University's schools participate, sharing their talents with over 750,000 "live" spectators annually and millions more on TV. Over the years the "Pride of the Southland Band" has proudly represented the University of Tennessee and the state at the inauguration of six U.S. presidents and has appeared at twelve different bowl games a total of 25 times. Its finest moment, however, has to be the one that is repeated each football gameday in Knoxville when the band forms up for "Running through the 'T'!"

"ROCKY TOP"
by Boudleaux Bryant and Felice Bryant

Wish that I was on ol' ROCKY TOP,
    down in the Tennessee hills;
Ain't no smoggy smoke on ROCKY TOP,
    ain't no telephone bills.
Once I had a girl on ROCKY TOP,
    half bear, other half cat;
Wild as mink, but sweet as soda pop,
    I still dream about that

CHORUS:
    ROCKY TOP, you'll always be home
        sweet home to me;
    Good ol' ROCKY TOP
        ROCKY TOP Tennessee.

Once two strangers climbed ol' ROCKY TOP
    looking for a moonshine still;
Strangers ain't come down from ROCKY TOP,
    reckon they never will.
Corn don't grow at all on ROCKY TOP,
    dirt's too rocky by far;
That's why all the folks on ROCKY TOP
    get their corn from a jar.

HERE'S TO OLD TENNESSEE
(Down the Field)

Here's to old Tennessee
Never we'll sever
We pledge our loyalty
Forever and ever
Backing our football team
Faltering never
Cheer and fight with all of your might
For Tennessee.

FIGHT, VOLS, FIGHT!

Fight, Vols fight with all you might,
For the Orange and White
Never falter, never yield
As we march on down the field
(Keep Marching!)
Let the Spirit of the Hill
Every Vol with courage fill
Your loyalty means our victory
So fight, Vols, fight!

UNIVERSITY OF TENNESSEE
"Alma Mater"

On a hallowed hill in Tennessee
Like a beacon shining bright
The stately walls of old U.T.
Rise glorious to the sight.

REFRAIN:
So here's to you, old Tennessee
Our Alma Mater true
We pledge to love and harmony
Our loyalty to you.
What torches kindled at that flame
Have passed from hand to hand
What hearts cemented in that name
Bind land to stranger land.

O, ever as we strive to rise
On life's unresting stream
Dear Alma Mater, may our eyes
Be lifted to that gleam.

Passing the baton . . . Dr. W. J. "Jay" Julian, the man who made "Rocky Top" UT's unofficial fight song, conducts the band in his final halftime show, after 31 years as director.

The Vol Navy at low tide . . . usually numbering around 200,
only a few nautical Vol fans ventured out on this grizzly game day.

The most "rabid" fans in the SEC are to be found at the University of Tennessee. They have a strong desire to win and with the help of their imposing stadium, intimidation is an important part of their game plan. SEC rivals agree (maybe with one exception) it is difficult to play the Vols on their home turf where it is large, loud and ORANGE!

We found that Vol fans are not here to enjoy the day . . . they come to win! However, they DO enjoy the experience. We found many, many Tennessee "fanatics" tailgating in spite of a rainy gameday. Hardy fans cooked under tents, ate from the back of their cars and trucks, and in front of their motorhomes. We were tempted with delicious chili, biscuits and smoked ham, fried chicken, barbecue, and even steak hot off the grill! If you care to try some local fare, UT fans suggest Bayou Bay Seafood House, Calhoun's, Chesapeakes, the Copper Cellar and Regas Restaurant.

One of the most unique traditions at UT is the Vol Navy which docks on the north bank of the Tennessee River between Neyland Stadium and Calhoun's Restaurant. Over 200 boats gather for most games. Many more fans gather at the park and in the restaurant for pre-game and post-game partying.

Many of the fans we interviewed said the "fan support" is what makes Tennessee unique in the SEC. That's not difficult to believe when you attend a game in Neyland Stadium. As John Cheek of Sparta, Tennessee, says "96,000 fans" is his favorite tradition and most of them are Vols like Lucian and Gene Scott of Lewisburg, Tennessee, who have not missed a home game in 21 years and have attended ALL games in 6 seasons! They travel in an orange and white van, with orange and white chairs, in orange and white clothes and meet their "Big Orange" friends for partying. Another fan even had the gridiron with its checkerboard end zones painted on the inside of her van. Rival fans agree that Tennessee fans are "unique" because of their ability to "pull out all the stops" when it comes to "psyching-out" their opponents. Vol fan Phillip L. Swanson of Madisonville, Tennessee, calls it that "true competitive zeal."

"The excitement!!! The fans, the team . . . everyone is pumped!" That's what Donna Morton enjoys most about UT games and we found it to be true. The "incredible excitement is contagious." Both fan and foe agree that excitement is a "tradition" associated with Vol football. There is no way one can remain calm and unaffected when playing the great Volunteers of Tennessee. Other important traditions are the "Vol Walk," the team "Running Through The 'T'" and the 3rd Saturday in October. Of course, "Rocky Top" is a beloved tradition to the consternation of rival fans.

Neyland Stadium, itself, is a tradition which impacts the game. It's size is immense, it's location on a major river lends itself to unique fan activity, and the trademark checkerboard end zones and giant letters spelling out "VOLS" identify this as "Big Orange" turf. Though it may seem intimidating, these authors believe that attending a game at UT is a must for all SEC fans. There is so much tradition, rivalry and atmosphere that one will certainly savor the memories and use them as a yardstick for other gameday experiences. UT fan, Jeff R. Greeley of Knoxville, reminds us of three reasons to visit the Vols on their home turf: "The Vol Navy, Vol fans and Vol parties." You may even agree with John Kreis, also of Knoxville, who says the hardest part about gameday at Tennessee is: "When it's over!"

Wearing their cold weather gear, the Vol cheerleaders fire up the fans in Nashville.

A panoramic view of Neyland Stadium, the Tennessee River and the skyline of Knoxville.

Head Coach

Phillip Fulmer (Tennessee, 1972)
Tennessee Assistant, 1972-73;
Wichita State Assistant, 1974-78;
Vanderbilt Assistant, 1979;
Tennessee Assistant, 1980-82;
Tennessee Interim Head Coach, 1992 (4 games);
Tennessee Head Coach, 1993-present.

| Birthday: | September 1, 1950 |
| Hometown: | Winchester TN |

Assistant Coaches

Kippy Brown (Memphis State, 1977)	Assistant Head Coach/Wide Receivers
David Cutcliffe (Alabama, 1976)	Offensive Coordinator/Quarterbacks
Larry Marmie (Eastern Kentucky, 1965)	Defensive Coordinator
Mark Bradley (Samford, 1969)	Tight Ends
Jacob Burney (UT-Chattanooga, 1981)	Defensive Line
Johnny Chavis (Tennessee, 1979)	Linebackers
Steve Marshall (Louisville, 1980)	Offensive Line
Randy Sanders (Tennessee, 1988)	Running Backs
Lovie Smith (Tulsa, 1979)	Defensive Backs

Neyland Stadium . . . Immense, Intimidating, Impressive!

Mystique, ambiance, awe, even reverence, are attitudes and feelings which are commonly experienced by football fans in and around Neyland Stadium. The setting, traditions and sheer intimidating size combine to create an environment as close to football heaven as any place on the planet.

Imagine a bright, crisp morning on a Saturday in October. You're in Knoxville at the foothills of the Smokeys, but the smoke today rises from a hundred charcoal grills ringing the huge stadium by the Tennessee River. The fires, tended by early arriving fans near their often orange vans and motor homes, infuse the already sharp atmosphere with the aromas of the day's delights, ranging from chili to scrambled eggs to barbecue.

Up on "The Hill" vehicles flying orange "Vol" flags and driven by orange clad fans, frantically maneuver to claim rapidly disappearing parking spaces. Fast food restaurant managers over on Cumberland Avenue, fretting that all of THEIR parking will be gobbled up by non-customers, make periodic forays like maniacal scarecrows shooing flocks of grackles. On Stadium Drive, vendors busily set up their food and souvenir stands. Down on the river, the "Vol Navy" swells in size to an even larger fleet as boat after boat cozies up to dock on the perimeter. The sounds of good times ripple across the water as boat hopping fans renew relationships and make new friends. Along the river bank and on the deck at Calhoun's, crowds savor the beauty of the day, reminisce about proud memories of Vol football and anxiously anticipate the excitement to come.

The focus of all the hubbub is venerable Neyland Stadium and the team which calls it home--the Tennessee Vols. Located on the north bank of the Tennessee, the stadium points its south end zone toward the river, one of only two college stadiums in the country located on a body of water (the other being Huskie Stadium at the University of Washington). The north end zone, kneeling at the foot of "The Hill," pays homage to the spiritual heart of the University of Tennessee.

The west side stands are commanded by the gigantic Neyland Stadium Press Box and Executive Suites which rises seven levels and stretches the length of the gridiron. The playing field sideline is a dizzying 194 feet from the lowest working level. The facility opened at the beginning of the 1987 season replacing one built twenty-five years earlier.

The University of Tennessee has played football at this hallowed site since 1921. It was in 1919 when Colonel W.S. Shields, a prominent Knoxville banker and UT Trustee, supplied the seed capital for construction of a football arena. When completed, the facility bore the name Shields-Watkins Field, after the donor and his wife, Alice Watkins-Shields. The name remained unchanged for forty-one years. In 1962, following the death of General Robert R. Neyland, long-time coach and Athletic Director and the man most responsible for the growth of the Tennessee football program, the complex received an expanded name: Neyland Stadium, Shields-Watkins Field.

Today, Neyland Stadium ranks as the third largest on-campus football facility in the nation after Michigan Stadium at the University of Michigan and Beaver Stadium at Penn State University. Even with a capacity of 91,902, the stadium consistently attracts overflow crowds and it may be only a matter of time before the upper deck is extended around the north end zone completing a double-decked bowl.

It is hard to believe that such a huge facility had humble beginnings. Originally, only 17 rows of the current west stands formed the entire stadium seating area with a capacity of 3,200. Since then the stands have been expanded and/or renovated 12 times as follows:

Year	Description	Total
1926	East stands, 17 rows, 3,600 seats	6,800
1929	West stands, 42 rows, 11,060 seats	17,860
1937	Section X, 1,500 seats	19,360
1938	East stands, 44 rows, 10,030 seats	31,390
1948	South stands (horseshoe) 15,000 seats	46,390
1962	West upper deck, press box, 5,837 seats	52,227
1966	North stands, end zone seats, 5,895	58,122
1968	East upper deck, 6,307 seats	64,429
1972	Southwest upper deck, 6,221 seats	70,650
1976	Southeast upper deck, 9,600 seats	80,250
1980	North stands (bowl), 16,944 total, 10,499 net	91,249
1987	Press Box and Executive Suites, net loss 139	91,110
1990	Seating adjustment	91,902

Unfortunately, the upper deck seats are constructed at a very steep angle with very little leg-room. Larger fans or those who have problems with vertigo should avoid these seats if possible.

Stadium Stats

First game:	September 24, 1921; Tennessee 27, Emory & Henry 0
Dedication game at Neyland Stadium:	October 20, 1962; Alabama 27, Tennessee 7
First game on artificial turf:	September 14, 1968; Tennessee 17, Georgia 17
First night game:	September 16, 1972; Tennessee 28, Penn State 21
Largest single game attendance:	97,731, September 28, 1991; vs Auburn
Consecutive home games without a loss:	55 (beginning 9/25/26 with a 13-0 win over Florida and ending 10/21/33 with a 12-6 loss to Alabama)
Consecutive home wins:	30 (beginning 12/8/28 with a 13-12 win over Florida and ending 10/21/33 with a 12-6 loss to Alabama)
Consecutive home losses:	4 (twice) 1) Beginning 11/13/54 with a 14-0 loss to Florida and ending 10/8/55 with a 13-0 win over Chattanooga; 2) Beginning 9/10/88 with a 31-26 loss to Duke and ending with a 10-7 win over Boston College, 11/5/88.
Winning seasons:	62 in 71 seasons at Neyland Stadium, Shields-Watkins Field (includes 30 undefeated seasons at home).
Last undefeated season at home:	1991 team (6-0-0)
Tennessee record at Neyland Stadium:	71 seasons; W -336 L-85 T-17 (Pct. .787)
Playing surface:	Artificial turf

Tennessee's Neyland Stadium

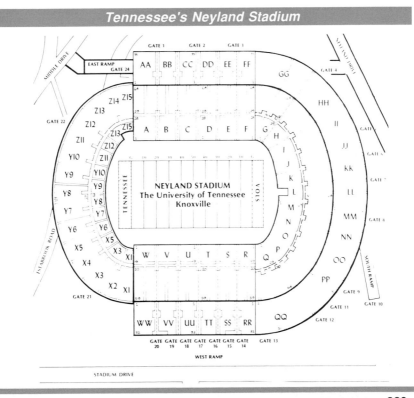

John Ward   -   Play-By-Play/"The Voice of the Vols"
Bill Anderson   -   Color Analyst

The Vol Radio Network

AM Stations

CITY	STATE	STATION	FREQUENCY	CITY	STATE	STATION	FREQUENCY
Atlanta	GA	WYNX	1550	Rockwood	TN	WOFE	580
Big Stone Gap	VA	WLSD	1220	Rogersville	TN	WRGS	1370
Brownsville	TN	WBHT	1520	Smithville	TN	WJLE	1480
Bryson City	NC	WBHN	1590	So. Pittsburg	TN	WEPG	910
Carthage	TN	WRKM	1350	Sparta	TN	WSMT	1050
Centerville	TN	WHLP	1570	Springfield	TN	WDBL	1590
Chattanooga	TN	WDEF	1370	Trenton	TN	WTNE	1500
Clarksville	TN	WDXN	540	Union City	TN	WENK	1240
Cleveland	TN	WBAC	1340	Wartburg	TN	WECO	940
Cleveland	TN	WCLE	1570	Winchester	TN	WCDT	1340
Columbia	TN	WMCP	1280				
Columbia	TN	WKRM	1340	**FM STATIONS**			
Cookeville	TN	WHUB	1400	Bristol	TN	WXBQ	96.9
Covington	TN	WKBL	1250	Brownsville	TN	WTBG	95.3
Cowan	TN	WZYX	1440	Camden	TN	WRJB	98.3
Crossville	TN	WAEW	1330	Carthage	TN	WUCZ	104.1
Decatur	AL	WAVD	1400	Centerville	TN	WHLP	96.7
Dyersburg	TN	WTRO	1330	Chattanooga	TN	WDEF	92.3
Erwin	TN	WEMB	1420	Covington	TN	WKBL	93.5
Franklin	TN	WAKM	950	Crossville	TN	WXVL	99.3
Gallatin	TN	WHIN	1010	Dickson	TN	WQCQ	102.0
Greeneville	TN	WGRV	1340	Erwin	TN	WXIS	103.9
Greenville	SC	WDAB	1580	Fayetteville	TN	WYTM	105.5
Harrogate	TN	WSVQ	740	Greeneville	TN	WIKQ	94.9
Jackson	TN	WDXI	1310	Jackson	TN	WMXX	103.1
Jellico	TN	WJJT	1540	Johnson City	TN	WUSJ	99.0
Johnson City	TN	WKTP	1590	Kingsport	TN	WKOS	104.9
Kingsport	TN	WKPT	1400	Knoxville	TN	WIVK	107.9
Knoxville	TN	WIVK	990	LaFollette	TN	WQLA	104.9
Lafayette	TN	WEEN	1460	Lawrenceburg	TN	WDXE	95.9
Lawrenceburg	TN	WDXE	1370	Lenoir City	TN	WLIL	93.5
Lenoir City	TN	WLIL	730	Lewisburg	TN	WJJM	94.3
Lewisburg	TN	WJJM	1490	Lobelville	TN	WIST	94.3
Livingston	TN	WLIV	920	Martin	TN	WCMT	101.7
Martin	TN	WCMT	1410	Nashville	TN	WYCQ	102.0
Memphis	TN	WREC	600	Oneida	TN	WBNT	105.5
McMinnville	TN	WAKI	1230	Paris	TN	WAKQ	105.5
Middlesboro	KY	WFXY	1490	Parsons	TN	WKJQ	97.3
Morristown	TN	WCRK	1150	Pulaski	TN	WINJ	98.3
Murfreesboro	TN	WMTS	810	Rockwood	TN	WOFE	105.7
Murphy	NC	WCVP	600	Rogersville	TN	WEYE	104.3
Newport	TN	WLIK	1270	Savannah	TN	WKWX	93.5
Oneida	TN	WBNT	1310	Selmer	TN	WSIB	105.5
Paris	TN	WTPR	710	Smithville	TN	WJLE	101.7
Parsons	TN	WKJQ	1550	Sparta	TN	WSMT	105.5
Pikeville	TN	WUAT	1110	Springfield	TN	WDBL	94.3
Pulaski	TN	WKSR	1420	Trenton	TN	WLOT	97.7
Ripley	TN	WTRB	1570	Wartburg	TN	WECO	101.3

*Ticket Information

UT Ticket Office: (615) 974-2491.

Games at Neyland Stadium are all sellouts, but tickets are still available. In Tennessee tickets are considered private property and there are no laws regulating ticket pricing. **Ticket scalping** is legal and is not discouraged by the University. Scalpers are allowed to conduct business any where including around the stadium. The best places to find individuals with tickets are "The Strip," an area of commercial eateries and businesses on Cumberland Avenue, and along Stadium Drive, especially around the University Center.

*Seating

The Tennessee Band sits in the bottom of section E. In 1993, in compliance with NCAA rules about crowd noise, the visitor's bench will be moved to the west (press box) side of the field. Tennessee will occupy the east side bench and sit near the band. Therefore, the "Running Through the T" tradition will be reversed with the team turning left at the head of the "T" instead of right.

Visiting bands sit in section Z-15 and visiting fans sit in sections Z-11, Z-12, Z-13, AB, AA and BB.

*Parking

Parking at UT can be a problem. With close to 100,000 people converging on an already highly developed and congested area the competition for parking is keen. The need to arrive early cannot be overstated! There are private lots within walking distance of the campus and stadium, but the steep terrain might be too challenging for some fans.

Parking costs are moderate, usually $3 to $5 in those areas. One alternative is to take the **shuttle bus** from the Auditorium Coliseum parking lot at the corner of Church Avenue and Mulvaney Street. This lot is located NE of the campus across the downtown area. As with almost all of the SEC campuses, the parking around Neyland Stadium is reserved for permitted vehicles. This includes RV's.

Non-permitted **motor homes** should park at the agriculture campus. For $3.00 RV operators get to park and ride a **shuttle** about a half mile to the stadium.

As kickoff approaches many fans simply pull their vehicles off roadsides and ramps and create their own parking areas. They should be cautioned that there is absolutely NO PARKING along Neyland Drive beside the stadium.

*ALL INFORMATION IS SUBJECT TO CHANGE.

Viewed from "The Hill," Neyland Stadium's press box is still massive.

~**The University of Tennessee Gallery Concourse** in the University Center, features twenty-one different shows and exhibitors annually including local, regional and national artists. Permanent arts and crafts collections displayed. Open Monday-Friday 8 AM - 10 PM. Admission free. (615) 974-5455.

~**The Frank H. McClung Museum** in Circle Park is a general interest museum with collections in anthropology, archaeology, decorative arts, medicine, local and natural history. Open Monday-Friday 9 AM - 5 PM, Sunday 2-5 PM. Admission free. (615) 974-2144.

~**The Hill** and **Ayres Hall**, two symbols of the University. The Hill is where the University started 199 years ago. Ayres Hall, constructed in 1919, dominates the campus with its majestic tower.

~**The Torchbearer** is another symbol of UT. Located at the entrance to Circle Park, the statue's live flame impresses visitors with the realization of how the University of Tennessee has done and meant so much to generation after generation in the Volunteer State.

~The thirty million dollar **John C. Hodges Library** has been called the most popular building on the UT campus. This state-of-the-art facility serves the needs of the Tennessee student body with the latest technology.

~UT's **Thompson-Boling Arena**, located at 1600 Stadium Drive, is the nation's second largest on-campus basketball facility with a seating capacity of 24,535. (615) 974-0953.

~**The Ewing Gallery of Art and Architecture,** at 1715 Volunteer Boulevard, features works of avant-garde artists and internationally known architects. Open Monday-Friday, 9:30AM 4:30PM; Monday-Thursday 7:00PM - 9:00PM; Sunday 1:00PM - 4:30 PM. Admission free. (615)974-3200.

~**Neyland Stadium** is legendary among college football both for its size and tradition. Located on Stadium Drive and Neyland Drive at the Tennessee River, it is the nation's second largest on-campus football facility and one of only two college stadiums located on a body of water.

The University of Tennessee
Football Parking Map

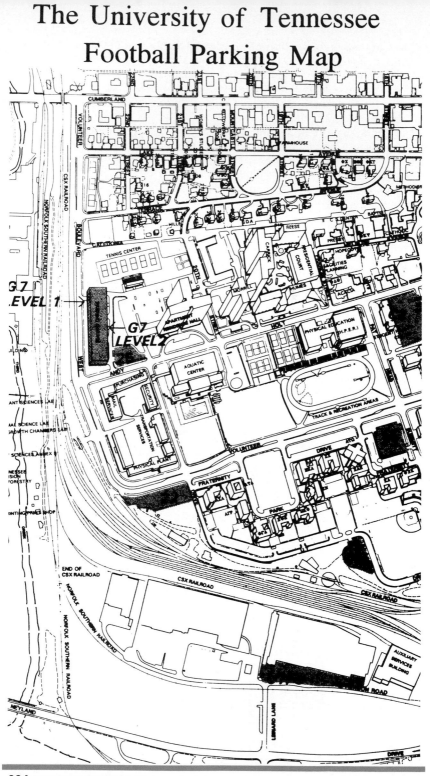

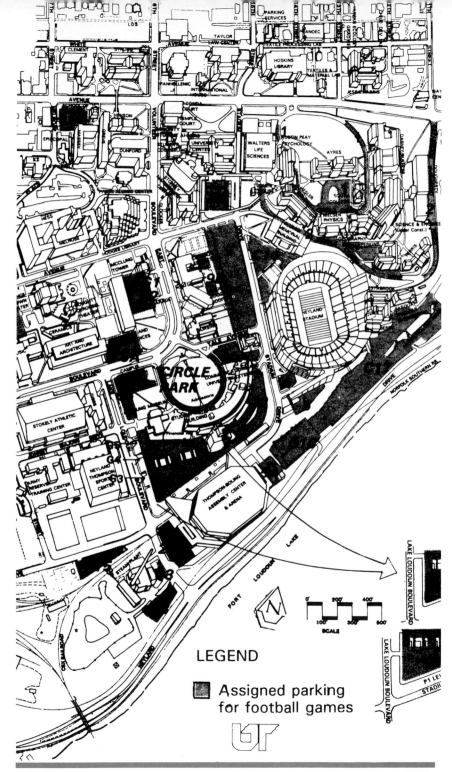

LEGEND

Assigned parking
for football games

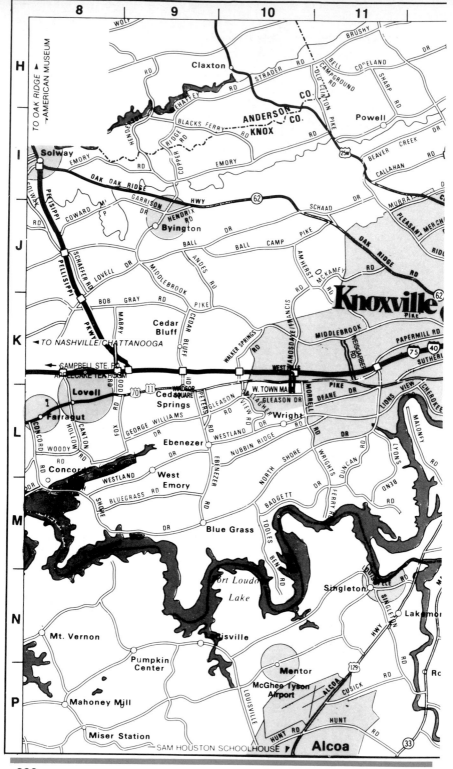

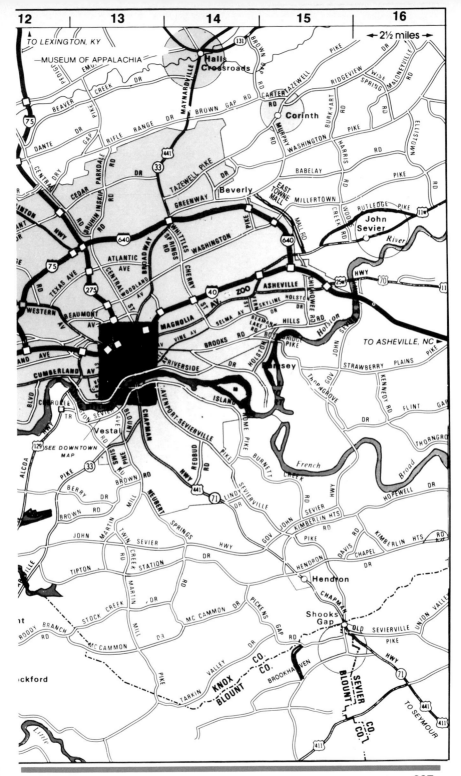

There are many attractions in East Tennessee which annually lure millions of tourists to that area. These include the Great Smoky Mountains National Park and the resort areas of Gatlinburg and Pigeon Forge. For complete information about the entire area contact:

Knoxville Convention & Visitors Bureau   (615) 523-2316
810 Clinch Avenue, P. O. Box 15012
Knoxville TN   37901

KNOXVOICE, constantly updated recording of Knoxville events,
(615) 525-9900

Tennessee Tourist Development   (615) 741-2158
P. O. Box 23170
Nashville TN   37202

Gatlinburg Chamber of Commerce   1-800-568-4748
P. O. Box 527
Gatlinburg TN   37738

Pigeon Forge Department of Tourism   (615) 453-8574 / 1-800-251-9100
P. O. Box 1390-G
Pigeon Forge TN   37868-1390

The James White Fort is actually a collection of several buildings dating back to 1786 and the founding of Knoxville. See how pioneers lived and worked. Located near downtown at 205 E. Hill Avenue. Open March 1-December 15, Monday-Saturday from 9:30 AM - 4:30 PM. Closed Sunday. Admission: adults $2.50, children under 12 $1.50, ages 6 and under free. Senior citizen discount. (615) 525-6514.

The Knoxville Zoological Gardens feature over 1,000 exotic animals, a petting zoo, "Zoo Choo" train rides, elephant and camel rides and bird, seal and sea lion shows. Located two miles east of downtown Knoxville. Take exit 392 off Interstate 40. Open 9:30 AM - 6:00 PM, April 1 through September 30, and 10:00 AM - 4:30 PM, October 1-March 31. Admission: adults (13+) $6.50, children (3-12) $4.00, children 2 and under free, senior citizens (62+) $4.00. (615) 637-5331.

The Blount Mansion, built in 1792, marked a great leap forward in home design and construction on the frontier. The mansion is furnished with authentic period pieces. The attraction includes the surrounding Colonial Revival gardens, Governor's office, detached kitchen and Visitor's Center with museum and gift shop. Located downtown at 200 W. Hill Street. Open March-October, Tuesday through Saturday from 9:30 AM - 4:30 PM, Sunday 2 - 4:30 PM; November-February, Tuesday through Friday, 9:30 AM - 4:30 PM. Weekends by pre-arranged groups only. Admission charged. (615) 525-2375.

The Museum of Appalachia, located in Norris, 16 miles north of Knoxville, is a living mountain village. Over 250,000 objects made and used by mountain folk are featured and demonstrated. Take exit 122 of Interstate 75. Open all year during daylight hours. Admission: adults $4.00, children (6-15) $2.50, children under 6 free, family rate (2 or more children) $12.00. (615) 494-7680.

Crescent Bend. The Armstrong-Lockett house dates from 1834 and is a beautifully restored and furnished farm home. It houses an outstanding collection of American and English furniture and English silver dating from 1640-1820. 2728 Kingston Pike (U.S. 11). Open Tuesday-Saturday from 10 AM - 4 PM, Sunday 1 - 4 PM. Admission charged. (615) 637-3163.

The American Museum of Science and Energy, 300 S. Tulane Avenue in Oak Ridge, tells the story of energy and the super secret of Oak Ridge during World War II. Features models, movies, demonstrations, etc., which will fascinate all age groups. Open Monday-Sunday, 9 AM - 5 PM. **Free** admission. (615) 576-3200.

The Star of Knoxville Riverboat Company, located at 300 Neyland Drive on Bicentennial Park, provides cruises on the Tennessee River in an authentic riverboat. (615) 522-4630.

Old City, located in the Jackson and Central Street area, encompasses a historic neighborhood brought back to life with restaurants, saloons, antiques, shops, etc.

Where to Eat and Sleep in the Knoxville Area

With a corporate population of 165,000 and a metro-census of 600,000, Knoxville is one of the largest host cities in the SEC, so there are plenty of places to eat and sleep, even on football weekends! Still, the region is large, and even though Knoxville's highway system is very good, travel time can be considerable, depending on location and traffic conditions.

For a complete listing of hotels/motels and dining information, including Bed & Breakfast Inns and campgrounds, contact:

Knoxville Conventions and Visitors Bureau
P. O. Box 15012
Knoxville, TN 37901
(615) 523-2316

Kirkland Hall, with its clock tower,
has become a symbol of Vanderbilt University.
Its unique roof line is repeated in the school's crest.

Vanderbilt is unique in the S.E.C. in at least two ways. It is the only private institution among the twelve member schools and it is the smallest in numbers, with a total student enrollment of 9,183 in 1992.

The University was founded in 1873 by Cornelius Vanderbilt, a wealthy industrialist, who donated one million dollars to start the school. His goal was to use education to bring the post Civil War nation together and reduce sectionalism.

Vanderbilt's campus encompasses 330 acres in an urban setting about a mile and a half southwest of downtown Nashville. It is bordered on the

Cornelius Vanderbilt's dream of ending sectional strife in the post-Civil War U.S. led to the founding of his namesake university, the only private institution in the SEC.

*Vanderbilt's library, where many Vandy players star off the field,
giving the school a national reputation for producing scholar athletes.*

northwest side by West End Avenue, which provides a convenient thorough-
fare linking downtown and I-440, as does 21st Avenue which flanks the school
on the east.

Vanderbilt has long been admired within the SEC and indeed, throughout
the nation, for academic excellence. In a recent evaluation of America's top
25 universities, "U.S. News and World Report" ranked Vanderbilt 19th.
Chancellor Joe. B. Wyatt said, commenting on the honor, "This list confirms
what we already know about Vanderbilt: we are a strong, national university
with extensive resources and outstanding students and faculty."

The tradition of academic excellence at Vanderbilt carries over to the
student-athlete. With a graduation rate of more than 90% for its football
players, Vanderbilt tops the Southeastern Conference and ranks among the
leading schools in the nation. The University is proud of its athlete support
program which closely tracks and tutors athletes in their academic endeavors.
Coach Gerry DiNardo claims,

**"Our mission at Vanderbilt is to create an atmosphere
where our student-athletes can achieve excellence both
in the classroom and on the playing field. Vanderbilt is
a place for the true student-athlete. Our Support
system....assures all of our players the opportunity to
excel as student-athletes."**

Certainly, Vanderbilt University is a class act!

The Vandy cheerleaders get the crowd up for a kickoff against in-state rival, Tennessee.

Black and Gold were chosen as Vanderbilt's colors by the school's first football team in 1890. These "commanding" colors are not surprising for a school named after a self-appointed Commodore! Vandy's gold is PMS Color #873.

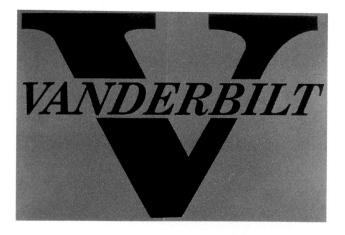

The nickname of Vanderbilt University's athletic teams, "Commodores," was inspired by the by the school's founder, Cornelius Vanderbilt, who himself was nicknamed "Commodore" due to his interest in steamboating.

The Commodore nickname was first applied to Vanderbilt teams in 1897 by Nashville newspaperman William E. "Billy" Beard who had played quarterback on the Vanderbilt team five years earlier. Sometimes the Commodore nickname is shortened to "Dores."

The nautical theme of Vanderbilt's mascot and nickname has been enhanced recently by the addition of a large ship's horn on top of the pressbox. It is sounded at important times before and during Vandy games.

The Commodore and cheerleaders "stand watch" as their team does battle.

*Mr. Commodore strikes a commanding pose
atop a pyramid of his peers.*

The fellow in the gold and black uniform, complete with shoulder epaulettes and gold fringed hat, seen stalking the sidelines at Vanderbilt football games is the "Fightin' Commodore," the school's mascot.

A Commodore is an old naval rank, no longer used in today's Navy. The Fightin' Commodore is part of Vanderbilt's cheerleader squad.

The Vanderbilt band, "The Spirit of Gold,"
adds color and warmth to a cold and gray late November day.

The Vanderbilt University Marching Band, "The Spirit of Gold," has experienced tremendous growth during the last six years, much to the delight of Commodore fans who witness the group's performances. From only 64 members then, the band has grown to 180 marchers today. Much of the credit goes to Dr. Dwayne Sagen, Director of Bands at Vandy, and his assistant, Dr. Joe Laird.

The band is proud of its on-field and academic accomplishments. Even in the academically challenged environment of Vanderbilt, the band maintains a higher composite GPA than the student body in general. This, when coupled with a demanding six hour per week rehearsal schedule, demonstrates the degree of dedication possessed by band members.

In addition to the Marching Band, the band program at Vanderbilt features the University Wind Ensemble, the Basketball Band, and the Jazz Ensemble.

VANDERBILT UNIVERSITY
"Alma Mater"

On the city's western border
Reared against the sky,
Proudly stands our Alma Mater
As the years roll by.

Forward ever be our watchword,
Conquer and prevail;
Hail to thee, our Alma Mater
Vanderbilt---all hail!
                    by Robert F. Vaughn, '07

VANDERBILT'S FIGHT SONG
"Dynamite" (When Vandy Starts to Fight)

Dynamite, Dynamite
When Vandy starts to fight
Down the field with blood to yield
If need be, save the shield.
If vic'try's won, when battle's done
Then Vandy's name will rise in fame,
But win or lose, the Fates will choose,
And Vandy's game will be the same
Dynamite, Dynamite
When Vandy starts to fight.
                    by Francis Craig, '24

Vandy fans show approval for the 'Dores play against Georgia.

Vanderbilt home games should be one of the toughest tickets in the SEC, so say these authors. There is easy access from I-440, easy parking, a great stadium in which to enjoy a hard-fought game and lots to see and do before and after the game.

Vandy is a charter member of the SEC and one of the most highly regarded schools according to our "Fan Scan" interviews.However, Vanderbilt does have a difficult time "staking out their turf" in middle Tennessee, especially since their in-state SEC rival is also the state's namesake and has a strong football team! On the other hand, Vanderbilt is a private school named for it's founder and is known more for its scholarship than football tradition. An example of this struggle for recognition could be heard on the radio before the Vandy-UT game in 1992. One caller reminded the DJ that there were "other fans in Nashville than Vandy fans" and she wanted some recognition. The DJ said he would oblige and played the "Green Acres" theme. Not all battles are won so easily for the Commodores.

The Dores are proud of their quality football program and believe their priorities are in order. There is an emphasis on the "whole person" and each of their players is considered a student athlete. Their rivals seem to agree since Vandy was chosen by a majority of fans whom we interviewed as the school they would most like for their child to attend other than their own. However, we must not forget that many individual Vanderbilt players hold SEC records as you can see from the superlative statistics we have included in the first section of this book. The determination to build a quality football team is evident in talking with fans and Coach DiNardo who anticipate the day when the Dores can win an SEC football championship as they did in basketball last year.

A new tradition at Vandy which we enjoyed is the "ship's horn" which calls the fans to the game and sounds-off at appropriate times during the game. It is quite impressive and will add to the whole gameday experience in Nashville. Other favorite traditions are tailgating, partying, the "black and gold" colors and the Commodore mascot, who is not just a "decoration" but is a true fan, as demonstrated by his animated reactions to events during the game.

Commodore fans are true "fanatics." We visited on a bitterly cold day with spitting snow and interviewed lots of fans who gathered with friends to tailgate. They gave us a genuinely "warm" welcome. However, as Mike Mullins of Franklin, Tennessee, told us, it's not easy to build a fan base for a small school. For example, if every living Vanderbilt alumnus bought a season ticket, it still would not fill up the stadium! That impressed us even more to meet such devoted fans with a determination to support their coaches and team. Many are concerned however, that the students do not support the team. They do attend the games, but as Retta Murray of Nashville pointed out, they often arrive late or not at all. Perhaps when the students read this guidebook and realize the strength and depth of their football team they will be more supportive!

The strongest rivalry for Vandy is, of course, Tennessee. It is the most important game for the Dores and they look forward to "beating the Big Orange" as Wayman and Sandra Hancock of Hermitage, Tennessee, told us. The rivalry is so intense that Bill and Colleen Grissom of Nashville said they would disown a child who chose to attend UT! However, Linda Rollins of Manchester, Tennessee, told us she would rather her child "remain illiterate than attend UT." Some other Vandy fans said, "What's the difference?" Well, this is a heated rivalry.

Though you will find ample space for tailgating when attending a game at Vanderbilt, there are many local restaurants for you to enjoy as well. Vandy fans recommend The Cooker, Stockyard, Houston's, Sperry's and Jimmy Kelley's.

Taken as a whole, with its modern facilities, ease of access and ample parking, availability of accommodations and restaurants, Vanderbilt should be high on every SEC fan's list of gameday destinations. You have to like these Commodores and hope they have as much success on the football field as they obviously have in the game of life!

Coach DiNardo has a tête-à-tête with his quarterback.

Head Coach

Gerry DiNardo (Notre Dame, 1975)
Maine Assistant, 1975-77
Eastern Michigan Assistant, 1978-81;
Colorado Assistant, 1982-90;
Vanderbilt Head Coach, 1990-present.

Birthday:	**November 10, 1953**
Hometown:	**Brooklyn NY**

Assistant Coaches

Ron Case (Carson-Newman, 1973)	Defensive Backs
Bill Elias (Massachusetts, 1977)	Outside Linebackers
Don Frease (Oregon, 1972)	Offensive Coordinator/ Wide Receivers/Split Ends
Hal Hunter (Northwestern, 1981)	Offensive Tackles/ Tight Ends
Ed Lambert (California State-Hayward, 1970)	Quarterbacks
Bob McConnell (Maine, 1973)	Running Backs
Jappy Oliver (Purdue, 1978)	Defensive Line
Carl Reese (Missouri, 1965)	Defensive Coordinator/ Inside Linebackers
Chris Symington (Colorado, 1988)	Centers/Guards

Fans funnel through the gate into Vanderbilt Stadium, the SEC's newest football facility.

Vanderbilt Stadium, "Home of the Commodores," is the SEC's newest football facility. The stadium was completed in 1981 on the site where Vanderbilt has played football for over 60 years.

The original stadium, Dudley Field, was the first facility built exclusively for college football in the South. It was placed in service in 1922 and named for Dr. William Dudley, long time Dean of the Vanderbilt Medical College and avid supporter of southern football. It was Dr. Dudley who had organized the Southern Intercollegiate Athletic Association in 1893 and in 1906 helped to begin the NCAA, an organization which he later served as vice-president.

The original capacity of Dudley Field was 20,000, large for its time. Over the years the stadium grew to its ultimate capacity of 34,000.

The construction process used on the new Vanderbilt Stadium is an interesting story in itself. While much of the old stadium was being demolished, portions of steel bleachers totaling 12,088 seats on both the East and West sides were being raised ten feet with massive hydraulic jacks, sandblasted, painted and outfitted with new aluminum seats. This raising of the seats above the playing field assures that no ones view is obstructed by the teams on the sidelines--every seat in the house is excellent! In our opinion, this fact, coupled with the intimate closeness to which the stands are constructed to the playing field, provide the best overall enjoyment for watching a game of all the stadiums in the SEC.

Above the horseshoe-shaped facility rises the magnificent four-level press box. With 17,000 square feet of floor space, the commodious structure comfortably accommodates two levels of donors, 15 luxury boxes, a working press area and a photo deck. Perhaps the most unique fixture in the press box is the huge ship's horn on the roof which was added during the 1992 season. I personally will never forget the first time it sounded when many members of the press were enjoying the hospitality of a pre-game meal. With coffee cups jitterbugging across the tables and the floor's vibrations shuddering up our spines, many must have thought, "earthquake" and fleetingly considered a dive beneath the nearest table. Seriously, we believe that the Commodores' ship's horn sounded at appropriate moments before and during the game, will become an enduring Vandy tradition!

Stadium Stats

Capacity: 41,000
First Game: September, 1981; Vanderbilt 23, Maryland 17
Playing surface: Astro-turf

A pair of Commodore cheerleaders demonstrate their acrobatic skills against the beautiful backdrop of Vanderbilt Stadium.

Vanderbilt Stadium

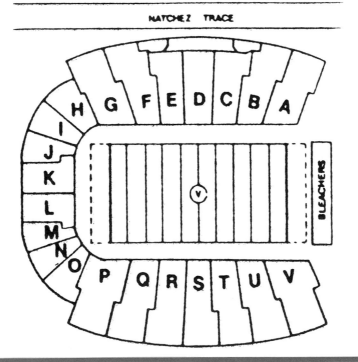

NATCHEZ TRACE

BLEACHERS

Wes Durham   -   Play-By-Play/"Voice of the Commodores"
Ralph Miranda   -   Analyst
Jim Fitzgerald   -   Sideline Reporter

Commodore Radio Network

AM Stations				FM Stations			
CITY	STATE	STATION	FREQUENCY	CITY	STATE	STATION	FREQUENCY
Ashland City	TN	WQSV	790	Alamo	TN	WNBE	93.1
Camden	TN	WFWL	1220	Columbia	TN	WKOM	101.7
Carthage	TN	WRKM	1350	Dresden	TN	WGNN	95.1
Clarksville	TN	WDXN	540	Jackson	TN	WBNE	93.1
Columbia	TN	WKRM	1340	Pulaski	TN	WINJ	98.3
Cooksville	TN	WPTN	780	Sparta	TN	WSMT	105.3
Fayetteville	TN	WEKR	1240				
Franklin	TN	WIZO	1380				
Lawrenceburg	TN	WDXE	1370				
Lewisburg	TN	WAXO	1220				
Memphis	TN	WHBQ	560				
Murfreesboro	TN	WMTS	810				
Nashville	TN	WLAC	1510				
Shelbyville	TN	WHAL	1400				
Springfield	TN	WDBL	1590				
Tullahoma	TN	WDFZ	740				
Waverly	TN	WPHC	1060				
Winchester	TN	WCDT	1340				

*Ticket Information

Ticket Office: (615) 322-3544.

Scalping is legal in Tennessee. Tickets are considered personal property and may be bought and sold for whatever value the parties agree.

The Commodore Band sits in section T of the stadium. The visiting band sits in section P and visiting fans sit in sections A, N, O and P.

*Parking Information

Parking is fairly simple at Vanderbilt Stadium. There are some lots adjacent to the facility where parking is available, but huge Centennial Park is across the street and easy convenient parking may be had for $3 to $5.

RV's may be parked at the corner of Capers Avenue and 25th Avenue South.

*ALL INFORMATION IS SUBJECT TO CHANGE.

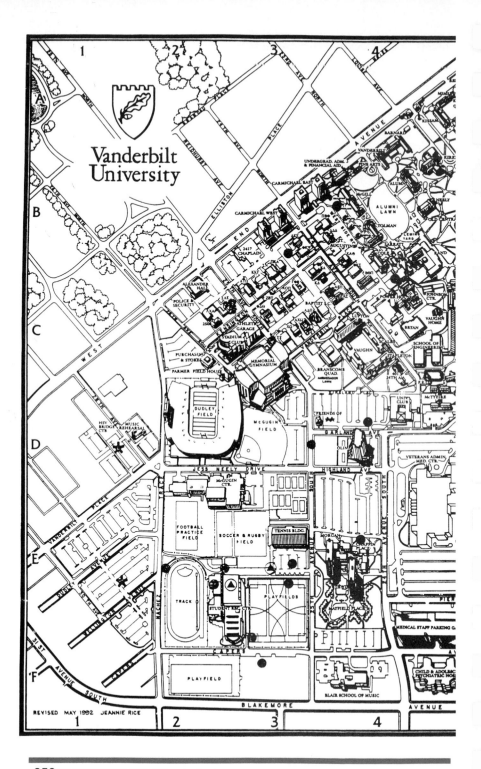

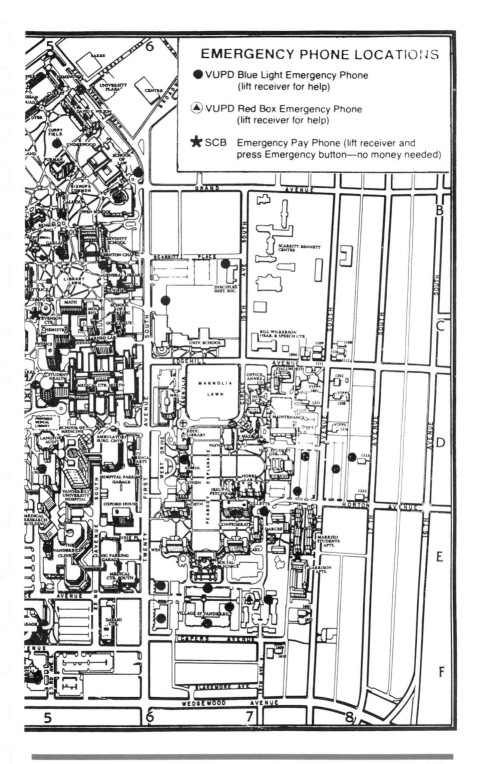

~**Auto Tour.** Circumnavigate the Vanderbilt University by car to get an overall impression of the urban campus environment. From Centennial Park, take West End Avenue toward downtown. Vanderbilt Stadium, home of the Commodores, looms on the right. Pass the University entrance with the statue of founder and benefactor, Cornelius Vanderbilt, just inside the gate. Note the Clock Tower beyond, an often-used symbol of the University. Turn right on 21st Avenue. Pass the Law School, library and Medical Center. Turn right on Blakemore Avenue and right again on Trace to return to your starting point.

~**Dudley Field.** A modern stadium seating 41,000 completed in 1981 on the long-time site of Commodore football.

~**Cornelius Vanderbilt Statue Area.** Statue of university founder with historical plaques. Walk around the horseshoe noting the beautiful variety of trees, tasteful landscaping and friendly squirrels. Kirkland Hall, the Administrative Building with its clock tower which is often used to symbolize Vanderbilt University, is located here.

~**Sarratt Student Center.** Vanderbilt Place and West Side Row, two blocks north of Memorial Gym. At the heart of the Vanderbilt Campus. Contains the Sarratt Gallery which features 10 exhibits a year of contemporary art. Also houses a cinema, Ticketmaster, gameroom and restaurant. (615) 322-2425.

~**Vanderbilt Fine Arts Gallery.** 23rd & West End Avenues. A constant variety of exhibits featuring various media from many cultures. (615) 322-0605.

Nashville has over 300 eateries from which to choose! Many are convenient to the Vanderbilt campus. When asking for information about location remember that those located on West End or 21st Avenues are the closest to the stadium.

There is also an abundance of motel/hotel rooms and we were able to find accommodations even at the last minute. However, advance planning is advised so that you can get the quality, price and location you desire. A complete listing, which includes bed & breakfast and campgrounds, can be found in the *"Music City Vacation Guide"* which is available from the Convention and Visitor's Bureau. Call **(615) 259-4700** for information.

While Nashville may be only the second largest city in Tennessee, it takes no backseat to Memphis or most other larger cities when it comes to the variety of interesting attractions it offers. Whether you are a music fan, history buff, bargain hunter or fun loving dare devil, Nashville has something for you.

For complete information contact:

The Nashville Convention & Visitors Bureau   (615) 259-4700
161 Fourth Avenue North
Nashville, TN 37219

Ask for the *"Music City Vacation Guide."*

~**Fort Nashborough,** 170 First Avenue, North (37201). Reconstruction of the original settlement of Nashville located in Riverfront Park. Free.

~**Grand Ole Opry,** 2804 Opryland Drive (37214). Country music shows performed by members of the Grand Ole Opry.

~**Opryland,** 2802 Opryland Drive (37214). Musical theme park: shows, rides, petting zoo, country music museums. Open daily until September 6. Weekends only, September 10-October 31. (615) 889-6611.

~**The Nashville Network,** 2806 Opryland Drive (37214). TNN offers visitors the chance to see television shows in production, including "Nashville Now" ($5.00 service charge), "Crook and Chase" and several others. Call TNN Viewer Services for production schedules and talent line-ups. (615) 883-7000.

~**The Parthenon,** West End and 25th Avenues in Centennial Park (37201). An authentic, full-scale replica of the beautiful Greek temple complete with a statue of Athena Parthenos, the largest indoor sculpture in the Western World. Gift Shop. Free parking. Handicapped accessible.

~**Ryman Auditorium and Museum,** 116 Fifth Avenue North (37219). Famous home of the Grand Ole Opry from 1943-1974. (615) 254-1445.

~**Tennessee State Capitol,** Charlotte Avenue between Sixth and Seventh Avenues. A unique and historic statehouse. Handicapped accessible. (615) 741-2692 / (615) 741-1621.

~**The Hermitage,** 4580 Rachel's Lane, Hermitage, TN 37076. Magnificent home of President Andrew Jackson. Admission includes theater, museum, two mansions and audiocassette tour. (615) 889-2941.

~**Music Row,** Demonbreun Street at 16th Avenue South (off Broadway). A collection of museums, gift shops and recording studios of the country music industry. (615) 256-8299.

~**Nashville Zoo,** take I-24 West to Exit 31; left on New Hope Road. A collection of over 800 animals from more than 150 species, many in natural settings. Admission: $5.00 adults, $3.00 children ages 3-12 and senior citizens (under 3 free). Open 9 AM - 6 PM Memorial Day through Labor Day; 10 AM - 5 PM remainder of year. (615) 370-3333.

Riverboat Excursions

**Belle Carol Riverboat Company, 106 First Avenue South, Riverfront Park (37201). Daytime cruise 2-1/2 hours. Includes historic commentary, $10.95. (615) 244-3430.

**The General Jackson Showboat, 2802 Opryland Drive (37214). Daytime cruise 2 hours, includes live entertainment, $14.95. (615) 889-6611.

**Both companies offer longer, evening cruises with meals.

NASHVILLE

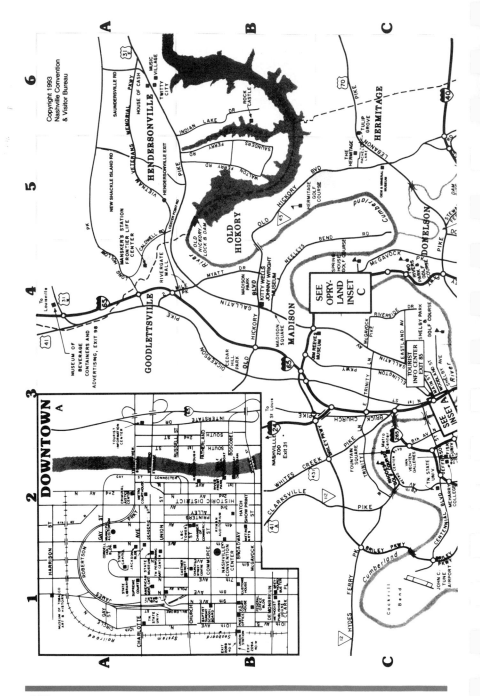

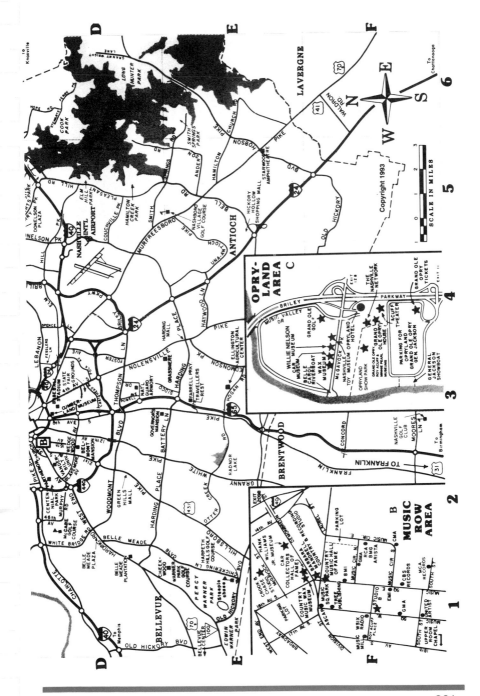

Sugar Bowl excitement spills outside the Superdome onto Poydras Street where Canes and Tide fans celebrate being "nearly there."

The 59th Classic played in the Louisiana Superdome on January 1, 1993, has to rank as one of the greatest of all time in the minds and hearts of SEC fans. Alabama, crowned League Champion in the first ever SEC Championship Game less than a month before, faced mighty Miami. It seemed only fitting that second ranked "Tide" and the number one "Hurricanes" should meet in the sound and fury of a National Championship Game with all the winds of opinion and the floodwaters of speculation swirling about. Who would survive in the aftermath and who would be washed into the sea of next year?

Even before the storm had passed, it was clear that this was Alabama's year to triumph, the SEC's time to shine. In a decisive 34-13 win, Bama silenced the rush of air coming from the South. In doing so, the naysayers who predicted that league expansion would mean the end of National Championships for the Southeastern Conference were proved wrong the first time out!

Sugar was never sweeter!

Watch out Big Al . . . somebody may be after your job. A proud poodle leads a parade of Bama Boosters through the streets of old New Orleans.

SEC fans filled French Quarter lounges, like this one, to cheer on the Tide. Here we found LSU, Mississippi State, Florida and Auburn fans united in support for their Conference Champion.

AND THE TRADITION . . .

CONTINUES . . . .

First . . . we want to encourage you **to travel** to see your favorite team play! It's a good opportunity to see new cities or areas of the Southeast. It's also an inexpensive way to take "mini-vacations" with your family or friends. Of course, it's also a great way to travel even if you don't have to worry about expenses. However, we traveled on a very tight budget and had some memorable weekends watching the best football in the USA!

Many hotels/motels now include a breakfast with the room and by picnicking or tailgating you can eat without a lot of expense. Do make reservations in advance so you won't spend lots of time searching for rooms.

We hope these tips help you enjoy your travel more and that you will send us your favorite tips . . . learned the hard way!

1. Make a list of your needs and keep it handy for last minute trips.
    Think before your pack. Make the trip in your mind to discover what you will need. Then make your list and assign responsibilities. Planning will eliminate forgotten items which can ruin a trip.
2. Don't duplicate items.
    Share shampoos, hair dryers, etc., so that you can pack more in less space.
3. Invest in a good ice chest and use it.
    Take into consideration the size which will fit into your trunk or cargo space. Evaluate the features. Look for compartments which hold small items and "shelves" keep meats out of the water. We carried 2: one large one for long-term needs (meats, veggies, milk, juice, etc.) and a small one to keep near us for short-term needs (cold drinks and snacks). This can save lots of money on cold drinks and snack foods.
4. Join a travel club.
    The $50.00 you spend will mean piece of mind and will be well worth it if you have a flat, run out of gas or need a tow. (We know from experience!)
5. To add to your enjoyment you will need: ·
    This guidebook
    Stadium cushions
    Binoculars
    Camera (take extra film, batteries, etc.)
    Sunglasses (spare contacts or eyeglasses can help, too!)
    Sunscreen
    Hat or visor
    Poncho (umbrellas are not allowed in stadiums)
    Tickets - but don't let the lack of them deter you!
6. Don't forget to pack medicines.
    Prescription and non-prescription medicines which can help for upset stomachs, travel sickness, fevers or allergies. This can really help save a trip so plan well. (Don't forget bandages, anti-bacterial creams, etc.)
7. Leave a number where you can be reached.
    Emergencies can happen and you may need to be reached by family or neighbors, so advise those you trust of your plans.

Each trip you make will be well worth the time and money you spend. So get out there and enjoy SEC football!